Roger Sherman and the Creation of the American Republic

Ralph Earl. *Roger Sherman (1721–1793), M. A. (Hon.) 1768.* Yale University Art Gallery. Gift of Roger Sherman White, B. A. 1859, LL.B. 1862.

Roger Sherman and the Creation of the American Republic

MARK DAVID HALL

OXFORD
UNIVERSITY PRESS

OXFORD
UNIVERSITY PRESS

Oxford University Press is a department of the University of Oxford.
It furthers the University's objective of excellence in research, scholarship,
and education by publishing worldwide.

Oxford   New York
Auckland   Cape Town   Dar es Salaam   Hong Kong   Karachi
Kuala Lumpur   Madrid   Melbourne   Mexico City   Nairobi
New Delhi   Shanghai   Taipei   Toronto

With offices in
Argentina   Austria   Brazil   Chile   Czech Republic   France   Greece
Guatemala   Hungary   Italy   Japan   Poland   Portugal   Singapore
South Korea   Switzerland   Thailand   Turkey   Ukraine   Vietnam

Oxford is a registered trade mark of Oxford University Press
in the UK and certain other countries.

Published in the United States of America by
Oxford University Press
198 Madison Avenue, New York, NY 10016

© Oxford University Press 2013

First issued as an Oxford University Press paperback, 2015.

Library of Congress Cataloging-in-Publication Data
Hall, Mark David, 1966–
Roger Sherman and the creation of the American republic / Mark David Hall.
p. cm.
Includes bibliographical references (p.).
ISBN 978–0–19–992984–9 (hardcover); 978–0–19–021870–6 (paperback)
1. Sherman, Roger, 1721–1793.   2. Statesmen—United States—Biography.
3. United States. Declaration of Independence—Signers—Biography.
4. United States. Continental Congress—Biography.   5. Connecticut—History—
Colonial period, ca. 1600–1775.   6. Connecticut—History—Revolution, 1775–1783.
7. United States—History—Revolution, 1775–1783.
8. United States—Politics and government—1775–1783.   I. Title.
E302.6.S5H35 2013
973.3092—dc23 [B]   2012018343

1 3 5 7 9 8 6 4 2

Printed in the United States of America
on acid-free paper

To my son, Joshua, of whom I am very proud.

Contents

Preface

I BEGAN THIS study with the belief that Roger Sherman's contributions to the founding of the American republic have been neglected, that he has been ignored as a political thinker, and that the significance of his religious convictions has been overlooked. Addressing these concerns remain at the core of this book. However, as the work progressed, I was intrigued by Sherman's extensive knowledge of, and commitment to, Reformed Christianity. ("Reformed," in this context, refers to the theological and broader cultural traditions that emerged from the Protestant Reformation, especially that branch of the Reformation associated with John Calvin. Accordingly, the terms "Reformed" and "Calvinist" are used interchangeably throughout this book.) As I delved into his correspondence and the world in which he lived, I became convinced that there was a larger story to tell. Sherman represents well the many founders influenced by the Reformed political tradition, a tradition that dominated New England and which had a significant presence throughout the rest of the nation.[1]

As this study evolved from being a narrow account of Sherman to include a broader argument for the influence of Reformed tradition in the American founding, I found it necessary to trace the development of Reformed political theory. Like many students of American political theory, I was trained broadly in political philosophy and so was familiar with great political philosophers such as Thomas Hobbes, John Locke, and Jean-Jacques Rousseau. Although I had read excerpts from Calvin's *Institutes* and Brutus's *Vindiciae, Contra Tyrannos*, I knew little about Reformed political theory. Perhaps it is as a result of this shortcoming, which I suspect is not uncommon among students of America's founding, that the influence of the Reformed tradition on American political theory is neglected. There are notable exceptions to this rule which will be discussed in the chapters to come, but these works are lost in a sea of books and articles contending that the founders were primarily influenced by some variation of a secular Lockean liberalism, classical republicanism, the Scottish Enlightenment, or other intellectual traditions—to say nothing of scholars who argue the founders were primarily motivated by personal, economic, state, or other interests.

In this book I contend that the political ideas of many leaders in the founding era are best understood in light of a long tradition of Calvinist reflection on politics. To make this argument, I focus on the political theory of Roger Sherman, but I attempt to demonstrate that he was representative of Reformed colleagues such as Samuel Adams, Isaac Backus, Abraham Baldwin, Elias Boudinot, Timothy Dwight, Eliphalet Dyer, Oliver Ellsworth, Matthew Griswold, John Hancock, Benjamin Huntington, Samuel Huntington, Richard Law, Joseph Montgomery, William Paterson, Jesse Root, Ezra Stiles, Richard Stockton, Jonathan Trumbull, William Williams, John Witherspoon, Oliver Wolcott, and many other founders. Because of space constraints, this broader argument can only be suggestive, although the narrower argument about Sherman is, I hope, definitive.

In speaking of the Reformed political tradition, I do not mean to suggest that all Calvinists approached politics in the same way or that the tradition did not develop over time. Moreover, I recognize that America's founders were influenced by practical concerns, including self-interest. As well, they read non-Calvinists, were affected by their arguments, and often used their works for rhetorical purposes. I am not arguing that Calvinism was the only influence on Sherman and his colleagues, simply that it was a very important influence that needs to be taken more seriously if we are to appreciate the political theory and actions of many of America's founders.

Works arguing for the influence of a particular theological tradition are often written by adherents to that tradition. I should therefore note that while I have a great deal of respect for many Reformed thinkers and theologians, I would not label myself a Calvinist and I am not a member of a Reformed church.

In writing this book, I have incurred many debts. As with all of my projects, I am profoundly grateful for my lovely wife, Miriam, and wonderful children Joshua, Lydia, and Anna. Without their patience and encouragement, I could not have completed the project. Similarly, my parents, David and Irene Hall, have been a constant source of love and support.

This is my first book written as the Herbert Hoover Distinguished Professor of Politics. I am grateful to the administrators and trustees of George Fox University for appointing me to this position and for granting me a sabbatical for the 2007–2008 school year. My teaching assistants,

Sergio Cisneros, Deanne Kastine, Janna McKee, Jay Miller, and Austin Schaefer, provided important research assistance and feedback. Thanks as well to the other politics majors, who make teaching at George Fox University such a joy. I also appreciate the support offered by the Institute for the Studies of Religion at Baylor University, where I serve as a Senior Fellow.

Critical outside funding for writing this volume was provided by the Earhart Foundation and the National Endowment for the Humanities. I am thankful for both of these institutions. Colleagues and friends including Jay Bruce, William Casto, Daniel Dreisbach, Gastón Espinosa, Greg Forster, Gregg Frazer, Tony Gill, Tommy Kidd, Peter Kozushko, Jeffry Morrison, Glenn Moots, Vincent Phillip Muñoz, Andrew Murphy, Paul Otto, Jonathan Rowe, Barry Shain, and two anonymous reviewers for Oxford University Press provided invaluable feedback. Richard Johnson and members of the Pacific Northwest Early Americanists colloquium were kind enough to comment on two different chapters. I am grateful as well to the editors and staff and Oxford University Press, especially Cynthia Read, Sasha Grossman, Erica Woods Tucker, India Gray, and Jessica Prudhomme, for their excellent work with the manuscript.

I would like to thank Hans Eicholz for encouraging me to direct a Liberty Fund colloquium on Roger Sherman and for the insights offered by its participants. Although I disagree with some of his interpretations, I have found Christopher Collier's work on Connecticut, generally, and his biography of Sherman, specifically, to be immensely useful. As well, I am profoundly grateful for the aid of archivists and librarians at the Library of Congress, Connecticut State Library, Yale University, New Haven Colonial Society, Connecticut Historical Society, Massachusetts Historical Society, and the Historical Society of Pennsylvania. Finally, I am obligated to the Yale University Art Gallery for permission to reproduce the portrait of Roger Sherman and The Boston Athanaeum for permission to reproduce the political cartoon "An Attempt to Land a Bishop in America."

Roger Sherman and the Creation
of the American Republic

I

The Old Puritan and a New Nation

ROGER SHERMAN WAS the only founder to help draft and sign the Declaration and Resolves (1774), the Articles of Association (1774), the Declaration of Independence (1776), the Articles of Confederation (1777, 1778), and the Constitution (1787). He served longer in the Continental and Confederation Congresses than all but four men, and he was regularly appointed to key committees, including those charged with drafting the Declaration of Independence and the Articles of Confederation. At the Constitutional Convention, Sherman often outmaneuvered Madison and, according to David Brian Robertson, the "political synergy between Madison and Sherman...may have been necessary for the Constitution's adoption." He was also a representative and senator in the new republic where, among other things, he played a significant role in drafting the Bill of Rights.[1]

Even as he was helping create and run a nation, Sherman served in a variety of state and local offices. These included overlapping terms as a member of Connecticut's General Assembly, judge of the Superior Court, member of the Council of Safety, and mayor of New Haven. Of particular significance, he and Richard Law revised the entire legal code of Connecticut in 1783. Although not as prolific a writer as some founders, Sherman penned essays defending hard currency, supporting the Articles of Confederation, and urging the ratification of the U.S. Constitution. His letters and a sermon contain some of the most sophisticated theological commentary by an American founder.

Sherman was held in high esteem by his contemporaries. In September of 1776, Sherman's Connecticut colleague William Williams observed to a friend:

If our Assembly rechose their Delegates, I hope They will be guided by Wisdom and Prudence. I must say that Mr. Sherman from his early acquaintance, his good sense, Judgment, Steadiness, & inflexible Integrity, has acquired much Respect & is an exceedingly valuable Member.

In 1780, Richard Henry Lee wrote to Sherman of the "very high sense that I entertain of your sound and virtuous patriotism."[2]

John Adams agreed with Williams and Lee, as indicated by his 1777 description of Sherman as "an old Puritan, as honest as an angel and as firm in the cause of American Independence as Mount Atlas." The following year he wrote to him from Europe requesting his advice about a possible alliance with France, noting that "[f]rom the long Series of arduous services, in which We have acted together, I have had Experience enough of your accurate judgment, in Cases of Difficulty, to wish very often that I could have the Benefit of it here." Forty-four years later, Adams wrote to John Sanderson that Sherman was "one of the most cordial friends which I ever had in my life. Destitute of all literary and scientific education, but such as he acquired by his own exertions, he was one of the most sensible men in the world. The clearest head and steadiest heart. It is praise enough to say that the late Chief Justice Ellsworth told me that he had made Mr. Sherman his model in his youth...[he] was one of the soundest and strongest pillars of the revolution." Patrick Henry remarked that Sherman and George Mason were "the greatest statesmen he ever knew" and that Washington, Richard Henry Lee, and Sherman were the "first men" in the Continental Congress.[3]

Thomas Jefferson, who was often at odds with both Adams and Henry, shared their admiration for Sherman, explaining to a visitor to the nation's temporary capital: "That is Mr. Sherman of Connecticut, a man who never said a foolish thing in his life." Similarly, Nathanial Macon, a Democratic-Republican from North Carolina who served with Sherman in the House of Representatives, remarked to a friend that "Roger Sherman had more common sense than any man he ever knew." Fisher Ames, a Federalist from Massachusetts in the same Congress, said that "if he happened to be out of his seat when a subject was discussed, and came in when the question was about to be taken, he always felt safe in voting as Mr. Sherman did; *for he always voted right.*" Timothy Pickering, another New England Federalist, referred to him as "a very sagacious man."[4]

Although Sherman had many strengths, oratory was not one of them. In 1774, John Adams observed that both Sherman and Eliphalet Dyer "speak often and long, but very heavily and clumsily." Similarly, Franklin Pierce of Georgia noted in his famous sketches of the delegates to the Constitutional Convention that Sherman

is awkward, un-meaning, and unaccountably strange in his manner. But in his train of thinking there is something regular, deep and comprehensive; yet the oddity of his address, the vulgarisms that accompany his public speaking, and that strange New England cant which runs through his public as well as private speaking make everything that is connected with him grotesque and laughable;-- and yet he deserves infinite praise—no Man has a better Heart or a clearer Head. If he cannot embellish he can furnish thoughts that are wise and useful.

In an age that valued eloquence, Sherman stood out as a significant leader who was rhetorically handicapped. Yet his good heart, clear head, and common sense earned him the respect of friends and enemies alike.[5]

Given this brief résumé and the high esteem in which he was held by his contemporaries, it is surprising that scholars have often neglected Sherman. Of course he is mentioned in passing in studies on the founding era, and American history and government texts often refer to him as an architect of the Connecticut Compromise. Yet few academics have considered his thoughts and actions in much depth. One exception is Christopher Collier, whose fine biography provides a rich account of Sherman's life in the context of state and national politics. Unfortunately, Collier does not carefully explore Sherman's political ideas, and he underestimates the significance of his theological convictions.[6]

Since the mid-1990s, students of the Constitutional Convention have come to recognize that Sherman was among the most effective delegates.[7] However, like Collier's work, their studies do not consider Sherman's political ideas or his religious views. Even with this recent scholarship, law professor Scott Gerber's assessment that Sherman "is arguably the most under appreciated, not to mention the most under-studied, political leader of the American Founding" remains correct. Indeed, a 2008 survey of more than one hundred historians, political scientists, and law professors ranked Sherman among the most important forgotten founders.[8]

Scholarly neglect of Sherman is particularly interesting in light of the attention academics have paid in recent years to the founders' religious beliefs.[9] A few historians have noted in passing that Sherman took his faith seriously, but none of them has explored its significance in any detail. Sydney Ahlstrom, in his magisterial *A Religious History of the American People*, points to Sherman as evidence that "theological maturity abounds" in the founding era. Similarly, Mark Noll, Nathan Hatch, and George Marsden refer to him as one of the few founders who "made lifelong efforts to base their personal lives on biblical teaching." More recently,

James H. Hutson, after noting that "many of the founders were recognized as religious specialists," comments that "[n]o one, perhaps, eclipsed Roger Sherman." Nevertheless,Sherman has been virtually ignored by scholars writing on the religious beliefs of the founders or their views of religious liberty and church-state relations.[10]

Sherman and Reformed Political Theory

In this volume, I offer the first systematic study of Sherman's contributions to the creation of the American republic that takes seriously his political theory and his theological commitments. I explore the development of his ideas over time and show how they influenced his political actions. Of course he was a practical politician, and he borrowed ideas and rhetoric from a variety of sources, but the principles that guided his civic engagement were rooted in a long and deep tradition of Calvinist reflections upon politics.

Because of his significance, Sherman's political theory and actions are worthy of study in their own right. In addition, he is an excellent representative of founders influenced by the Reformed political tradition, a tradition that dominated New England and was well represented throughout the nation. Although the days of *Locke et praeterea nihil* should be long gone, students of politics, law, and history are still too wont to attribute references to natural rights, religious liberty, consent, and the right to resist tyrannical governments to John Locke.[11] In doing so, they neglect the reality that for many founders, these and other political principles were derived from Calvinist thought—and that in each case that they were present in Reformed communities long before Locke wrote the *Second Treatise.*[12]

More than forty years ago, Alan Heimert complained that the "contribution of eighteenth-century Calvinism to the making of the American public mind has been allowed to remain unappreciated." In spite of his work, and more recent volumes such as Barry Alan Shain's *The Myth of American Individualism: The Protestant Origins of American Political Thought*, the influence of Calvinism on American political theory in the founding era is still too often neglected or relegated to footnotes.[13] An excellent example of this phenomenon is Alan Gibson's survey of the literature on America's founding, which has chapters dedicated to progressive, liberal, classical republican, Scottish, multiple traditions, and the politically correct interpretations of the founding. He mentions only in passing the possibility that Protestantism may have had an influence on America's founders.[14]

Of course it is inaccurate to say that religion has been ignored by students of the founding. There are excellent works that explore the influence of Christianity in the era, particularly with respect to the American Revolution.[15] As well, there are important books and essays that recognize Christianity as one of several strains of thought from which the founders drew.[16] Students of individual founders often neglect the significance of their subject's religious commitments, but there are notable exceptions to this rule.[17] Finally, there are excellent studies on ministers in this era, although these works seldom attempt to make clear connections between these men and the political theory of civic leaders.[18] In sum, while there are useful works on the subject, the intellectual influence of Christianity, generally, and Calvinism, more specifically, on the political theory and actions of America's founders has not been given sufficient attention. One goal of this study is to help remedy this situation by tracing the influence of Calvinist political theory on Sherman and his colleagues.

Sherman on Church and State

A major theme of *Roger Sherman and the Creation of the American Republic* is Sherman's approach to religious liberty and church-state relations. Like many of his Reformed colleagues, he had come to embrace a fairly expansive notion of religious liberty, but continued to believe that it is appropriate for civic authorities to encourage and support Christianity. However, his views have been largely ignored because of the tendency of scholars and jurists writing on these issues to focus on the views of a few elites. Inevitably, these founders are the ones most influenced by deism and the most likely to embrace something approximating contemporary notions of the separation of church and state. The two men regularly discussed, Thomas Jefferson and James Madison, are undoubtedly important, but their theological beliefs and their views on church-state relations are among the *least* representative of the founders. Other founders often covered in these studies include Benjamin Franklin, Thomas Paine, George Washington, John Adams, and Alexander Hamilton, some of whom were heterodox in their religious beliefs and who, with the exception of Washington, Adams, and Hamilton, were more likely to support something approximating modern notions of the separation of church and state.[19]

A good example of this tendency is Edwin S. Gaustad's *Faith of Our Fathers*, which explores the founders' attitudes toward religion by carefully considering only the views of Jefferson, Madison, Franklin, Adams, and Washington.[20] More recently, Steven Waldman's *Founding Faith: Providence, Politics, and the Birth of Religious Freedom in America* also focuses on these "five main characters."[21] David L. Holmes's *The Religion of the Founding Fathers* dedicates individual chapters to the same five men, with an additional chapter on James Monroe. In a revised edition, retitled *The Faiths of the Founding Fathers*, perhaps chastened by criticism of his narrow definition of the founders, Holmes includes chapters on "Wives and Daughters" and "three orthodox Christians." Popular author Brooke Allen, in *Moral Minority: Our Skeptical Founding Fathers*, likewise devotes chapters to Franklin, Washington, Adams, Jefferson, and Madison—although she includes a chapter on Alexander Hamilton as well. A similar approach is taken by Frank Lambert, Richard Hughes, Steven J. Keillor, Geoffrey Stone, and many others.[22]

These authors typically concede that not all Americans in the founding era were as "enlightened" as these famous founders, but then they proceed to attribute the views of these select elites to the entire founding generation. More orthodox founders, and those who desired closer cooperation between religion and the polity, are largely ignored. The net result of this selective approach to history is the distortion of the founders' collective views on religion, religious liberty, and church-state relations.

Such concerns might be only of academic interest except that the views of the American founders carry significant weight in contemporary political and legal discourse. To provide one concrete example, United States Supreme Court justices have made it clear that "[n]o provision of the Constitution is more closely tied to or given content by its generating history than the religious clause of the First Amendment. It is at once the refined product and the terse summation of that history." Overall, 76% of the justices who have written at least one religion-clause opinion have appealed to the founders or founding era history to shine light on the meaning of the religion clauses, and every one of the twenty-three justices who have authored more than four religion-clause opinions have done so. Yet, like the scholars mentioned earlier, justices have tended to be selective in the founders to whom they appeal. When United States Supreme Court justices have used history to interpret the First Amendment's religion clauses, they have made 112 distinct references to Jefferson but have only mentioned Sherman three times. This is particularly striking because Sherman helped draft the First Amendment whereas Jefferson was in France at the time![23]

The proclivity of justices and students of the founding era to focus on a relatively narrow range of founders when it comes to religion and church-state issues is understandable in some respects. Jefferson, Madison, Adams, Washington, Franklin, and Paine are among the more interesting founders, and some of them—particularly Jefferson and Madison—are arguably so influential as to justify detailed study and debate. Moreover, these founders all left a tremendous paper trail with which scholars can work. If one is interested specifically in the seeds of modern separationism or in a very eloquent discussion of these issues, it may make sense to focus on them. However, these men are not representative of the founders as a whole.[24]

Sherman's theological views are different from the founders mentioned above, and he favored closer cooperation between church and state than Jefferson, Madison, Franklin, and Paine. Although all of these individuals embraced religious liberty, unlike the few founders influenced significantly by Enlightenment thought, Sherman's commitment to religious liberty was informed by his Reformed faith. If scholars and jurists are really interested in "the founders'" approach to these subjects, surely Sherman's views, along with those of his fellow Calvinists, should be taken into account.

Plan of the Book

Studying American political theory in the founding era is difficult because most founders were so busy *doing* things that they rarely wrote about their political ideas in a systematic manner. Works such as Jefferson's *Notes on Virginia*, John Adams's *Thoughts on Government*, James Wilson's *Lectures on Law*, and Publius's *The Federalist Papers* are partial exceptions to this rule, but even these texts had practical purposes and are hardly systematic treatments of the basic issues of political philosophy. Indeed, if we consider political *philosophy* to be the most systematic and abstract reflection upon perennial questions concerning politics, it is probably inaccurate to describe any of the founders as political philosophers. However, many founders developed well-formed and interconnected political ideas, so it is reasonable to consider at least some of them to be political theorists.[25]

In this book, I explore Sherman's political ideas and actions, with particular focus on his contributions to the founding of the American republic. Although tracing intellectual influence is always difficult, I argue his political theory is best understood in light of Reformed political thought. Sherman was interested in abstract theological, moral, and political questions, but he spent little time thinking about metaphysics and epistemology, so readers interested in founders who wrote on these subjects should look elsewhere (perhaps John Witherspoon or James Wilson). Like most founders, he did not write political treatises, so it is necessary to piece together his political ideas by carefully considering his essays, letters, speeches, and actions.

I begin *Roger Sherman and the Creation of the American Republic* by providing an overview of the Calvinist world into which Sherman was born and raised. Because some readers may be unfamiliar with Reformed political theory, I offer a brief introduction to this tradition and sketch its transmission from Europe to America. I then turn to Sherman and demonstrate, contrary to assertions by most scholars who have studied him, that he was a serious Calvinist.

This book is not a biography, but I generally approach Sherman in a chronological fashion and discuss the development of his ideas over time. In chapter 3, I consider his early state service and his contributions to America's movement toward independence. I show that he and many of his Reformed colleagues shared similar concerns—concerns that are often overlooked by scholars who concentrate on founders like Jefferson and Paine. Chapter 4 focuses on Sherman's work in the Continental Congress, particularly his role in drafting and defending the Articles of Confederation. The chapter also explores his revision of Connecticut's statutes, especially those provisions related to slavery and religion.

In chapter 5, I consider in detail Sherman's contributions at the Federal Convention of 1787. I highlight his views on the proper scope of the federal government, the relationship between the national and state governments, the extent to which the powers of national institutions should be separated, and the respective roles of each institution. I also explore his defense of the proposed Constitution in the ratification debates. The penultimate chapter examines Sherman's actions as a member of Congress, particularly with respect to the issues heatedly debated earlier in the Constitutional Convention. As well, I discuss his contributions to the creation of the Bill of Rights, especially the religion clauses of the First Amendment. I conclude the book by reflecting on the extent to which Sherman represents other founders and whether his ideas are relevant today.

A significant theme of this study is that the political theory of many founders is best understood in light of Calvinist political thought. To support this argument, I focus on Sherman's political ideas and actions, and I attempt to show that he is representative of many of his colleagues—men such as Samuel Adams, Isaac Backus, Abraham Baldwin, Elias Boudinot, Timothy Dwight, Eliphalet Dyer, Oliver Ellsworth, Matthew Griswold, John Hancock, Benjamin Huntington, Samuel Huntington, Richard Law, Joseph Montgomery, William Paterson, Tapping Reeve, Jesse Root, Ezra Stiles, Richard Stockton, John Treadwell, Jonathan Trumbull, William Williams, John Witherspoon, and Oliver Wolcott. Of course some of these men were better Calvinists than others, and all were influenced by other ideologies and political, legal, and economic interests. My argument regarding the influence of the Reformed political tradition is strongest for Sherman, strong with respect to his colleagues from New England, but primarily suggestive regarding Calvinists in other regions and founders who were not members of Reformed churches but who may have been influenced by the tradition in other ways. If other scholars find my analysis convincing, I hope this book will encourage additional work on the influence of the Reformed tradition in the American founding.

A Life in Brief

Because many readers of this volume are likely unfamiliar with Sherman, a brief overview of his life may be of service. Sherman was born in Massachusetts in 1721 to Mehetabel and William Sherman. William was a farmer and cobbler, and like most of his fellow citizens he was Congregationalist. William died in 1741, and shortly thereafter Roger moved to New Milford, Connecticut, where he worked as a cobbler, surveyor, and store owner. Sherman never went to college, but he was a voracious reader. He taught himself advanced mathematics and, in 1750, he began publishing a popular almanac that was issued annually or biannually until 1761. Sherman later studied law and was admitted to the Litchfield bar in 1754. Under the guidance of Roger and his older brother, the two younger Sherman brothers, Nathaniel and Josiah, attended the College of New Jersey (Princeton), from which they graduated in 1753 and 1754 respectively. They both became Congregational ministers.[26]

As Sherman prospered professionally, he was selected for a variety of local offices and was elected to several six-month terms in the lower house of Connecticut's General Assembly. In 1760, after the death of his first wife (with whom he had seven children), Sherman moved to New Haven. There he opened a store next to Yale College and sold general merchandise, provisions, and books. Sherman married Rebecca Prescott three years later, and the two had eight children. Once again he was elected to local offices and to the lower house of the General Assembly. In 1766, Connecticut voters chose him to be one of the twelve members of the upper house, or Council of Assistants. Traditionally, four assistants were selected by the General Assembly to serve with the deputy governor as judges on Connecticut's Superior Court. Sherman was appointed to this court in 1766, and he held both offices until 1785, when he resigned as an assistant to retain his position as a judge as a result of a 1784 law that prohibited individuals from holding both offices. He remained a Superior Court judge until he became a member of the U.S. House of Representatives in 1789.

Beginning in 1774, Sherman accepted multiple appointments to the Continental Congress. Collectively, he served 1,543 days in that body, and he helped draft and signed virtually every significant document produced by it (the primary exception being the Northwest Ordinance).[27] He served on many committees, including those charged with drafting the Declaration of Independence and the Articles of Confederation. In 1783, Sherman and the aptly named Richard Law accepted the task of revising *all* of Connecticut's statutes.[28] Four years later he was appointed to the Federal Constitutional Convention. In spite of his age, Sherman was an active member, speaking more often than all but three delegates and serving as the driving force behind the Connecticut Compromise. He was also a leader in Connecticut's ratification convention, and he wrote six "Letters" for the *New Haven Gazette* responding to objections from anti-Federalists.[29]

Under the new Constitution, Sherman was elected first to the House of Representatives (1789–1791) and then appointed to the U.S. Senate to fill the unexpired term of William Samuel Johnson. In Congress, he played important roles in debates over the Bill of Rights, the assumption of state debts, and the creation of a national bank. Sherman served in the Senate until his death on July 23, 1793. His life is summed up well by Yale President Timothy Dwight:

> Mr. Sherman possessed a powerful mind; and habits of industry, which no difficulties could discourage, and no toil impair. In early life he began to apply himself, with inextinguishable zeal, to the

acquisition of knowledge. In this pursuit, although he was always actively engaged in business, he spent more hours than most of those, who are professedly students. In his progress he became extensively acquainted with Mathematical science, with Natural philosophy, with Moral and Metaphysical philosophy, with History, Logic and Theology. As a lawyer, and a statesman, he was eminent. The late Judge Ingersoll, who has been already mentioned, once observed to me, that, in his opinion, the views which Mr. Sherman formed of political subjects, were more profound, just, and comprehensive, than those of almost any other man, with whom he had been acquainted on this continent. His mind was remarkably clear and penetrating; and, more than almost any other man, looked from the beginning of a subject to the end. Nothing satisfied him but proof; or where that was impossible, the predominant probability which equally controls the conduct of a wise man. He had no fashionable opinions, and could never be persuaded to swim with the tide. Independent of every thing but argument, he judged for himself; and rarely failed to convince others, that he judged right.

As a man, as a patriot, and as a Christian, Mr. Sherman left behind him an unspotted name. Profoundly versed in Theology, he held firmly to the doctrines of the Reformation. Few men understood them so well; and few were equally able to defend them. What he believed, he practiced. It can excite no wonder, therefore, that he died with bright hopes of a glorious immortality.[30]

2

Reformed Political Theory in the American Founding

IN *ORIGINAL MEANINGS*, Jack Rakove observes that the "larger intellectual world within which the Constitution is often located—the Enlightened world of Locke and Montesquieu, Hume and Blackstone, plain whigs and real whigs, common lawyers and Continental jurists—has been the subject of extensive analysis." It is noteworthy that he does not mention religion in this context. Historians are better than political scientists and law professors at recognizing that faith mattered to many Americans in the founding era, but even they have a tendency to treat America's founders as deists who embraced a rationalist approach to politics and who produced secular documents such as the Declaration of Independence, Constitution, and Bill of Rights. Although there are important exceptions, scholars are still prone to neglect the significant influence of Christianity, generally, and the Reformed tradition, specifically, on many of America's founders.[1]

One reason Calvinism is overlooked is that students of the founding often view the era through the eyes of southern Anglican gentlemen: Thomas Jefferson, James Madison, and George Washington; men born outside America: Alexander Hamilton and Thomas Paine; and the cosmopolitan Benjamin Franklin, who lived most of the last thirty-five years of his life in Europe. As adults, Franklin and Hamilton were nominal Anglicans, which means five of the seven famous founders (71%) were Episcopalians (compared to 16% of all Americans in that era). The only member of a Congregational or Presbyterian church among the famous founders is John Adams, but like a few of his fellow Congregationalists (primarily in and around Boston) he was moving rapidly toward Unitarianism. These men were brilliant and influential, but they are not representative of the many American leaders who were firmly rooted in the Reformed tradition.[2]

Even with respect to Sherman, scholars have not paid sufficient attention to the significance of his faith. In some instances, this neglect is a result of the questions scholars bring to their subjects. However, because of the Reformed tradition's influence in eighteenth-century America (dominant in New England and significant elsewhere), scholars like John Murrin who contend that "by virtually any standard of doctrinal orthodoxy" hardly any of the founders were orthodox, and that "[q]uite possibly not a single delegate [to the Constitutional Convention] accepted Calvinist orthodoxy on original sin" miss an important piece of the story.[3]

Reformed Political Theory

Reformed political theory is a branch of Christian political theory, so it is not surprising to find significant overlap between how Calvinists and other Christians view politics. General Christian propositions with implications for politics include the ideas that humans are created in the image of God; that men and women are sinful; and that God has established different institutions for various purposes, notably, the family, church, and state. Virtually all Christian political thinkers recognize that civil governments and civil magistrates are ordained by God and that there is a biblical obligation to obey them, but that the obligation is not absolute. Although generalizations are always dangerous, it is fair to say that between Constantine and the Protestant Reformation many Christians who thought about politics assumed that monarchy was the ideal form of government, saw rulers as playing an important role in promoting the common good, and paid little attention to individual rights. While they believed that Christians should refuse to obey an unjust law, virtually none of them contended that the people had a right to revolt against unjust rulers.[4]

Reformed political theory broke in significant ways from previous Christian views. Of course Reformed thinkers borrowed from earlier thinkers, and the tradition developed over time. However, in the same way that scholars are comfortable speaking of a "liberal tradition" that includes John Locke, John Stuart Mill, John Rawls, and, according to numerous scholars, most of the founders, so too is it possible to speak of a Reformed tradition that includes John Calvin, Theodore Beza, John Knox, Samuel Rutherford, John Winthrop, Thomas Hooker, and Roger Sherman.[5] Because some readers, even sophisticated students of the American founding, may be unfamiliar with this tradition, I offer a brief introduction in this chapter. Obviously, a few pages on a tradition that spans centuries and involves a contentious and wordy people cannot do it justice, but it allows me to introduce ideas that had a significant impact in the era.

The Protestant Reformation was a wide-ranging movement opposed to perceived abuses by the Roman Catholic Church. It may be conveniently dated to 1517, when Martin Luther (1483–1546) nailed his Ninety-Five Theses to the Wittenberg castle church door. For our purposes, the work of John Calvin (1509–64), whose followers comprise what is considered to be the Reformed tradition, is of particular interest. Calvin was born in France but lived most of his adult life in Geneva, Switzerland, which he helped govern between 1536–1538 and 1541–1564. In 1536 he published the first edition of his *Institutes of the Christian Religion*, a volume that he revised several times until its final 1559 edition. The work, along with his voluminous biblical commentaries, has proven enormously influential among his followers, who were represented most prominently in America by the Puritans.[6]

Calvin's work echoed the great battle cries of the Reformation such as *sola fide* and *sola scriptura*, and it reinforced the seminal notion of the priesthood of all believers. Reformers rejected the ideas that the church and its priests were necessary intermediaries between common persons and God, and that the church as an institution possessed the authority to speak for Him. Individuals were told that they were responsible for their relationship with God, and that His will for them is most clearly revealed in the holy scriptures. This belief led to a heavy emphasis on literacy and a commitment to translating and printing the Bible in the vernacular.[7] These views and practices helped undermine existing hierarchies and paved the way for the growth of self-government. Although ecclesiastical structures varied, Reformed churches leaned heavily toward democratic forms of government; nowhere was this truer than among the Calvinists who immigrated to America. New England Calvinists debated the relative merits of pure congregationalism versus more presbyterian forms of church governance, but under both models church members played critical roles in governing themselves.[8]

Particularly significant within the Reformed tradition is the insistence that God is sovereign over all of creation. Reformers attempted to apply their faith to all elements of life, including are as such as raising children, conducting business, and participating in politics. This "sanctification" of every part of human existence contributed to the tremendous economic and social development that marked most Protestant countries.[9] From their earliest days in power, Calvinists were concerned with creating Christian political institutions and practices. Yet they were not theocrats, and they even expanded distinctions between church and state. Reformers believed that both institutions were divinely mandated and that the two should work closely together to create a Christian society. Because only God is sovereign, and because of their commitment to the doctrine of total depravity, they insisted that both ecclesiastical and civil authority be limited. As well, they remained committed to the traditional Christian idea that governments should promote the common good.[10]

Calvinist movements sprang up throughout Europe and were particularly successful in Switzerland, Holland, Scotland, and England. In these and other countries—notably France, where the Huguenots were a persecuted minority—they faced hostile regimes. Although the Reformers initially advocated passive obedience, they rapidly developed a resistance ideology unlike anything ever seen on a widespread level in Christendom. Calvin, one of the most politically conservative of the Reformers, contended that in some cases inferior magistrates might resist an ungodly ruler.[11] However, Reformers such as John Knox (1505–72), George Buchanan (1506–82), and Samuel Rutherford (1600–1661) of Scotland, Theodore Beza (1519–1605) of France and Switzerland, David Pareus (1548–1622) of Germany, and Christopher Goodman (1520–1603) and John Ponet (1516–1556) of England argued that inferior magistrates must resist unjust rulers and even permitted or *required* citizens to do so.[12]

Among the most famous pieces of resistance literature is Stephanus-Junius Brutus's *Vindiciae, Contra Tyrannos* (1579). Written by a Huguenot, probably Philippe du Plessis Mornay (1549–1623) or Hubert Languet (1518–1581), the *Vindiciae* contends that men originally exist in a state of natural liberty and that "the natural law [*ius Naturale*] teaches us to preserve and protect our life and liberty—without which life is scarcely life at all—against all force and injustice." Humans are "free by nature, impatient of servitude," and they create governments to promote the common good. Legitimate rulers are established only by virtue of a twofold covenant (*duplex foedus*). The first of these, between God, king, and people, commits the people and ruler to obey God. If either the king or the people turn from God and so violate this covenant, it is void. The second covenant, which is between the ruler and the people, stipulates that the consent of the people is necessary for government to be legitimate. The people promise to obey the king as long as he rules justly. Rulers who are illegitimate, negligent, unjust, or tyrannical break this covenant and forfeit their right to rule. When the people resist ungodly or unjust rulers, they are "procuring that which is their natural right [*droit naturel*]."[13]

For Reformers, families, churches, and civil governments should be grounded in agreements between humans that are witnessed and enforced by God. Of course, they did not invent covenants, but they significantly emphasized their use and significance, particularly with respect to civil and ecclesiastical authorities. Moreover, as represented well by Brutus's first covenant, they believed that God makes covenants with peoples, much as He did with the ancient Jews. These covenanted people then have an important role to play in God's plan to bring about His kingdom on earth. Failure to keep these covenants, clergy routinely warned in sermons known as jeremiads, would result in divine punishment. The rights and responsibilities associated with such covenants would have an important influence in America.[14]

One might object that nothing in the preceding section is distinctive to the Reformed tradition. Indeed, Quentin Skinner has argued that Protestant resistance literature is not "specifically Calvinist at all" but that these ideas are borrowed from Scholastic authors.[15] As a matter of the genealogy of ideas this may be the case, but what is critical for the purposes of this book is that these ideas were most extensively developed, defended, and applied within the Reformed tradition. Within a generation of Calvin, virtually every Reformed civil and ecclesiastical leader was convinced that the Bible taught that governments should be limited, that they should be based on the consent of the governed, that rulers should promote the common good and the Christian faith, and that unjust or ungodly rulers should be resisted or even overthrown. These ideas are not unique to Calvinists, but the Reformed tradition became a major means by which they became a part of American political culture.[16]

Reformed Political Theory in Early New England

Protestantism's progress began inauspiciously in England when Henry VIII severed ties with Rome and created the Church of England in 1534. However, this institution remained too "popish" for many Calvinists, who became known as Puritans for their desire to completely purify this church. Some Separatists eventually gave up hope for reformation of the English church and, facing increasing persecution in their homeland, fled to Holland in 1608 and then to America in 1620. Before they disembarked from the *Mayflower*, they created a covenant that represents important aspects of early Puritan political thought. This agreement, known today as the Mayflower Compact, committed the people and the rulers to "the Glory of God, and the Advancement of the Christian Faith, and the Honour of our King and Country." Its legitimacy stemmed from the consent of the forty-one men heading households on the *Mayflower*, and it required rulers to govern justly.[17]

The Mayflower Compact is the most famous early civil covenant made in America, but it is not unique. As David A. Weir illustrates in his exhaustively researched book, *Early New England: A Covenanted Society*, hundreds of ecclesiastical and civil covenants were created whereby people joined together before the eyes of God to pursue specific ends ultimately aimed at glorifying God.[18] Each of these covenants reinforced the idea that governments are legitimate and binding because they were established by the consent of the governed. This view is reflected well by Henry Wolcott's notes of a 1638 election sermon by one of Connecticut's founders, Thomas Hooker:

> Doctrine. I. That the choice of public magistrates belongs unto the people by God's own allowance.
>
> II. The privilege of election, which belongs to the people, therefore must not be exercised according to their humors, but according to the blessed will and law of God.
>
> III. They who have the power to appoint officers and magistrates, it is in their power also to set the bounds and limitations of power and place unto which they call them.
>
> Reasons. 1. Because the foundation of authority is laid, firstly, in the free consent of the people.[19]

Not only did the people consent to the original form of government, but most men could also participate in town meetings and freemen could be elected representatives of the General Court. Of course there was an expectation that citizens would elect and defer to godly, talented magistrates. John Winthrop famously lectured Massachusetts Bay's General Court on this point in 1645, and thirty-five years later Connecticut's Samuel Willis reiterated the sentiment with a greater emphasis on class when he declared that "[t]he making of rulers of the lower sort of people will issue in contempt, let their opinion be what it will." Such statements have led some scholars to overemphasize the importance of social class in the era, but others, such as Joy and Robert Gilsdorf, have persuasively argued that eighteenth-century Connecticut citizens were more concerned with competence (and, I would add, godliness) than social standing or wealth. Moreover, the colonies clearly grew more democratic in the seventeenth and eighteenth centuries, and Connecticut and Rhode Island were always the most democratic colonies in North America.[20]

Early Puritan societies are often described as theocracies, and their founders and leaders wanted to create thoroughly Christian social and political institutions. This mission is illustrated well by the 1672 declaration by the Connecticut General Court: "We have endeavoured not only to ground our capital laws upon the Word of God, but also all other laws upon the justice and equity held forth in that Word, which is a most perfect rule." However, within these societies the institutions of church and state were kept separate and distinct. In early Massachusetts, clergy could not hold political offices or otherwise serve in a civil capacity (this restriction was eventually lifted), and the Massachusetts Body of Liberties (1641) specifically banned European practices such as ecclesiastical courts and made it clear that sanctions such as excommunication have no impact upon holding civil office. Civil magistrates were to be "nursing fathers" to the church (a phrase taken from Isaiah 49:23), by creating a society that encouraged true Christianity. Throughout New England, the Congregational church was supported financially through taxation, there were religious tests for office holders, and statutes required church attendance and punished vice. Protestant dissenters in the region were tolerated if they remained quiet and did not disturb the public order. However, vocal and disorderly dissenters such as the Quakers and perceived troublemakers including Roger Williams (1636) and Anne Hutchinson (1638) were banned, exiled, or, on rare occasions, hanged.[21]

The Puritan conviction that rulers should promote true religion might suggest a powerful state, but this possibility was tempered by the view that civil power should be strictly limited. Fear of arbitrary power exercised by fallen human actors led the Puritans to devise and adopt a variety of democratic institution and checks on rulers. Among the most significant innovations was the 1641 Massachusetts Body of Liberties. These statutes contained many protections later found in the American Bill of Rights, including prohibitions against double jeopardy, torture, and "in-humane Barbarous or cruell" bodily punishments. Seven years later these laws were revised and published as *The Book of the General Lawes and Liberties Concerning the Inhabitants of Massachusetts*. This was one of the first times a legal code had ever been printed in the western world—a practice that made it possible to distribute the laws more widely than if they were copied by hand.[22]

More broadly, Puritans believed the power of the state was also constrained by what John Davenport called in 1669 the "Law of Nature" which is "God's law."[23] Rulers who violate natural law may legitimately be resisted. A striking expression of this idea is found in a 1678 sermon by Massachusetts's Samuel Nowell entitled "Abraham in Arms," where he contended that the "Law of nature . . . teachth men self-preservation." Moreover, he proclaimed that there "is such a thing as Liberty and Property given to us, both by the Laws of God & Men, when these are invaded, we may defend our selves."[24] Puritans were less likely to make natural rights arguments than later Calvinists, but the essential elements for such arguments were all present in earlier Reformed political theory.[25]

Long before the War for Independence, Reformed Americans had experience resisting tyrannical political power. New England Puritans supported Parliament against abuses of the British Crown during the English Civil War, and John Cotton even preached a sermon defending the execution of Charles I. After the Restoration, England attempted to "improve" the governance of New England by combining all of the colonies into a single entity know as the Dominion of New England (1686–89). The first governor of the new entity, Sir Edmund Andros, immediately made himself unpopular by demanding that a Congregational meeting house in Boston be made available for Anglican services and by restricting town meetings. On April 18, 1689, shortly after news of the Glorious Revolution reached Boston, colonial leaders arrested Andros and returned him to England for trial. The new monarchs and Lords of Trade wisely abandoned the Dominion, but the new Massachusetts charter did require toleration of other Protestants.[26]

Like their descendants, Puritans were concerned with "liberty," but it is critical to recognize that they never understood the concept to include the excessively individualistic idea that men and women are free to do anything except physically harm others. They distinguished between liberty and personal license. Puritans were primarily interested with freedom from sin, but they also understood liberty as the ability of a people to govern themselves and to do what God requires of them. They came closest to embracing modern notions of liberty with respect to freedom of conscience, but even here religiously motivated *actions* judged to be disruptive by the community could still be restricted. As Barry Alan Shain has demonstrated, this constrained understanding of liberty remained dominant in America until well into the eighteenth century.[27]

David D. Hall argues in *A Reforming People: Puritanism and the Transformation of Public Life in New England* that Calvinists in seventeenth-century New England had greater freedom to reform ecclesiastical and civil governments than they did elsewhere. He makes a persuasive case that they created political institutions that were far more democratic than any the world had ever seen and that they strictly limited civic leaders by law. Notably, he points out that these Calvinists had an "animus against 'tyranny' and 'arbitrary' power that pervaded virtually every sermon and political statement." Of course, Puritan New England was hardly a modern, liberal democracy, but many of the ideas scholars associate with liberalism were prevalent there. To be sure, civic authorities continued to play an important role in supporting Christianity and Christian morality, but in that era, they were hardly alone in doing so.[28]

Few scholars question the influence of the Reformed tradition on the early Puritans, but some have argued it declined rapidly.[29] Clearly the way New England colonists thought about society and politics changed in response to increased prosperity and events like the English Civil War, the Restoration, the Glorious Revolution, the Great Awakening, and the Seven Years' War. In spite of a variety of significant changes, leaders in the Reformed tradition remained committed to the political principles discussed above, and many became more convinced that America had a special role to play God's advancing kingdom.[30] The Great Awakening, it is true, introduced unwanted seeds of discord into Congregational and Presbyterian churches, but in many cases, advocates of the Awakening were more concerned about orthodoxy and piety than those who opposed it. Moreover, well into the eighteenth century, Reformed ministers in New England remained the best educated and the most influential members of their communities. Their influence began to decline toward the end of the century, and there were a few ministers who were beginning to lean in the direction of Unitarianism. However, even among these ministers—to speak nothing of their more orthodox brothers—there was a firm commitment to Reformed political theory.[31]

What about John Locke?

Tracing intellectual influence is difficult, and it is certainly possible that even if late eighteenth-century Calvinists remained committed to their faith that their political views were shaped by other traditions. A variety of political ideas were available to the founders, but it does not follow that all ideas were equally influential. An important argument of this volume is that Sherman and other Calvinists in the era were heavily influenced by the Reformed political tradition. Yet many scholars argue that the founders were motivated by a version of John Locke's political philosophy that is at odds with this tradition.

In his 1922 book on the Declaration of Independence, Carl L. Becker famously remarked that most revolutionary era Americans "had absorbed Locke's works as a kind of political gospel." Almost seventy years later, Isaac Kramnick echoed Becker's conclusion that "Locke lurks behind its [the Declaration's] every phrase." More recently, Scott Gerber has argued that the primary purpose of the U.S. Constitution is to protect a Lockean understanding of natural rights, and Barbara McGraw has asserted that "Lockean fundamentals...shaped the conscience of the American founders" with respect to the role of religion in public life. Numerous scholars, writers, and activists have made similar arguments.[32]

In many instance, academics making claims about Locke's influence simply attribute any reference by the founders to individual rights, government by consent, and the right to resist tyrannical authority to Locke, apparently unaware that Reformed thinkers had been making similar arguments long before Locke wrote his *Second Treatise*. In doing so, they ignore the possibility that Locke's political philosophy is best understood as a logical extension of Protestant resistance literature rather than as a radical departure from it. Obviously, if this interpretation is correct (and I am very sympathetic to it), any amount of influence Locke had on Reformed founders would be unproblematic for the thesis of this book. Locke's influence would be cooperative with the influence of the Reformed tradition rather than competing with it.[33]

However, a number of prominent scholars have argued that Locke is a secular political thinker who grounded his theory of politics on the natural rights of individuals.[34] In the context of the American founding, for instance, Michael Zuckert has contended that key documents like the Declaration of Independence must be understood in light of this secularized Lockean liberalism. In *The Natural Rights Republic*, he supports this position by showing that Jefferson's political ideas were different from those held by the Puritans. In doing so, he virtually ignores the development consent, natural rights, religious toleration, and resistance within the Reformed tradition.[35] As well, it is not self-evident that the Declaration of Independence should be understood in light of Jefferson's views, particularly as Jefferson claimed that he was "[n]ot to find out new principles, or new arguments" but that all "its authority rests on the harmonizing sentiments of the day."[36]

Zuckert may be correct in his observation that Jefferson, in the Declaration, traced "rights to the creator, that is, nature." However, there is little reason to think that Sherman or other Reformed signers of the Declaration, such as Josiah Bartlett, William Whipple, Matthew Thornton, John Hancock, Samuel Adams, John Adams, Robert Treat Paine, William Ellery, William Floyd, Philip Livingston, Richard Stockton, John Witherspoon, John Hart, Abraham Clark, James Smith, James Wilson, Thomas McKean, and Lyman Hall, thought the Declaration's "Creator" was anything other than the God of Abraham, Isaac, and Jacob.[37] And they certainly did not think they were signing a document that "mandates" a "secular politics" or affirms that "governments exists for the sake of securing rights and only for that." As Supreme Court Justice Antonin Scalia remarked in a different context, the Constitution cannot be interpreted according to "secret or technical meanings that would not have been known to ordinary citizens in the founding generation."[38]

Assuming for the sake of argument that there is a significant difference between Reformed political theory and Locke's political ideas, the question remains, how influential was Locke in early America? With very few exceptions, Locke's works were not available in America until 1714, when bulky three-volume editions of his writings began appearing in university libraries. Even then, American elites were primarily interested in his *Essay on Human Understanding*, and there is no evidence that Locke's *Second Treatise* was a part of any college curriculum until the War for Independence.[39] The first American edition of one of Locke's works was published by the senior class at Yale in 1742. This group of seventeen men, ten of whom went on to become ministers in Reformed churches, apparently hoped publication of *A Letter Concerning Toleration* would encourage Connecticut's General Assembly to be more accepting of New Light Calvinists (who were more theologically conservative than the Old Lights). This essay was used with some regularity by dissenters seeking greater religious liberty.[40]

By the 1760s and 1770s, American patriots cited Locke with some regularity to support American resistance to Great Britain. Yet, as Donald S. Lutz has shown, the Bible was referenced far more often than Locke's works—indeed, more often than the works of all Enlightenment thinkers combined (34% to 22%). Moreover, only 2.9% of the citations to individual authors between 1760–1805 were to Locke (by contrast, 8.3% were to

Montesquieu). That Americans' interest in Locke was not boundless is suggested as well by the facts that the *Second Treatise* was not published in America until 1773 and that it was not republished in the United States until 1937.[41]

If Locke's works were late to arrive on America's shores, the Bible was virtually omnipresent from the first days of the Puritan settlements. As Daniel L. Dreisbach has demonstrated, the Bible retained its cultural dominance well into the founding era. Many founders continued to look to it for moral guidance, and virtually all of them referenced it regularly in their public and private speeches and writings. This reality is often overlooked because founders assumed a familiarity with scripture and so did not include textual citations. As Benjamin Franklin explained to Samuel Cooper in 1781:

> It was not necessary in New England, where every body reads the Bible, and is acquainted with Scripture phrases, that you should note the texts from which you took them; but I have observed in England as well as in France, that verses and expressions taken from the sacred writings, and not known to be such, appear very strange and awkward to some readers; and I shall therefore in my edition take the liberty of marking the quoted texts in the margin.[42]

In addition to the Bible, books containing the essential elements of Reformed political thought were accessible to political and ecclesiastical elites from the colonies' inception. A thorough and systematic study of which Reformed books were available at what time has yet to be attempted, but Herbert D. Foster has documented the availability of classic texts by John Calvin, John Knox, Theodore Beza, Stephanus Junius Brutus, Peter Martyr, and others.[43] The respect early Puritan leaders had for their European predecessors is reflected well by John Cotton's (1585–1652) statement that "I have read the fathers and the school-men, and Calvin too; but I find that he that has Calvin has them all." Yet, as Perry Miller pointed out, "[i]f we were to measure by the number of times a writer is cited and the degrees of familiarity shown with his works, Beza exerted more influence than Calvin, and David Pareus still more than Beza."[44] This is significant for our purposes because the latter two thinkers had significantly more radical theories of resistance than did John Calvin.

Moving to the founding era, political leaders generally, but particularly those from New England, often owned or referred to Reformed literature.

It is not surprising that Princeton President John Witherspoon owned Calvin's *Institutes*, Beza's *Rights of Magistrates* (1757), and Buchanan's *The Law of Scottish Kingship* (1579). More intriguing is that the Unitarian-leaning John Adams declared that John Poynet's *Short Treatise on Politike Power* (1556) contains "all the essential principles of liberty, which were afterwards dilated on by Sidney and Locke." He also noted the significance of *Vindiciae Contra Tyrannos*.[45] Similarly, late in life, Adams wrote, "I love and revere the memories of Huss Wickliff Luther Calvin Zwinglius Melancton and all the other reformers how muchsoever I may differ from them all in many theological metaphysical & philosophical points. As you justly observe, without their great exertions & severe sufferings, the USA had never existed."[46]

Unlike his cousin John but like Roger Sherman, Samuel Adams was a latter-day Puritan. In 1740, well before the *Second Treatise* was popular in America, he returned to Harvard to defend the thesis that "it is lawful to resist the Supreme Magistrate, if the Commonwealth cannot be otherwise preserved" in order to receive his master's degree. Twenty-eight years later, he wrote three essays for the *Boston Gazette* under the pseudonym of "a Puritan." In them, he urged Americans to guard their rights carefully and to beware of British attempts to appoint a Bishop for America lest the nation be subjected to "Popery." The following year, the famous political cartoon "An Attempt to Land a Bishop in America" was published in *The Political Register*. It represented a bishop who is not allowed to disembark in America because of a rioting mob wielding works by Locke and Sidney. Notably, the bishop is about to be struck in the head by a copy of *Calvin's Works*, which had apparently been thrown at him by a member of the mob (see figure 2.1). In 1766, George Buchanan's *De Jure Regni: Or the Due Right of Government* was reprinted in Philadelphia—seven years before the *Second Treatise* was printed in America. Finally, at the Constitutional Convention, Luther Martin (who, in spite of his name, was hardly an exemplar of the Protestant Reformation), read passages from "Locke & Vattel, and also Rutherford [presumably *Lex, Rex*]" to show that states, like people, are equal. There is no shortage of evidence that civic leaders in the founding era were aware of Reformed political thinkers and their major doctrines.[47]

As suggested by the examples in the preceding paragraph, by the 1760s, American leaders were familiar with Locke, but few thought his political philosophy was at odds with traditional Christian or Calvinist political ideas. This is indicated by the willingness of Reformed clergy

FIGURE 2.1 "An Attempt to Land a Bishop in America." *Political Register,* September 1768. Boston Athenaeum.

to appeal to him as an authority in sermons and pamphlets. For example, in his 1776 election day sermon to the Connecticut General Assembly, Judah Champion urged state leaders to resist British oppression. The vast majority of his sermon relied on biblical and theological arguments, such as when he contended that "liberty and freedom" belong "to us, not merely as men, originally created in God's image, holding a distinguished rank in his creation, but also as christians redeemed by the Blood of CHRIST." Yet this indisputably orthodox Congregationalist did not hesitate to cite Locke's *Second Treatise* on the origin of government.[48]

Michael Zuckert suggests that the clergy's use of Locke is evidence of "a Lockean conquest, or at least assimilation, of Puritan political thought."[49] However, if one recognizes that Calvinists had long advocated political ideas similar to those later articulated by Locke, and that most New England ministers were by any measure orthodox Christians, it is more plausible to conclude that these ministers viewed Locke as an ally to be cited to defend concepts well within the bounds of Reformed Christianity. Most Reformed ministers in this era were well-educated and sensitive (perhaps too sensitive) to any hint of theological heterodoxy.[50] If Lockean and Reformed political theories are really as different as Zuckert suggests, is it not odd that virtually no Reformed minister objected to the use of Locke by his fellow Calvinists?[51]

By comparing Lockean and Reformed political theories, I do not mean to suggest that these are the only intellectual traditions present in the founding era. I make the comparison because a secularized version of Locke's ideas is most obviously at odds with Reformed political theory. Many aspects of Whig, classical republican, and Scottish Enlightenment thought, to name just three other widely discussed intellectual influences on the founders, seem clearly informed by or compatible with Reformed thought.[52] For instance, Robert Middlekauff notes that "Radical Whig perceptions of politics attracted widespread support in America because they revived the traditional concerns of a Protestant culture that had always verged on Puritanism."[53] Similarly, many concerns often attributed to the classical republican tradition, such as fear of corruption and concentrated powers and the belief that the state should promote virtue, seem to be more readily explained by Christian commitments.[54] Many founders read, learned from, and admired the classics, but this is a far cry from embracing their values and ideas.[55] And, of course, they were motivated, to one degree or another, by political, economic, and other interests.

This is not the place to provide a critique of the many works arguing for different intellectual influences on America's founders. My central concern here is to provide a sketch of an intellectual tradition that has been too often ignored by students of American political thought. If nothing else, I hope to have shown that simplistically assigning all references to natural rights, consent, limited government, and a right to rebel to the influence of John Locke is problematic. Given the political culture of eighteenth-century New England, there is a strong prima facie case that such appeals were based on Reformed political theory. A similar case can be made for Calvinists in other parts of the nation. To be sure, it is unlikely that many citizens read Reformed political thinkers directly, but neither did they read Locke, Rousseau, or Blackstone. However, in New England approximately 85% of them attended churches where they at least occasionally heard Calvinist political ideas from their well-educated ministers. Moreover, many political leaders throughout the nation graduated from Harvard, Yale, or Princeton—which in that era were Reformed institutions.[56]

Calvinism in the American Founding

In 1781, François de Marbois, the secretary of the French legation in Philadelphia, sent a set of queries to a variety of American civic leaders. Only Thomas Jefferson responded with a book-length manuscript (known today as *Notes on Virginia*). Sherman, like the rest of his colleagues who wrote to Marbois, offered shorter answers. Of particular relevance for this book is his description of religion in Connecticut:

> The Religion professed by the people in General is in matters of Faith the same as the Presbyterians, in Scotland, as to Church Govt. & Discipline they are congregational. [O]f these some are consociated & some Independents. There are also a number of Episcopal Churches the same as in England & some anabaptists and a very few Quakers.

By "anabaptists" Sherman meant Baptists, who at that time were, with few exceptions, Calvinists. Although he does not offer statistics, he paints a portrait of a state populated by citizens in the Reformed tradition. This image has been reinforced by modern scholarship.[57]

Sydney Ahlstrom, in his magisterial history of religion in America, estimates that the Reformed tradition was "the religious heritage of three-fourths of the American people in 1776." Similarly, Yale historian Harry Stout states that prior to the War for Independence "three out of four colonists were connected with Reformed denominations (mostly Congregational and Presbyterian)." These figures may be high—neither scholar explains or defends them—but a plethora of studies make it clear that Calvinist churches dominated New England and were well represented throughout the rest of the nation.[58] In 1776, 63% of New England churches were Congregationalist, 15.3% were Baptist, and 5.5% were Presbyterian. Thus 84% of the region's churches were in the Reformed tradition, and these tended to have larger and more influential congregations. This estimate corresponds well with the 1790 U.S. Census Bureau's finding that only 20% of Connecticut citizens were dissenters (most of whom were Anglicans or Baptists).[59]

Among Congregational churches, 95% of ministers were college graduates—usually from Harvard or Yale—and they were among the most educated and influential members of their communities.[60] Within these churches, congregants would gather twice on Sunday to hear theologically and exegetically rich sermons lasting about one-and-a-half hours and to engage in other acts of worship. As well, they would regularly meet on Thursday evening for an additional sermon or "lecture." Harry S. Stout calculates that the "average 70-year old colonial churchgoer would have listened to some 7,000 sermons in his or her lifetime totaling nearly 10,000 hours of concentrated listening. This is the number of classroom hours it would take to receive ten separate undergraduate degrees in a modern university, without even repeating the same course!"[61]

But did New Englanders hear these sermons? Ever since W. W. Sweet famously estimated that only 20% of New Englanders in this era took their faith seriously, some scholars have questioned the religiosity of founding era Americans. In recent years, the most important advocates of this position are sociologists Roger Finke and Rodney Stark, who claim that on "the eve of the Revolution only about 17 percent of Americans were churched." Such assertions have made their way into polemical literature, as evidenced by Isaac Kramnick and R. Laurence Moore's statement that "Americans in the era of the Revolution were a distinctly unchurched people. The highest estimates from the late eighteenth century make only about 10–15 percent of the population church members." Although all of these authors acknowledge that "adherence" rates varied by region, Finke and Stark still conclude that New England adherence rates were no more than 20% of the total population.[62]

James Hutson, chief of the Manuscripts Division at the Library of Congress, has demonstrated that Finke and Stark make numerous factual, methodological, and historical errors. For instance, they misstate Ezra Stiles's estimate of the population of New England in 1760, and they ignore the best calculations of the American population in 1776. Most significantly, by relying on church-membership rates in an era and for denominations where it was exceedingly difficult to formally join a church (particularly in New England), they grossly undercount the number of Americans who were active in their churches. As well, Hutson notes that much of Finke and Stark's data comes from decades after the era about which they write and that fledgling denominations, such as Methodists, were included.[63] Using their methodology, but the more reliable data offered by Ezra Stiles, Hutson contends that 82% of New Englanders were involved in Congregational churches—and this does not include New Englanders who were active in Baptist, Anglican, or other churches.[64] Patricia U. Bonomi and Peter R. Eisenstadt similarly conclude that in late eighteenth-century America "from 56 to 80 percent of the [white] population were churched, with the southern colonies occupying the lower end of the scale and the northern colonies the upper end."[65]

Outside of New England, Calvinism was less dominant, but by 1776, Reformed congregations accounted for 51% and 58% of the churches in the middle and southern colonies respectively. Particularly noteworthy in these regions were Scottish and Scotch-Irish immigrants, most of whom were Presbyterian. In Pennsylvania, for instance, Presbyterians accounted for 30% of the population by 1790 and held 44% of the seats in the state legislature by the late 1770s. In the South, most political elites were Anglicans, but in the late eighteenth century, Presbyterianism was the fastest growing faith in the region, and its adherents were rapidly becoming a significant factor in state politics. J. C. D. Clark points out that well over a majority of the leaders of North Carolina's militia were Presbyterian elders and that Presbyterians dominated the proceedings that produced the famous Mecklenburg Resolves, which reportedly declared that "all Laws and Commissions confirmed by, or derived from the Authority of the King or Parliament, are annulled and vacated" more than a year before the Declaration of Independence was adopted by the Continental Congress.[66]

Not only were more than a majority of all Americans in the founding era associated with Calvinist churches, adherents to the tradition exercised significant influence through a variety of venues. New England was the intellectual and cultural center of America until well into the nineteenth century. Literally millions of Americans learned to read using the explicitly Calvinist *The New-England Primer* (more than two million copies were printed in the eighteenth century alone, and, in spite of its name, the text was used throughout America).[67] As well, many pedagogues throughout the nation were members of Reformed faiths. For instance, James Madison was educated by the Scottish Presbyterian minister Donald Robertson (about whom he later said, "all that I have been in life I owe largely to that man"); the Anglican rector Thomas Martin (a graduate of the Presbyterian College of New Jersey); and the Presbyterian minister John Witherspoon. Under President Witherspoon, the College of New Jersey produced "five delegates to the Constitutional Convention; one U.S. President (Madison); a vice president (the notorious Aaron Burr), forty-nine U.S. representatives; twenty-eight U.S. senators; three Supreme Court Justices; eight U.S. district judges; one secretary of state; three attorneys general; and two foreign ministers." It is noteworthy that only two of the 178 students who studied under Witherspoon between 1769 and 1775 became Loyalists.[68]

As in any age, it is difficult to determine the extent to which parishioners took their faith seriously or might have attended church simply because of societal expectations or pressures. However, there are good reasons to believe that many Calvinists in the era were quite serious about their faith. This is especially evident in the close partnership between Reformed churches and civil governments throughout New England. Particularly relevant for this study is the close connection between church and state in Sherman's adopted state of Connecticut.

In 1636, Puritan minister Thomas Hooker led part of his congregation from Massachusetts to Connecticut where he founded the town of Hartford. In 1639, representatives from Hartford joined with those from Windsor and Wethersfield and agreed to the Fundamental Orders of Connecticut, the primary purpose of which was to establish a government to "mayntayne and prsearue the liberty and purity of the gospell of our Lord Jesus wch we now prfesse, as also the discipline of the Churches, wch according to the truth of the said gospel is now practiced amongst us." Over the next century, the relationship between church and state changed as a result of internal and external pressures, but when Sherman was first elected to the General Assembly in 1755, Connecticut remained a society dominated by Reformed Christians who drew heavily from a long tradition of Calvinist political ideas and practices.[69]

The primary church-state dispute in Connecticut in 1755 was not whether the state should support the Congregational church, but whether it should support more than one such church in the same geographic area. The colony was divided into different districts, called societies, each responsible for taxing its residents to support the local Congregational church. However, during the Great Awakening, some Congregationalists rejected the Half-Way Covenant, which allowed baptized but unconverted parents to bring their infants forward for baptism. Persons baptized in this manner were considered to have partial church membership, but a conversion experience was still required for full church membership and participation in the Lord's Supper. New Lights, on the other hand, insisted that only infants of full church members should be baptized. Although "New" implies "progressive," in this case it meant embracing a stricter and more enthusiastic version of Calvinism. By 1754, New Lights had obtained majorities in all but two of Connecticut's associations and con-sociations (regional groups of Congregational churches).[70]

If the "established" Congregational church in a town was controlled by Old Lights, New Lights often formed separate churches. Initially, they were harassed, and severe limits were placed on ministers' ability to preach the gospel unless they gained approval from the established society. As the New Lights gained strength, the more repressive measures were repealed, and dissenters were given permission to tax their own members to support their new church. However, the established Congregational society retained the ability to tax all citizens who were not members of approved churches. Because of Parliament's 1689 Act of Toleration, it was possible for members of approved Anglican, Quaker, and Baptist churches to avoid paying taxes to support Congregational churches, but in practice it was often difficult to take advantage of this right.

Congregationalism's dominance within Connecticut is reflected well by the traditional New England practice of election sermons. From at least 1674 until 1830, Connecticut's General Court invited a minister to preach an election sermon in May, on the first day the legislature met. Prior to 1818, these ministers were always Congregationalists. The sermons, which were attended by the full General Court and other notables, were often printed and distributed at state expense. In them, clergy would remind civil leaders that men are sinful, that civil government is ordained by God to promote the common good, that the state should promote true Christianity, and that civil government is limited and must not be arbitrary. On election night, legislators would attend a dinner paid for by the state to which every Standing Order minister in the state—but no dissenters—was invited.[71]

Connecticut laws in this era also reflect the influence of Christianity, generally, and Reformed thought, specifically. Like most legal codes throughout the colonies, a variety of vices were punished as a matter of law, including adultery, drunkenness, card playing, dice throwing, swearing, and cursing. Offenses against God, such as blasphemy and Sabbath breaking, were illegal as well. On the positive side, select men were required "from Time to Time" to

> make diligent Enquiry of all House-holders, within their respective Towns, how they are Stor'd with Bibles; and if upon such Enquiry, if any such House-holder be found without One Bible at least; then the said Select-men shall warn the said House-holder forthwith to procure One Bible at least, for the Use and Benefit of the said Family... and that all those Families as are numerous, and whose Circumstances will allow thereof, shall be supplied with a consider-able number of Bibles, according to the Number of persons in such Families; And they shall see that all such Families be Furnished with suitable Numbers of Orthodox Catechisms, and other good Books of Practical Godliness, viz. Such especially as Treat on, Encourage, and duly Prepare for the right Attendance on that great Duty of the Lord's Supper.

Connecticut required families to own Bibles, and it demanded that towns have schools so that citizens would be able to read them. The colony, like the rest of New England, had one of the highest literacy rates the world had ever seen. Moreover, the General Assembly provided significant support for the Congregationalist Yale College. The primary mission of this school was to supply well-educated Congregational min-isters for the state.[72]

Church and state cooperated closely in eighteenth-century Connecticut. Of course, there were significant arguments about how they should work together, and political leaders were motivated by a variety of concerns—from the frivolous to the noble. Nevertheless, the basic political theory of Connecticut's leaders, such as Roger Sherman, Eliphalet Dyer, Oliver Ellsworth, Matthew Griswold, Benjamin Huntington, Samuel Huntington, Richard Law, Tapping Reeve, Jesse Root, Ezra Stiles, Jonathan Trumbull, William Williams, and Oliver Wolcott, differed little. In each instance they were influenced signifi-cantly by Reformed political ideas.[73]

Sherman's Faith

Throughout this chapter, I have written much about Calvinism and Calvinist political theory, but I have spent little time on Sherman. No one denies that he was a Congregationalist, but most scholars who have written about him at any length have dismissed the significance of his religious beliefs. Christopher Collier, for instance, contends that Sherman "was more than anything else an ambitious man, but second only to that quality, his unemotional, concise rationality is most striking." Although he mentions Sherman's religious views in passing, he does not consider them in detail until a brief section in the last chapter of his biography where he writes, "one of Roger Sherman's most prominent characteristics was his compromising temper. Indeed, expedience is a hallmark of his political career. His lapses from flexibility were few. Perhaps, however, it is to be expected that a man over seventy would develop some rigidities, especially in religion, and Sherman's part in the New Divinity fracas that rumbled through Connecticut in the late eighties and nineties is most uncharacteristic." Similarly, John Rommel contends that Sherman joined a New Light church for political rather than theological reasons, and James D. German describes him as an "[a]mbitious, acquisitive, avaricious," man who "shifted his own opinions to suit those of his constituents."[74]

Collier may have concluded that Sherman did not take theology seriously until the end of his life because the most extensive documents he penned on the subject were written after 1789. Relatively few of Sherman's early papers have survived, but there is enough evidence to indicate that he was concerned with theological matters throughout his life. Moreover, careful consideration of the corpus of his writings, in addition to his life and actions, provides abundant support for the conclusion of Ezra Stiles, president of Yale and Sherman's neighbor, that he was "an exemplary for Piety & serious Religion."[75]

Sherman was raised in a Congregational church in Stoughton, Massachusetts. His modern biographers all mention that he was likely educated, at least to some extent, by its minister, Samuel Dunbar. However, they neglect the implications of this possibility or the significance of Dunbar's ministerial influence on Sherman's spiritual and intellectual formation. Dunbar (1704–1783), a protégé of Cotton Mather and a 1723 graduate of Harvard, was fluent in Latin and Greek, and, like many ministers in that era, he likely supplemented his income by teaching. He arrived in Stoughton to pastor the Congregational church in 1727, and he remained there until his death. Because the town's first school was not established until 1735, by which time Sherman was fourteen years old, it is probable that he was educated, at least in part, by Dunbar.[76] This would help explain how a cobbler had the educational foundation to teach himself surveying, publishing, and law; and eventually rise to be one of the founding era's most significant statesmen.

Even if Dunbar did not serve as Sherman's schoolmaster, he was his minister, and, in an eighteenth-century Congregational church, this role included a great deal of teaching. George F. Piper noted that a sermon written by Dunbar in the forty-ninth year of his ministry is numbered 8,059, which suggests he composed an average of 164 sermons a year, or more than three a week. If this figure is accurate, before he moved to New Milford, Sherman could have heard as many as 2,460 of Dunbar's sermons.[77]

But what sort of man was Dunbar? According to Jason Haven, who preached his funeral sermon, Dunbar was

> a zealous defender of what he took to be "the faith once delivered to the saints." He treated much on what have been called the peculiar doctrines of grace; these he considered as doctrines according to godliness.... He was, on proper occasions, a *Son of Thunder*, endeavoring, by these terrors of the law, to awaken secure and hardened sinners, to point out to them the dreadful danger of a course of sin and impenitency. But he knew how happily to change his voice, and to become a Son of Consolation, and by the soft winning charms of the gospel to lead weary souls to Christ for rest and to comfort those that are cast down.

Dunbar's surviving sermons demonstrate that he was a conservative Calvinist who emphasized the sovereignty of God and the sinfulness of man. He opposed the revivalism of the Great Awakening because he thought it put too much emphasis on human agency. Like all Calvinists of the era, he believed ministers should provide guidance on political matters. He served as chaplain for a regiment in the Seven Years' War in 1755, and he quickly joined American opposition to what he deemed tyrannical British actions in the 1770s.[78]

Dunbar, like most Congregationalist clergy, was serious about his faith, embraced Reformed theology, and was extremely sensitive about the possibility of ungodly rulers infringing upon colonial liberties. Of course, one cannot simply impute the views of a pastor/teacher onto a parishioner/student, but, at a minimum, Dunbar's ministry shines light on the environment in which Sherman was raised. Moreover, in the context of the pattern of evidence described later, it is reasonable to attribute at least part of Sherman's commitment to a Reformed understanding of Christianity and politics to his early minister and teacher.

A few months after joining Dunbar's church, Sherman moved to New Milford, Connecticut, and transferred his church membership to the local Congregational church. Joining a Congregational church in the mid-eighteenth century was not simply a formality, and church members made every effort to elect only pious men to be church leaders (unlike Anglican churches in the South, where local gentry were routinely appointed to be church leaders regardless of their devotion to the faith). Sherman was by all appearances an active member of the church and a godly man. He was chosen "Deacon upon trial" in 1755 and "was established Deacon" in 1757. He was regularly elected clerk of the ecclesiastical society and served on the school and other committees.[79]

After moving to New Haven in 1761, Sherman transferred his church membership to White Haven, a New Light Congregational church, where he was "by the vote of the Church received to full communion in Gospel Ordinances and Privileges." Jonathan Edwards Jr. was chosen as minister of this church in 1768. Like his more famous father, Edwards's emphasis on theology and concern for piety had a tendency to drive away parishioners. Ezra Stiles estimated that White Haven had 480 members in 1772, but by 1789 the congregation had shrunk to "nineteen men and their families." Edwards's biographer contends that "the major reason he was not dismissed in the late 1780's or early 1790's was the fact that he received strong support from Roger Sherman." Among other things, Sherman wrote several letters defending Edwards's theological positions and his conduct.[80]

As in Connecticut's churches, divisions between New and Old Lights were prominent at Yale College in the 1760s. After President Thomas Clap switched allegiances to the New Lights, he appointed Roger Sherman to be Yale's treasurer. Sherman served in this position from 1765 to 1776. Like other officers of the college, Sherman presumably had to subscribe to the Westminster Catechism, the Saybrook Confession of Faith, and, particularly, "give Satisfaction to them [the trustees] of the Soundness of their Faith in opposition to Armenian [sic] and prelaitical Corruptions or any other Dangerous Consequence to the Purity and Peace of our Churches." According to Ezra Stiles, Yale's president from 1778–1795, Sherman was "ever a Friend to its [Yale's] Interests, & to its being &

continuing in the Hands of the Clergy, whom he judged the most proper to have the Superintendend[y] of a *religious* as well as a *scientific* College." Sherman's last public act was presiding over laying a foundation stone for a new building at Yale on April 15, 1793.[81]

In addition to his active involvement in churches and Yale, Sherman's writings give no reason to doubt his commitment to orthodox Christianity or, more specifically, the Reformed tradition. Of course, many of these writings are not explicitly religious. For instance, among Sherman's earliest surviving publications are his almanacs.[82] These primarily contain mathematical charts concerning agriculture and the weather, but, like other almanacs, they also have a healthy dose of proverbs—many with moral and/or religious overtones. Sherman borrowed most of these from elsewhere, although he may have composed some himself. Examples include:

> The Times wherein we live are very bad:
>   Let's every one mend our Ways, and we shall soon see better Days. (1751)
>   A faithful man in pubic is a Pillar in a Nation. (1751)
>   Self Interest will turn some mens opinions as certainly as the wind will a weather cock. (1753)
>   Profaness Intemperance & Injustice presage Calamitious Times. (1753)
>   A timely Reformation,
>   Wo'd save our Land & Nation. (1758)
>   All seek Happiness; but many take wrong Courses to obtain it. (1761)[83]

Sherman's last almanac was published in 1761, and many of his surviving writings between thatdate and 1789 concern political topics. A careful reading of these texts reveals the influence of his faith on his political ideas and actions. This is not to say, however, that all of Sherman's early writings lack an interest in theology proper. For example, in 1772 he wrote a letter to theologian Joseph Bellamy criticizing his view that "the covenant between a Minister & People" lasts only at the "people[']s pleasure." Instead, Sherman argued on legal, scriptural, and moral grounds that the covenant between a minister and his congregation cannot be broken except by mutual consent, unless the minister is unable to fulfill his duties or for reasons of "*Apostasy, Heresy,* and *Immorality.*" Similarly, a later exchange of letters with Princeton

President John Witherspoon demonstrates that Sherman had a covenantal rather than a contractual view of marriage.[84]

Notwithstanding Sherman's letter to Bellamy, it is the case that Sherman's later writings are more explicitly theological than his early ones. Most significant among these are his 1789 "A Short Sermon on the Duty of Self Examination, *Preparatory to Receiving the* Lord's Supper," his 1791 letter to Dr. Nathan Williams on infant baptism and church membership, and his 1790 debate with Samuel Hopkins. Sherman's sermon, which according to President Stiles was published but never preached, addressed the question of how a believer should examine himself or herself before receiving the communion. He made five major points, which he summarized in a passage worth quoting at length:

> If upon a careful examination we find, that we have a competent understanding of the gospel way of life by Jesus Christ, and of the nature, use and design of this holy institution of the supper:—If we do heartily repent of all our sins, bewailing them before God, with a deep rooted hatred of, and turning from them to the Lord, and the practice of his commandments: If we sincerely acknowledge Jesus Christ to be our Lord and master, believing him to be an all sufficient and infinitely suitable Saviour, as well as unspeakably willing even for us, and do earnestly desire as be interested in, and devoted to him upon the terms of the gospel: with a cheerful confidence in his power and grace for salvation.—If we have reason to think we have that love to God and Christ which is a spring of charity and obedience and at the same time are of a charitable, forgiving obliging disposition toward our fellow-men and especially our fellow christians; if we are conscious that we use our honest endeavors to live in obedience to all God's commands; and if we have any due sense of our spiritual wants, that we are in ourselves, poor and miserable, wretched and blind and naked. I say, if we can answer such enquiries as these in the affirmative ... we ought to come and eat of this bread and drink of this wine.[85]

In this passage, and throughout the thirteen-page sermon, Sherman's commitment to Reformed Christianity is clear. He leaves no doubt that he believed humans are in "a state of depravity, guilt and misery, exposed to the eternal curse of the law;—dead in trespass and sins;—by nature prone to evil and adverse to good, and unable to deliver ourselves." He contended that the only hope humans have for deliverance is "faith in Jesus," by which he meant that "we receive it for an undoubted truth that Jesus Christ was made an atoning sacrifice for sin." Christians are required to act in a moral manner, but their ability to do so is a result of having been redeemed by Christ's work; it is not a cause of their salvation. Like Jonathan Edwards Sr., he discussed morality in terms of a "love of benevolence" that "is due to all mankind, but in an especial manner" to Christian brothers and sisters.[86]

Sherman attached to his sermon extracts from the *Works* of the English Puritan Richard Baxter (1615–1691). In these excerpts Baxter argued that infant baptism makes one a member of the church, but that it is necessary for adults to make a profession of faith in order to receive communion.[87] Dr. Nathan Williams wrote a nineteen-page letter to Sherman objecting to a number of elements in these excerpts, but, most significantly, to the necessity of adults making a profession of faith in order to be admitted to the Lord's Supper and other privileges of adult members of the church.[88] Sherman responded that "Dr. Witherspoon, Dr. Stiles, Dr. Wales and several other Ministers" had raised no concern about the extracts, and that they are in accord with "the general usage of the Congregational Churches in New England." He proceeded to argue that Baxter fleshed out his argument significantly but stipulated that "I do not think that his, or any other man's opinion is of any authority in the case, unless supported by the word of God." He then spent three-and-a-half single-spaced pages making scriptural arguments to support Baxter's claims. The details of these arguments need not concern us; the significant point is that Sherman, like all good Reformed Christians, relied on the Bible which is, as he noted in an earlier letter, "the only rule of faith in matters of religion."[89]

The most sophisticated theological discussion in which Sherman participated was with Jonathan Edwards's disciple Samuel Hopkins, founder of the school of theology that bears his name, but perhaps better known as the elderly minister in Harriet Beecher Stowe's *The Minister's Wooing* (1859). In 1790, Sherman wrote Hopkins a letter dissenting from two points in his *An Inquiry into the Nature of True Holiness* (1773). Notably, he disagreed with Hopkins's characterization of self-love and his proposition that "it is the duty of a person to be *willing* to give up his eternal interest for the Glory of God." In his criticisms, Sherman demonstrated the ability to engage one of America's most prominent theologians in a sophisticated debate about nuances of Reformed theology. This assertion is best supported by reading the exchange in full, but it is illustrated by the following passage from one of Sherman's letters:

> You do not here distinguish between *occasion and positive cause* though you make a material distinction between them in your sermons on "Sin the *occasion* of great good." President Edwards I think has illustrated this point in his answer to Dr. Taylor on original sin, and in a sermon published with this life, on the enquiry, why natural men are enemies to God. He supposes original righteousness in man was a supernatural principle which was withdrawn on his first transgression, and his natural principles of agency remaining, were exercised wrong, and his affections set on wrong objects in consequence of such withdrawment.[90]

This brief excerpt reveals that Sherman was familiar with key analytical distinctions in Edwards's and Hopkins's works, and that he was interested in theology proper (not just religious ideas or scriptural exegesis; although he was concerned with these as well). His interest in these subjects is illustrated by the list of books contained in his library at the time of his death, of which about a third (about fifty books) consists of Bibles, concordances, catechisms, confessions of faith, volumes of sermons, and works by prominent Reformed theologians (notably, Jonathan Edwards). Although Sherman was not an academic theologian, he demonstrated, in the words of Sydney Ahlstrom, "theological maturity." It seems highly unlikely that Sherman developed this grasp of scripture and theology merely in his waning days. Moreover, glimpses of his life recorded by others suggest that he made a lifelong effort to live by his convictions.[91]

Sherman's faith affected his political ideas and actions in significant ways, and it influenced his day-to-day life in ways that may seem quaint today. For instance, in 1774, Silas Deane, Sherman's fellow delegate to the Continental Congress, observed, much to his annoyance, that Sherman "is against sending our carriages over the ferry this evening, because it is Sunday; so we shall have a scorching sun to drive forty miles in to-morrow." Similarly, Benjamin Rush recorded that Sherman "once objected to a motion for Congress sitting on a Sunday upon an occasion which he thought did not require it, and gave as a reason for his objection, a regard of the commands of his Maker." Rush also recalled what seems to be an attempt at biblical humor by Sherman: "Upon hearing of the defeat of the American army on Long Island, where they were entrenched and fortified by a chain of hills, he said to me in coming out of Congress 'Truly in vain is salvation hoped for from the hills, and from the multitude of mountains' (Jeremiah xii, 23)."[92]

In summary, Sherman was born into a pious Congregational family in which two of the four sons grew up to be ministers. He came of age under the tutelage of the Reverend Samuel Dunbar, a solid, Old Light Calvinist. He was elected to be an elder in his church and was appointed treasurer of Congregationalist Yale College. He engaged ministers and theologians in sophisticated theological debates, and he remained supportive of Jonathan Edwards Jr. after most of his church abandoned him. There is little reason to conclude that Sherman simply turned to religion as an old man. Far more accurate is Yale President Timothy Dwight's view, penned in 1811:

> As a man, as a patriot, and as a Christian, Mr. Sherman left behind him an unspotted name. Profoundly versed in Theology, he held firmly to the doctrines of the Reformation. Few men understood them so well; and few were equally able to defend them. What he believed, he practiced. It can excite no wonder, therefore, that he died with bright hopes of a glorious immortality.[93]

3

Connecticut Politics and American Independence

I BEGIN THIS chapter by offering a brief overview of Connecticut politics in the eighteenth century. After discussing Sherman's first significant publication, "A Caveat against Injustice," I describe his rise to prominence as a civic leader in the state. The bulk of the chapter focuses on his role in America's move toward independence. A central thesis is that Sherman and his Calvinist colleagues were significantly influenced by religious concerns and the Reformed political tradition.

Connecticut Politics in the Eighteenth Century

The Fundamental Orders of Connecticut was the first constitution written to ensure popular self-government. Under it, inhabitants of towns governed themselves in most matters, and twice each year freemen in towns elected representatives to a General Court to address matters affecting the whole colony. This court met in May to elect a governor and other magistrates, and then in October to revise and pass legislation. As well, the General Court served as the highest judicial body in the colony. In 1662, King Charles II granted Connecticut a royal charter; one drafted by the General Court that retained civic institutions similar to those established in the Fundamental Orders. The major change effected by the charter was to incorporate, against its will, New Haven into Connecticut's borders. The colony remained almost completely self-governing, and the Crown exercised virtually no oversight of the colony. Over the next century, the number of towns in the colony increased rapidly, and in 1698 it adopted a bicameral legislature, but political and ecclesiastical structures remained stable. Upon independence, the legislature, now referred to as the General Assembly, simply removed all references to the Crown from its 1662 charter. This document functioned as the state's constitution for another forty-two years.[1]

When Sherman entered colonial politics in 1755, freemen in each town chose two representatives to serve in the lower house of the General Assembly. As well, each voter could nominate up to twenty men to serve in the upper house, or Council of Assistants. The top nominees were placed on a list, with the current and ex-assistants listed first. Freemen then cast twelve votes for members of the Council. This system had the effect of virtually guaranteeing the reelection of current assistants, for although they could theoretically be voted out of office in any given year, only a highly coordinated effort would succeed in doing so. The governor and deputy governor were elected at large, but if no candidate received a majority of the votes the General Assembly filled the positions.

Connecticut had a bicameral legislature, but separation of powers was minimal by modern standards. The chief executive was an ex officio member of the Council and had little independent power. He possessed no veto, appointed only minor officials, and could not pardon criminals. Members of the General Assembly regularly accepted administrative and judicial responsibilities, and the legislature remained the final arbiter of judicial disputes until 1819. Throughout most of Sherman's life, Connecticut's highest judicial tribunal was the Superior Court, which consisted of a chief judge (after 1715 always the deputy governor) and four members appointed by the Assembly. Although most anyone could be appointed to this court, judges were always members of the upper house, until 1785, when the legislature prohibited Superior Court judges from holding other high state or national offices. The General Assembly retained the power to review and overturn any judicial decision until 1819.[2]

Connecticut was governed by an unofficial alliance between Congregational ministers and godly magistrates known as the Standing Order. Political leaders were almost always members of Reformed churches, although there were exceptions, such as William Samuel Johnson who, in 1766, became the first Anglican elected to the upper house of the General Assembly. These leaders worked closely with clergy on matters involving religion and morality. Of course, political leaders had disputes about specific policies, and, as in any political body, there were petty jealousies and rivalries. Yet there was a great deal of agreement on broader issues, such as the nature of man, the existence and content of moral standards, the appropriate role of civil government, and the virtues of state support for Christianity. Throughout the eighteenth century, Connecticut society and politics became less deferential and slightly more diverse, but the colony generally lived up to its reputation as "the land of steady habits."[3]

Sherman did not come from a prominent Connecticut family, but he gradually worked his way into the colony's political structure. In 1748, five years after moving to New Milford, he became a "freeman." This status could be granted to males "twenty-one years of age, in possession of a freehold estate of the value of forty shillings per annum, or of forty pounds personal estate in the general assessment lists of that year, and 'of a quiet and peaceable Behaviour, and Civil Conversation.'" As a freeman, Sherman was eligible to vote and hold civic offices. In 1749 he became a grand jury-man, which was followed by appointments as list-taker, leather sealer, society clerk, fence viewer, and surveyor. In 1753 he was elected selectman, and in 1755 he was chosen to represent New Milford in the lower house of the General Assembly. Representatives routinely served as local justices of the peace, and Sherman was accordingly appointed to this office. Around this time he turned to the study of law, likely at the urging of William Samuel Johnson, and he was admitted to the Litchfield bar in 1754.[4]

"A Caveat against Injustice"

Prior to his election to the General Assembly, Sherman wrote "A Caveat against Injustice, or an Inquiry into the Evil Consequences of a Fluctuating Medium of Exchange," which was published in 1752 under the pseudonym of Philoeunomos (lover of good law). The pamphlet addressed problems resulting from every New England colony issuing their own bills of credit. All of these bills depreciated over time, but those from Rhode Island and New Hampshire lost value with alarming speed. To compound the diffi-culties created by this dynamic, some debtors argued that because mer-chants had traditionally accepted bills of credit from other colonies, there was now a common law requirement for them to do so.[5]

Sherman responded to this legal argument by contending that mer-chants had only accepted bills of credit from other colonies by "voluntary Consent." Moreover, they never took the bills at face value, but only according to their "Extrinsical Value"—that is, what they were actually worth. For courts or the legislature to require merchants to accept bills at face value even though they were worth less would violate the principle that

no Government has a Right to impose on its Subjects any foreign Currency to be received in Payments as Money which is not of intrinsick Value; unless such Government will assume and under-take to secure to make Good to the Possessor of such Currency the full Value which they oblige him to receive it for. Because in so doing they would oblige Men to part with their Estates for that which is worth nothing in itself and which they don't know will ever procure him any Thing.[6]

Sherman's essay illustrates his commitment to the ideas that individuals have a right to private property that cannot be violated by *any* government and that citizens properly expect governments to defend and secure this property. He noted that the right to private property is protected by the "Laws of Man," but he cited no legal texts to support this point. Instead, Sherman relied primarily on arguments based on reason, justice, and the "Law of God." He contended, for instance, that requiring merchants to receive a fluctuating medium of exchange "is no better than unjust Weights and Measures, both which are condemn'd by the Laws of God and Man," an indirect reference to Proverbs 20:10 which states: "Divers weights, and divers measures, both of them alike abomination to the LORD."[7]

Sherman also addressed the possibility that permitting merchants to refuse currency from other colonies would adversely affect trade. If so, he contended that "we had better die in a good Cause than live in a bad one." However, he was optimistic that the colony would thrive because they "are seated on a very fruitful Soil, the Product whereof, with our Labour and Industry, and the Divine Blessing thereon, would sufficiently furnish us with, and procure us all the Necessaries of Life and as good a *Medium of Exchange* as any People in the World have or can desire." Most of the items brought into the colony could be produced in Connecticut, and many "we had much better be without, especially the Spirituous Liquors of which vast Quantities are consumed in this Colony every Year, unnecessarily to the Great Destruction of the Estates, Morals, Health and even the Lives of many of the Inhabitants."[8]

Sherman concluded his essay by proposing that the General Assembly ban recently issued bills from Rhode Island and set a future date when no bills of credit from Rhode Island or New Hampshire could be used in Connecticut. As well, he suggested that it would benefit the "Publick Good" to "Lay a large Excise upon all Rum imported into this Colony, or distilled therein, thereby effectually to restrain the excessive use thereof, which is such a growing Evil among us and is leading to almost all other Vices." Like most Calvinists, Sherman did not abstain from alcohol, but he believed that the excessive use of hard liquor was causing significant damage to the community. Throughout his political career, he evinced a willingness to use the power of the state to promote the common good by promoting virtue and prohibiting (or taxing) vice.[9]

"A Caveat against Injustice" contains a significant, early argument by an American founder about the evils of paper money. As well, it reveals Sherman's commitment to the principle that men have a natural right to private property that even governments must respect. He did not address the validity of taxes in detail, but later writings and actions make it clear that he thought they were legitimate only if people consented to them. Given the views expressed in the pamphlet, it should come as no surprise that he was an early and vocal opponent of Parliament's attempt to tax the colonists.[10]

Sherman's Early Legislative Career

Sherman was elected to the lower house of the General Assembly three years after "A Caveat against Injustice" was published. The May 1755 session of the General Assembly focused on electing officers, appointing judges and other officials, and dealing with memorials. In a special August session, the Assembly raised revenue and troops for the Seven Years' War—and noted its desire to be reimbursed by the Crown for the expense![11] The first substantial law passed in the fall session prohibited Connecticut's citizens from accepting bills of credit issued by New Hampshire or Rhode Island after December 5, 1749. The second provided for stricter regulation of liquor retailers and an excise tax on liquor to be paid by tavern keepers. There are no records of who introduced, promoted, or voted for these laws, but given the similarities between them and those proposed in "A Caveat against Injustice," it seems likely that Sherman was behind these statutes.[12]

Sherman was not returned to the General Assembly for its 1756 sessions, but he was elected again in October 1758. Although he moved to New Haven in 1760, he continued to represent New Milford in the lower house until March 1761.[13] In addition to the usual business of appointments and dealing with memorials and petitions, much of the legislature's work during these years involved the war with France and her Native American allies. The General Assembly passed legislation raising troops; required the quartering of His Majesty's soldiers; and, finally, called for a day of thanksgiving to return "gratitude to Almighty God" for the "termination of a bloody and expensive war."[14]

In New Haven, Sherman opened a store next to Yale College and quickly established himself as one of the town's leading citizens. He was again elected to local offices and was chosen to represent the town in the lower house of the General Assembly in October of 1764. In May 1766, voters moved him to the upper house, in large part because of his opposition to the Stamp Act. He was immediately appointed to the Superior Court as well, and he served in both capacities until he resigned as an assistant in 1785.[15]

During his years in the Assembly, numerous acts and decisions reveal the influence of Reformed Protestantism on Sherman and in the colony. For instance, the Assembly often passed laws or dealt with memorials on subjects such as the promotion of education, the punishment of vice, and the maintenance of established Congregational churches.[16] During this era, greater toleration was extended to separatists, but the colony's leaders remained profoundly suspicious of Roman Catholicism. This is illustrated well by the legislature's adoption in 1766 of oaths originally "provided by an act of Parliament" that required individuals to swear, among other things, that "I do from my heart abhor, detest and abjure, as impious and heretical, that damnable doctrine and position, that princes excommunicated or deprived by the Pope, or any authority of the See of Rome, may be deposed or murthered by their subjects" and that "I do believe that in the sacrament of the Lord's Supper there is not any transubstantiation of the elements of bread and wine into the body and blood of Christ."[17]

One of the most significant issues running through Sherman's political career concerned Connecticut's claim to land in the Wyoming Valley along the Susquehannah River. The territory in question was physically separated from the rest of Connecticut by the colony of New York. Nevertheless, it was apparently granted to both Pennsylvania and Connecticut by charters issued by Charles II. For many years, the potential for conflict remained just that—potential. However, in 1753 the Susquehannah Company was founded in Connecticut to "Spread Christianity" and "to promote our own Temporal Interest." The company purchased land in the Wyoming Valley from Native Americans and encouraged the settlement of Connecticut citizens in the region. Numerous towns were populated by these settlers in the mid-to-late 1750s. Pennsylvania proprietor Thomas Penn objected to the settlements and in 1763 was able to secure an order from the Crown requiring settlers to leave the Wyoming valley. Connecticut citizens refused to leave and, indeed, continued moving to the territory.[18]

Sherman's involvement with the issue began in 1769 when he was appointed representative for the Council on a joint committee investigating the controversy. He quickly convinced himself of the justice of Connecticut's claim and became a steadfast advocate for the Susquehannah Company. In 1774, he voted with the General Assembly to grant a charter to the town of Westmoreland in the disputed territory. In the same year, Sherman wrote a private legal brief and published an essay in the *Connecticut Journal* arguing the colony's position based on prior charter rights, the legality of purchases from Native Americans, and settlement. In the public essay, he criticized his fellow citizens who opposed the colony's claims, contending that "every *kingdom divided against itself is brought to desolation*" and charging opposition leaders such as Jared Ingersoll with being gentlemen "who love to monopolize wealth and power, think it best for land to be in a few hands, and that the common people should be their tenants[,] but it will not be easy to persuade the people of this colony, who know the value of freedom, and of enjoying fee-simple estates." Sherman thought that concentrated land ownership promoted aristocracy, whereas widespread ownership was necessary for creating freemen who could be good, republican citizens.[19]

During the War for Independence, the Susquehannah Company ceased planting new settlements, although controversies about existing ones continued. In 1782, a court of commissioners established under Article IX of the Articles of Confederation resolved the dispute in Pennsylvania's favor. Even then, cases concerning specific property claims were heard into the nineteenth century, and Connecticut did not give up all of its western land claims until it was compensated with approximately 3.5 million acres in Ohio—land which was eventually sold to support public education in the state.[20]

Judge Sherman

Sherman served on Connecticut's Superior Court from 1766 until 1789. Unfortunately, judicial decisions were not formally reported until the end of Sherman's career.[21] From the records and unofficial accounts that are available, it appears that most cases adjudicated by Sherman and his colleagues involved mundane criminal, civil, and procedural issues. Some of these reflect the political culture of late eighteenth-century Connecticut. For instance, divorces were granted only for causes like desertion and cruelty, and an ecclesiastical society was denied the ability to fire a minister who had not violated the "covenant" between him and the society. One case involved "a Presentment of Grandjury against Drake for Defaming Mr. P. a Clergyman viz. for charging him for being an Arminian, unfit to be a Minister of the Gospel." None of the judges who heard the case denied that such an accusation was slander, but the lower court decision was overturned on a procedural issue.[22]

At the very end of Sherman's judicial service, a few of his votes and a handful of individual opinions were reported by "the first full-fledged official law report in the country," Ephraim Kirby's *Reports of Cases Adjudged in the Superior Court of the State of Connecticut, from the Year 1785, to May, 1788*. As a matter of legal trivia, it is worth noting that Sherman wrote the first dissenting opinion published in an American law report. Similarly, he was on the court that issued the first reported search and seizure case. In the decision, he joined his colleagues in declaring that a general warrant "to search all places, and arrest all persons" to be "clearly illegal." The few additional cases of interest decided by Superior Court judges while Sherman was on the court are addressed in subsequent chapters.[23]

Sherman and the Move Toward Independence

For centuries, Calvinists had warned about the dangers of rulers exceeding their lawful authority. They regularly insisted that legitimate governments must be based on the consent of the governed, that civil government should be limited, and that individuals possess rights against the state. Following the conclusion of the Seven Years' War, Parliament for the first time attempted to raise money by directly taxing American colonists. Although the taxes were not high, in many American minds they were clearly unconstitutional and to pay them would encourage arbitrary government. As the conflict with Great Britain escalated, American patriots produced a host of documents against perceived abuses. Many specific legal, constitutional, or political complaints were not based on Reformed theology per se, although Calvinist concerns about tyrannical rulers informed many citizens' responses to perceived violations of their rights. In some cases, such as the possible appointment of an Anglican bishop and the Quebec Act, recognizing that many Americans were serious Calvinists helps explain why they were so alarmed by these seemingly innocuous policies.[24]

Of all the direct taxes passed by Parliament, particularly imprudent was the Stamp Act of 1765, which "fell particularly hard on two categories of men skilled in circulating grievances—publicans (who had to pay a registration fee of £1 a year) and newspapers (who had to print on stamped paper.)" Sherman, like many patriots, objected to the statute because he believed Parliament had no power to tax the colonists. He led a New Haven town meeting that instructed the city's delegates, himself, and Samuel Bishop to oppose the act. In the General Assembly, Sherman served on a committee that drew up a petition to the king and instructions for Connecticut's agent in Great Britain that insisted that the colonists had not forfeited the "sacred and inviolable" rights of Englishmen, so they could not be taxed without their consent. All but five members of the General Assembly voted to approve these instructions, a vote that helps illustrate the consensus among the colony's political class (virtually all of whom were members of Reformed churches). This agreement apparently went well beyond Connecticut's leadership, as suggested by G.A. Gilbert's and Oscar Zeichner's estimates that only 8% of adult males in Connecticut were Loyalists—and that most of these were Anglicans who lived in the western part of the colony.[25]

Parliament repealed the Stamp Act in March 1766, but it immediately passed the Declaratory Act, which asserted that Parliament had the authority to make laws binding colonists "in all cases whatsoever," a claim Americans found to be both remarkable and dangerous. As if to further provoke the colonists, Parliament also passed the Quartering Act and, in 1767, the Townshend Acts. Sherman again helped craft a petition to the king challenging the legality of the legislation. In a personal letter written on June 25, 1768, to William Samuel Johnson, who was then serving as Connecticut's agent in Great Britain, he reiterated his argument that no "Colonial Assembly on this continent will ever concede that the Parliament has authority to Tax the colonies."[26]

After the colonial boycott of British goods forced Parliament to largely repeal the Townshend Acts in 1770, some merchants began to waiver in their commitment to the boycott. Throughout America, meetings were held in towns to encourage the colonists to persevere. A New Haven committee consisting of Sherman and five colleagues sent a letter to merchants at Weatherfield and Hartford urging them to not forsake the cause of liberty for "the prospect of a little wealth." The broader issue, they contended, was that if Parliament was not checked it would open the door for tyrannical legislation that would result in "slavery."[27]

Sherman was convinced from a relatively early date that Parliament's constitutional authority extended only to geographic areas represented in the body. In 1772, he wrote to Thomas Cushing that it

> is a Fundamental principle in the British Constitution and I think must be in every free State, That no Laws bind the people but such as they consent to be governed by, therefore so far as the people of the Colonies are Bound by Laws made without their consent, they must be in a state of Slavery or absolute Subjection to the Will of others... And tho' some general Regulations of Trade &c. may be necessary for the general interest of the nation[,] is there any Constitutional way to Establish such Regulations so as to be legally binding upon the people of the several distinct Dominions which compose the British Empire, but by consent of the Legislature of each Government[?][28]

Since 1765, many Americans had come to deny Parliament the power to tax colonists, but even many patriots conceded that it could regulate external colonial affairs. Sherman denied even this power, insisting that external regulations must be agreed upon by each local legislature. James Wilson, followed by Jefferson and Adams, popularized this argument in 1774.[29] While there is no evidence that these founders were influenced by Sherman, it is clear that he arrived at this position before their prominent essays were published. Indeed, in August of 1774—five months before the publication of his first Novanglus essay—John Adams met Sherman on his way to Congress and noted in his diary that he is "a solid, sensible man. He said he read Mr. Otis's Rights &c in 1764, and thought that he had conceded away the rights of America. He thought the reverse of the declaratory act was true, namely, that the parliament of Great Britain had authority to make laws for America in no case whatever."[30]

Even more directly tied to Sherman's Reformed commitments was his concern that Parliament and the Crown intended to restrict the colonists' freedom of worship. Notably, he and his colleagues worried that the king planned to appoint a bishop for the American colonies. The Puritans and their descendents had always been in the precarious position of maintaining what was in effect a dissenting establishment. They feared that a bishop would attempt to take over all colonial churches and set up oppressive ecclesiastical courts. The latest recent episode in the long-running pamphlet war concerning an American episcopate had erupted in 1763. Two years later, Parliament passed the Stamp Act, which contained a reference to courts "exercising ecclesiastical jurisdiction within the said colonies." This was taken by partisans on both sides to imply that a bishop would be sent shortly and that for the first time ecclesiastical courts would operate in the American colonies. As Sherman pointed out in a 1768 letter to William Samuel Johnson, the problem was

> not that we are of intolerant principles, nor do we envy the Episcopalian church of the privileges of a Bishop for the purposes of ordination, confirmation, and inspecting the morals of their clergy, provided they have no kind of superiority over, nor power in any way to affect the civil or religious interest of other denominations, or derive any support from them.

He went on to note: "Many of the first inhabitants of these Colonies were obliged to seek an asylum among savages in this wilderness in order to escape the tyranny of Archbishop Laud and others of his stamp...We dread the consequences as oft we think of this danger [ecclesiastical tyranny]."[31]

Sherman's fears may seem excessive today, but to an eighteenth-century Calvinist they made perfect sense. Calvinists had often struggled against unfriendly governments, and New England Puritans had come to America precisely because they were unable to reform completely the Church of England. Throughout the eighteenth century, some American Anglicans continued to argue that the Congregationalist and Presbyterian churches were not "true" churches because their ministers had not been ordained by bishops. The extent to which Anglican leaders in England supported the plans of Americans such as Samuel Johnson, the father of William Samuel Johnson, has been extensively debated by scholars, but there is little reason to doubt that Reformed Christians genuinely feared an Anglican episcopate. Ill-conceived actions by the Church of England such as founding a "mission" in Cambridge, Massachusetts, in 1759 did little to calm their fears.[32]

Carl Bridenbaugh, in his classic work on the debate over an American bishop, identified Noah Welles, Noah Hobart, Ezra Stiles, and Francis Alison as some of the most committed ministerial opponents of an Anglican episcopate.[33] Sherman must have known Welles from his time in New Milford, when Welles had been a candidate for a church there. Personal friend or not, in 1767 he paid for the publication of Welles's sermon defending Presbyterian ordination.[34] As well, Sherman was a longtime neighbor and close friend of Ezra Stiles. That both Welles and Stiles preached election day sermons before the Connecticut Assembly while Sherman served there helps illustrate the tight-knit community that comprised the Standing Order.[35] Yet concern over a bishop was not limited to elites, as indicated by John Adams's recollection that "the apprehension of Episcopacy contributed...as much as any other cause, to arouse the attention, not only of the inquiring mind, but of the common people, and urge them to close thinking on the constitutional authority of parliament over the colonies."[36]

Sherman was motivated by fear of Anglican aggression rather than religious bigotry. In fact, he got along well with Anglicans in the colony. This is suggested as early as 1750 when, to the consternation of some of his readers, he inserted observable days of the Church of England into his almanacs. When several customers complained, Sherman responded that while he felt free to not observe such days:

> as I take Liberty in these Matters to judge for myself, so I think it reasonable that Others should have the same Liberty; and since my Design in this Performance is to serve the Publick, and the inserting of those observable Days does not croud out any Thing that might be more serviceable, I hope none of my Readers will be displeased with it for the Future.[37]

Throughout his life, Sherman had good relations with his Anglican neighbors—particularly his frequent collaborator and correspondent William Samuel Johnson.

Sherman and his colleagues were troubled by the possible appointment of a bishop, but they were incensed by the Quebec Act of 1774. From Parliament's perspective, this innocuous piece of legislation simply provided for the efficient governing of territory won from France after the Seven Years' War. However, the act extended the colony of Quebec into what is now the American Midwest, permitted the use of French civil law, and allowed Catholics to freely practice their faith and take oaths without reference to Protestantism. To many Protestants (especially Calvinists), these steps constituted a significant retreat for the kingdom of God in North America and profound victories for "Papists" and arbitrary government. Reformed Protestants of the era considered Roman Catholics, at best, seriously deceived and, at worst, in league with Satan. Connecticut minister

Samuel Sherwood reflected the views of many Calvinists when he interpreted the Quebec Act as attempting "the establishment of popery" and as part of a pattern of "violent and cruel attempts of a tyrannical and persecuting power," the main goal of which was the destruction of Protestant Christianity.[38]

Reformed Christians had long been on their guard against tyrannical rulers desiring to stamp out the true gospel. Although they recognized that God is sovereign, they were haunted by events like the massacres of French Huguenots where evil rulers seemed to succeed. When tyrants had failed it was, from a human perspective, because Protestants had resisted them with arguments, laws, and force. As Sherman and his colleagues began to perceive a pattern of tyranny by Parliament and the Crown, they reacted forcefully against the threat. They would not sit idly by while their sacred rights were violated by ungodly tyrants.

Sherman and the Declaration of Independence

The influence of Reformed political ideas on American patriots is often ignored because students of the era focus on the Declaration of Independence as *the* statement of why separation from Great Britain was justified. Moreover, they read the document in light of the views of its primary drafter, Thomas Jefferson, who was more influenced by the Enlightenment than virtually any other American. The Declaration of Independence is compatible with Reformed political theory, but the tradition's influence is even more evident in other public documents stating the colonists' case. These texts are not narrowly Reformed—indeed, to the extent to which they are explicitly religious, they might be better characterized as articulating Protestant concerns. However, a majority of Protestants in America at the time were, in fact, Calvinists, and these Protestants were more likely to support the patriot cause and use such language than, say, Anglicans. Because texts like the Suffolk Resolves, the Declaration of Rights, and the Declaration of the Causes and Necessity of Taking up Arms are relatively unknown, in the following section I quote from them more extensively than from better-known and readily available documents.

In 1774, the General Assembly appointed Sherman to be one of Connecticut's delegates to the Continental Congress. He arrived in Philadelphia on September 1 with his fellow representatives Eliphalet Dyer and Silas Deane.[39] Congress convened four days later, and, shortly thereafter, Sherman was appointed to a committee to draft a statement of colonial rights. Although the committee reached no agreement and its work was postponed, his fellow committee member John Adams later recalled that the central debate concerned whether colonists should rely primarily on constitutional and/or natural law arguments. In addition, they attempted to discern what authority, if any, should be conceded to Parliament. Adams noted that in these discussions Sherman contended: "There is no other legislative over the Colonies but their respective assemblies. The Colonies adopt the common law, not as the common law, but as the highest reason."[40]

On September 17, Paul Revere delivered the Suffolk Resolves to the Continental Congress. It is an interesting coincidence illustrative of the relatively small world of colonial New England that the Suffolk Resolves were adopted in Sherman's childhood hometown at a meeting opened in prayer by his old pastor, Samuel Dunbar. One contemporary witness observed that Dunbar offered "the most extraordinary liberty-prayer that I ever heard. He appeared to have a most divine, if not prophetical, enthusiasm in favor of our rights."[41] The Resolves recognized the sovereignty of King George, but challenged the legality of recent acts and practices by the British Parliament. The convention also proclaimed

> [t]hat it is an indispensable duty which we owe to God, our country, ourselves and posterity, by all lawful ways and means in our power to maintain, defend and preserve those civil and religious rights and liberties, for which many of our fathers fought, bled and died, and to hand them down entire to future generations.

As well, they condemned

> the late act of parliament for establishing the Roman Catholic religion and the French laws in that extensive country, now called Canada, is dangerous in an extreme degree to the Protestant religion and to the civil rights and liberties of all America; and, therefore, as men and Protestant Christians, we are indispensably obliged to take all proper measures for our security.[42]

The Suffolk Resolves played a significant role in encouraging Congress to take a strong stand against Parliament and in adopting a meaningful statement of colonial rights.[43] Sherman's fellow delegates were not prepared to go as far as he would have liked, but the final version of the Declaration of Rights did condemn Parliament for passing the Intolerable Acts, which were called "impolitic, unjust, and cruel, as well as unconstitutional, and most dangerous and destructive of American rights." It went on to assert:

> That the inhabitants of the English Colonies in North America, by the immutable laws of nature, the principles of the English constitution, and the several charters or compacts, have the following Rights:
>
> *Resolved* N. C. D. 1. That they are entitled to life, liberty, and property, and they have never ceded to any sovereign power whatever, a right to dispose of either without their consent.[44]

Congress also claimed that Parliament has no authority to tax the colonies, although to Sherman's chagrin it conceded that Parliament could regulate them. As well, the declaration protested other violations of rights, including denying colonists the right to be "tried by peers of the vicinage," to assemble, and to petition the king. Delegates complained about Parliament's attempt to keep a "Standing Army in these colonies in times a peace"—a sure sign of tyranny. Reformed members of Congress were particularly supportive of Congress's objection to the act passed

> for establishing the Roman Catholick Religion in the province of Quebec, abolishing the equitable system of English laws, and erecting a tyranny there, to the great danger, from so total a dissimilarity of Religion, law, and government of the neighbouring British colonies, by the assistance of those whose blood and treasure the said country was conquered from France.[45]

After declaring their rights and petitioning the king, Congress passed the Articles of Association wherein delegates agreed on behalf of the colonies not to import and consume goods from Great Britain or Ireland, or to export goods to them. The Articles provided for the creation of committees in each county, city, and town to enforce the terms of the association. Sherman signed this agreement, and he was later moderator at New Haven's town meeting which formed the committee to implement the Articles in the city. He occasionally chaired this body, but was unable to do so when attending Congress. It is noteworthy that Congress's act was patterned after an earlier nonimportation agreement by Boston's committee of correspondence called a "Solemn League and Covenant," a reference to an agreement between the Scottish Covenanters and the leaders of the English Parliament, where the latter pledged to preserve the Reformed faith in Scotland and spur the reformation of Christianity in England and Ireland in exchange for the former's support against Charles I.[46]

Of particular interest for our purposes is Congress's appeal to the people of Great Britain. The document reiterated many of the arguments in the Declaration of Rights, but expanded on the significance of the Quebec Act. Congress contended that

> we think the Legislature of Great-Britain is not authorized by the constitution to establish a religion, fraught with sanguinary and impious tenets, or, to erect an arbitrary form of government, in any quarter of the globe. These rights, we, as well as you, deem sacred. And yet sacred as they are, they have, with many others been repeatedly and flagrantly violated.

Several pages later, delegates reemphasized the significance of the issue when they declared that by the Quebec Act

> the dominion of Canada is to be so extended, modelled, and governed, as that by being disunited from us, detached from our interests, by civil as well as religious prejudices, that by their numbers daily swelling with Catholic emigrants from Europe, and by their devotion to Administration, so friendly to their religion, they might become formidable to us, and on occasion, be fit instruments in the hands of power, to reduce the ancient free Protestant Colonies to the same state of slavery with themselves.[47]

These quotations highlight issues that are only vaguely represented in the Declaration of Independence. Many delegates to the first Continental Congress were profoundly concerned about the establishment of the Catholic faith in Quebec, and they often spoke specifically as "Protestants." By contrast, the Declaration of Independence mentions only "abolishing the free System of English Laws in a neighboring Province." The difference has something to do with the person who drafted the document, but even more to do with the intended audience. Jefferson was obviously not a Calvinist, and a critical audience for the Declaration was Roman Catholic

France. The eventual intervention of France on the patriots' side did much to diminish the vehement anti-Catholicism of many Americans in this era, but suspicion of "Papists" remained a powerful force in the American imagination well into the twentieth century.[48]

An excellent illustration of the seriousness with which Sherman took the perceived Catholic threat is found in a 1766 letter from him to William Samuel Johnson, where he asked, "If the Succession according to the present Establishment Should cease for want of an Heir or if the Parliament should alter it and admit a Papist to the Crown, would not the Colonies be at Liberty to joyn with Brittain or not[?]"[49] In posing this hypothetical, Sherman could have chosen a variety of constitutional violations or immoral actions. It is telling that the worst scenario he could imagine was Parliament permitting a Papist to become king.

Sherman was returned to Congress in May of 1775, and he continued to advocate American independence. Notably, he voted for and signed Congress's the Declaration of the Causes and Necessity of Taking up Arms. Originally drafted by Jefferson for a committee consisting of himself, John Rutledge, William Livingston, Benjamin Franklin, John Jay, and Thomas Johnson, it was revised significantly by John Dickinson and then amended and approved by Congress. The document began by providing the following theoretical foundation:

> If it was possible for men, who exercise their reason, to believe, that the Divine Author of our existence intended a part of the human race to hold an absolute property in, and an unbounded power over others, marked out by his infinite goodness and wisdom, as the objects of a legal domination never rightfully resistible, however severe and oppressive, the inhabitants of these Colonies might at least require from the parliament of Great Britain some evidence, that this dreadful authority over them, has been granted to that body. But a reverence for our Creator, principles of humanity, and the dictates of common sense, must convince all those who reflect upon the subject, that government was instituted to promote the welfare of mankind, and ought to be administered for the attainment of that end.[50]

This paragraph reflects well some of the basic tenets of Reformed political theory. God is the author of freedom, and He ordains limited governments to promote the common good. The document goes on to proclaim that

Parliament's actions must be resisted, not because of the particular harm of any one policy, but because its ultimate aim is to enslave the colonies. Congress emphasized Parliament's overreaching claims, particularly its extravagant assertion that it could "make laws to bind us IN ALL CASES WHATSOEVER." After listing a number of specific grievances against Parliament and the king's officials, such as the "unprovoked assault" on Lexington and Concord, the burning of Charles-Town, and the instigation of Indian attacks, the delegates proclaimed:

> Our cause is just. Our union is perfect. Our internal resources are great, and, if necessary, foreign assistance is undoubtedly attainable.—We gratefully acknowledge, as signal instances of the Divine favour towards us, that his Providence would not permit us to be called into this severe controversy, until we were grown up to our present strength, had been previously exercised in warlike operation, and possessed of the means of defending ourselves. With hearts fortified with these animating reflections, we most solemnly, before God and the world, declare, that, exerting the utmost energy of those powers, which our beneficent Creator hath graciously bestowed upon us, the arms we have been compelled by our enemies to assume, we will, in defiance of every hazard, with unabating firmness and perseverence, employ for the preservation of our liberties; being with our [one] mind resolved to die freemen rather than to live slaves.

This declaration, passed a little less than a year before its more famous cousin, falls short of requiring separation from Great Britain. Instead, it concludes "[w]ith an humble confidence in the mercies of the supreme and impartial Judge and Ruler of the Universe, we most devoutly implore his divine goodness to protect us happily through this great conflict, to dispose our adversaries to reconciliation on reasonable terms, and thereby to relieve the empire from the calamities of civil war." It is interesting for our purposes because it more obviously reflects the concerns and language of Reformed Protestants. Because this text is often neglected by students of the era, the intellectual influence of Calvinist political thought is less apparent than it might otherwise be.[51]

Throughout the 1770s, Sherman steadfastly denied that Parliament had any authority whatsoever over the colonies. Their only allegiance was to the Crown, and in his mind the king had clearly removed the colonists from his protection. When it came time to appoint a committee to write a declaration of independence, Sherman was a logical candidate. On June 11, 1776, Congress appointed Benjamin Franklin, John Adams, Thomas Jefferson, Robert Livingston, and Roger Sherman to such a committee. Unfortunately for Sherman's future fame, the very next day he was also appointed to the committee to draft what became the Articles of Confederation (Livingston was the only other delegate to serve on both committees). Two days later, he was appointed to the Board of War. He was the only member of Congress to serve on all three of these committees.[52]

According to John Adams, the committee on the declaration "had several meetings, in which were proposed the articles of which the declaration was to consist and minutes made of them. The committee then appointed Mr. Jefferson and me to draw them into form, and clothe them in a proper dress." As Adams recalled the story, he insisted Jefferson write the draft, the committee met to discuss it, and Franklin and Sherman declined to criticize anything because of the press of time. Jefferson's account varies slightly from Adams's, but not significantly with respect to Sherman's participation.[53] Nevertheless, although none of the changes in the draft declarations are made in Sherman's hand, Julian P. Boyd reasonably asked how "can we be certain whether some of these corrections and changes...were not suggested by Adams or Franklin—or even by Roger Sherman, a very wise man, or by Robert R. Livingston, an intelligent youngster?"[54] Similarly, Pauline Maier emphasizes that "[i]n the end, the efforts of these five men produced a workable draft that the Congress itself, sitting as the Committee of the Whole, made into a distinguished document by an act of group editing that has to be one of the great marvels of history."[55] And there is certainly no reason to suspect that Sherman did not wholeheartedly support the Declaration, including its famous assertions that

> all men are created equal; that they are endowed by their Creator with certain unalienable rights; that among these are life, liberty, and the pursuit of happiness; that, to secure these rights, governments are instituted among men, deriving their just powers from the consent of the governed; that whenever any form of government becomes destructive of these ends, it is the right of the people to alter or to abolish it, and to institute new government, laying its foundation on such principles, and organizing its powers in such form, as to them shall seem most likely to effect their safety and happiness.[56]

These words reflect arguments long made by patriots in New England, many of whom likely never read Locke and almost all of whom were serious Calvinists. Of course, Jefferson definitely read Locke and was most certainly not a Calvinist, but he later noted that he was not attempting to "find out new principles, or new arguments," but that the Declaration's authority rests "on the harmonizing sentiments of the day." Jefferson indisputably borrowed language from Locke, but for Sherman and his Reformed colleagues the ideas to which he referred predated Locke by years. There is simply no evidence that Sherman and the delegates from Connecticut—William Williams, Samuel Huntington, and Oliver Wolcott—or other delegates from Reformed backgrounds: Josiah Bartlett, William Whipple, Matthew Thornton, John Hancock, Samuel Adams, John Adams, Robert Treat Paine, William Ellery, William Floyd, Philip Livingston, Richard Stockton, John Witherspoon, John Hart, Abraham Clark, James Smith, James Wilson, Thomas McKean, and Lyman Hall understood the "Creator" to be "nature" or thought they were approving a document that mandated a "secular politics" when they approved the Declaration.[57]

Some scholars have argued that the use of "distant" words for God or "vague and generic God-language" like "Nature's God," "Creator," and "Providence" in the Declaration is evidence that the founders were deists. However, indisputably orthodox Christians regularly used such appellations. For instance, the Westminster Standards (a classic Reformed confession of faith), both in the original 1647 version and the 1788 American revision, refer to the deity as "the Supreme Judge," "the great Creator of all things," "the first cause," "righteous judge," "God the Creator," and "the supreme Law and King of all the world." They also regularly reference God's providence and even proclaim that "[t]he light of nature showeth that there is a God." Similarly, Isaac Watts, the "father of English Hymnody," referred to the deity as "nature's God" in a poem about Psalm 148: 10. Jeffry H. Morrison has argued persuasively that the Declaration's references to "'divine Providence' and 'the Supreme Judge of the World' would have been quite acceptable to Reformed Americans in 1776, and conjured up images of the 'distinctly biblical God' when they heard or read the Declaration."[58]

As an additional point of reference, it is instructive to look beyond Congress to the Connecticut General Assembly. On June 15, 1776, that body proclaimed that the king and Parliament had repeatedly violated the colonies' "antient just and constitutional rights," ignored their "frequent humble, decent and dutiful petitions for redress of grievances," and "have declared us out of the King's protection." The only appropriate response to this pattern of tyrannical behavior was to appeal to God,

> who knows the secrets of all hearts for the sincerity of former declarations of our desire to preserve our antient and constitutional relation to that nation, and protesting solemnly against their oppression and injustice, which have driven us from them and compelled us to use such means as God in his providence hath put in our power for our necessary defence and preservation.

In practical terms, the General Assembly "resolved unanimously" that "the Delegates of this Colony in General Congress, be and they are hereby instructed to propose to that respectable body, to declare the United American Colonies Free and Independent States, absolved from all allegiance to the King of Great Britain, and to give the assent of this colony to such declaration when they shall judge it expedient and best."[59]

Of course, Connecticut was not the only colony to give such instructions; indeed, the colony drew from an earlier resolution from Virginia. The critical point for present purposes is that it is implausible to think the General Assembly *unanimously* approved these instructions because of a sudden conversion to a secularized Lockean liberalism.[60] Sherman's old colleagues such as William Williams, Eliphalet Dyer, and William Pitkin were staunch Calvinists, and it is far more reasonable to conclude that they were influenced Reformed political theory. This conclusion is supported as well by Governor Jonathan Trumbull's proclamation (which was approved by the General Assembly) issued three days later. It began with a lengthy argument defending the colonists' cause that reached back to the dawn of human history:

> The Race of Mankind was made in a State of Innocence and Freedom, subjected only to the Laws of GOD the CREATOR, and through his rich Goodness, designed for virtuous Liberty and Happiness here and forever.

After tracing the fall of mankind, the institution of government, the glories of the British constitution, and the recent tyrannical acts of Great Britain, the proclamation encouraged all citizens to fight the "Tyrant of *Britain*," to defend their "Liberty, and every thing they hold sacred and dear, to defend the Cause of their Country, their Religion and their God." It concluded with the recommendation that the ministers and people meet together for "Prayer to ALMIGHTY GOD, for the out-pouring of his blessed Spirit upon this guilty Land—That he would awaken his People to Righteousness and Repentance." The proclamation, which is well worth reading in full, is reprinted in appendix one.[61]

In a 1775 speech urging reconciliation between Great Britain and the colonies, Edmund Burke warned his fellow members of Parliament that Americans "are Protestants; and of that kind which is the most adverse to all implicit submission of mind and opinion. This is a persuasion not only favorable to liberty, but built upon it." A few months later, British Major Harry Rooke confiscated a presumably Calvinist book from prisoners taken at Bunker Hill and remarked, "It is your G-d Damned Religion of this Country that ruins the Country; Damn your religion." Similarly, the Loyalist Peter Oliver railed against "Mr. *Otis's* black Regiment, *the dissenting Clergy*, who took so active a part in the Rebellion." King George himself reportedly referred to the War for Independence as "a Presbyterian Rebellion," a sentiment echoed by a Hessian soldier who described it as "an Irish-Scotch Presbyterian rebellion." In 1780, Anglican clergy in New York wrote, "Dissenters in general, and particularly Presbyterians and Congregationalists were the active Promoters of the Rebellion" because "from their infancy [they] imbibe Republican, levelling Principles." Historians have long recognized that there was an "almost unanimous and persistent critical attitude of the Congregational and Presbyterian ministers toward the British imperial policy." Connecticut citizens and their political leaders agreed with their ministers. The General Assembly was not in session when the Continental Congress voted to adopt the Declaration of Independence, but, when it reconvened in October 1776, its first act was to unanimously approve the document.[62]

Sherman and his Reformed colleagues were part of a tradition that had long held that individuals possess natural rights, that governments should be based on the consent of the people, that civil authority should be limited, and that the people have a right to overthrow tyrannical regimes. Students of American political theory underestimate the influence of this tradition because of their proclivity to focus on only a few select documents and founders. As scholars expand the conversation beyond Jefferson, they may well find that Sherman is a better representative of the American political class than his more eloquent colleague from Virginia.

4

Achieving Independence

STUDENTS OF AMERICAN political theory often skip over the Continental and Confederation Congresses as they rush from the Declaration of Independence to the Constitution. If they slow down, it is generally to note that Congress created and the states ratified an inefficient national constitution—the Articles of Confederation. Space constraints prohibit consideration of all the documents and policies Sherman helped craft during his 1,543 days of service in America's first national government, but an exploration of several key texts and issues shines light on his political ideas and actions. Without denying the interplay of practical and other ideological influences, this chapter reinforces my thesis that Sherman and many of his colleagues were significantly influenced by the Reformed tradition.[1]

Economics and the War for Independence

Perhaps the most difficult duty for Sherman-the-advocate-of-hard-money was serving in a body notorious for issuing nearly worthless "Continentals." His longstanding opposition to depreciating paper money was reinforced when he read George Whatley's "Principles of Trade...Containing Reflections of God, Silver and Paper Passing as Money," around 1776. Originally published in 1774, the pamphlet offers a spirited defense of both hard money and free markets. However, in the midst of the War for Independence, Sherman could do little to prevent Congress from printing paper money or to find sources of revenue to support the value of its bills. Throughout the war he encouraged Congress and the states to "sink" rapidly depreciating paper money. For instance, a June 14, 1779, Treasury Committee report in Sherman's handwriting strongly recommended that Congress cease to print paper money and redeem Continental bonds with gold or silver. The measure failed six states to five. Sherman was a bit more successful in Connecticut, one of the few states to support its emissions of paper money with sufficient tax revenue.[2]

Sherman believed in the virtues of hard money and, generally, free markets, but he was not an advocate of laissez-faire economics. During the war he argued that inflation could be contained and the common good promoted by restricting the cost of goods and labor. Connecticut was the first state to pass price controls in November 1776, and New England states held a convention shortly thereafter aimed at regulating prices in the region. Sherman was not at this meeting, but he served on a congressional committee with Richard Henry Lee, James Wilson, Samuel Chase, and John Adams that recommended approving the proposed price controls. After significant debate, Congress agreed. Sherman did attend a July 1777 convention in Springfield, Massachusetts, as a delegate from Connecticut. According to Christopher Collier, he was "a dominant figure" in that body which, among other things, called on the states to "draw in and sink bills of credit issued by the several states."[3]

In response to the Springfield convention's report, Congress urged all of the northern states to send delegates to a January 1778 meeting in New Haven. New Hampshire, Massachusetts, Rhode Island, New York, New Jersey, Pennsylvania, and Connecticut complied with the request, and the latter appointed Sherman, William Hillhouse, and Benjamin Huntington to represent the state. The convention elected Sherman chairman, and, after a week of meetings,instructed him, Robert Treat Paine, Nathaniel Peabody, and Benjamin Huntington to "draw up a report of the doings of this Convention."[4] Sherman's account book contains the only known draft of this report. It is in Sherman's handwriting and is dated January 29, one day before the final report was approved by the convention. There is little doubt that he played a major role in drafting the text. The document illustrates well the influence of Calvinism on Sherman and his colleagues. It begins by reminding readers:

When we see *self-love*, that first principle planted in the humane breast, by the All-Wise Creator for our benefit and preservation, through Misapplication and corruption, perverted to our destruction, we feel the necessity of correcting so pernicious an error & directing the operation of it in such a manner as that our self and social love may be the same. The application of this remark to the present state of our public affairs in obvious.

The freeborn Inhabitants of America, oppressed by the Tyranny of Great Britain found it necessary for the support of their Liberties to declare themselves *Independent*. To support that *Independence* it was necessary to raise and maintain an expensive Army and to Issue large emissions of paper Bills to defray the expenses: Upon the support & success of this Army, under *God*, depends the whole we are contending for: and on the Credit of our currency depends immediately the support of our Army; when therefore the principle of *self-love* impels the individuals of a Community, to exact & receive for their services or commodities such prices as exceed that proportion of price at which the Army was raised & Established . . . Is it not evident that their *self-love* and attention to their supposed self Interest have exceeded their true bounds, and tend not only to the destruction of the Welfare of the community, but also of the individuals?[5]

James D. German has argued that Sherman and his colleagues were capitalists who "licensed the frankest pursuit of self-interest." Such a position is difficult to maintain in light of the corpus of Sherman's writings. It is true that he spoke of an appropriate "self-love" here and elsewhere. For instance, in his 1753 almanac, Sherman printed the following lines from Alexander Pope's *Essay on Man*: "Reason & passion answer one great Aim,/And true self love & social are the same."[6] Similarly, late in life, he challenged Samuel Hopkins's assertion that every form of self-love is sinful. Sherman agreed that "selfishness in a depraved being" is wrong, but contended that there is a proper self-love which "exists in beings perfectly holy, which by the moral law is made the measure of our love to our neighbor." He contended that if one agrees with the Westminster Catechism that "Man's chief end is to glorify God, and enjoy him forever," one should recognize that "when a person seeks his own highest good and happiness in the enjoyment of God, and in connection with his glory, he answers the end of his creation."[7]

Sherman believed that acting in one's own interest—properly understood—promoted an individual's own good and, as an added benefit, contributed to the common good. However, as he wrote in the New Haven report, problems arise by the "misapplication and corruption" of this principle. Sherman and his fellow Calvinists believed that unregenerate humans were totally depraved and that even Christians continued to struggle with sin. Moreover, virtually all of them agreed that it was appropriate for governments to pass laws requiring men and women to act morally in some circumstances. In this case, to restrain greed and aid the war effort, they concluded that it was necessary to limit wages and prices.

To "those who are actuated by no better principle than contracted *self love*," such restrictions "may be considered as infringing the principles of Trade & Liberty." However, they are "nevertheless a salutary measure in conjunction with the others, and practiced by all the states."[8]

Sherman had little patience with those who complained about state regulations. "Why" he asked,

> do we complain of a partial infringement of liberty, manifestly tend-
> ing to the preservation of the whole? Must the Lunatick run uncon-
> trolled, to the destruction of himself and Neighbours, merely
> because he is under the operation of medicines which may in time
> work his cure? And indeed without the use of those medicines will
> the confinement cure him?

In Sherman's mind, and in the minds of his fellow delegates, Americans were pursuing a common and moral end that justified restrictions on liberty. Not only would these restrictions lead to success, they would also promote true self-love. Thus they benefit both the community and individuals; including those men and women who were taking advantage of the current crises.[9]

The New Haven convention proposed strict limitations on wages and prices, approved a letter urging Congress to redeem Continental bills, and expressed disappointment that Delaware did not send delegates to the meeting. The details of the proposals are not important for a number of reasons, including the fact that Congress acknowledged but refused to act on the report. Connecticut did respond to the convention by adopting restrictions, perhaps owing to Sherman's influence in the Assembly.[10] Practically speaking, the wage and price controls were both ineffective and counterproductive. However, the report is still noteworthy in that it illustrates Sherman's conviction that humans are sinful and that governments may restrict harmful activities both for the good of the community *and* the individuals involved.

Another controversy that reveals something about Sherman's political ideas arose from the desire of citizens living in the New Hampshire Grants to form what is now the state of Vermont. Because the area was claimed by both New Hampshire and New York, and populated by people with little love for either state, the issue was extremely divisive. In 1777, Sherman introduced to Congress a petition from settlers in the region requesting recognition as an independent state. The next year, when several towns clearly within New Hampshire's borders attempted to join the new republic, Sherman wrote Elisha Payne, noting that for these towns "to separate without the consent of the State to which they belong appears to me a very unjustifiable violation of the social compact, and pregnant with the most ruinous consequences." He acknowledged that the New Hampshire constitution was not perfect, but suggested that the solution was for citizens from these towns to seek to amend it. This letter underlines the tensions between Sherman's commitment to government by the consent of the governed, his concern for states' rights, and his love of order.[11]

On August 7, 1781, Sherman and four colleagues presented a report to Congress defining Vermont's boundaries and recommending the appointment of a committee to discuss admitting the republic into the "federal union." Congress accepted the report, but opposition from a variety of quarters kept Vermont out of the union until 1790. During this time Sherman remained a consistent advocate for the state. Notably, in the Constitutional Convention he proposed an alteration to what became Article IV, Section 3 to make it easier to admit Vermont.[12]

Throughout the war Sherman often served on congressional committees charged with providing troops with supplies and war material. He was regularly at odds with members of the Commissary General, who often cared more about lining their own pockets than hungry troops. As well, he was on Congress's Board of War, "a Grand Committee to report a requisition on the States for the payment of interest on the National Debt," and on a variety of ad hoc committees. He also participated extensively in debates over, and voted to approve, the precursor of the Northwest Ordinance. In his last year in the Confederation Congress, he voted to ratify the Treaty of Paris, and he left the body for good on June 4, 1784.[13]

Congress and Religion

Because of its limited authority, the Continental and Confederation Congresses seldom addressed issues involving religious liberty or church-state relations. Yet Sherman's faith often influenced his arguments and votes in the new national government. Moreover, Congress did on occasion take actions that indicate how he and many of his colleagues thought church and state should be related. Of course, there were occasionally disagreements on these subjects, but delegates from New England were remarkably consistent in supporting congressional actions that encouraged Christianity and Christian morality.

To begin with obvious examples, Sherman occasionally appealed directly to the Bible when making political decisions and arguments. For instance, he opposed a congressional committee's proposal to increase the maximum number of lashes allowed for military discipline from one hundred to five hundred. John Sullivan reported in a letter to George Washington that "though a Great Majority of Congress were for it, the question was Lost" due to "principles Laid down by Levitical Law Strongly urged by Roger Shearman Esqr and Co."[14] Although the record does not specify it, Sherman's objection almost certainly stemmed from Deuteronomy 25:3, "Forty stripes he may give him, and not exceed: lest, if he should exceed, and beat him above these with many stripes, then thy brother should seem vile unto thee."

Sherman and his colleagues regularly supported congressional calls for prayer, fasting, and thanksgiving. In 1781, Sherman was appointed to a committee with John Witherspoon, Joseph Montgomery, and James Varnum to write a proclamation recommending a day be set aside for public thanksgiving. The final proclamation, in Witherspoon's handwriting, was adopted by Congress. It requested that states set apart December 13, 1781:

> To be religiously observed as a Day of Thanksgiving and Prayer; that all the people may assemble on that day, with grateful hearts, to celebrate the praises of our gracious Benefactor; to confess our manifold sins; to offer up our most fervent supplications to the God of all grace, that it may please Him to pardon our offences, and incline our hearts for the future to keep all his laws ... and cause the knowledge of God to cover the earth, as the waters cover the seas.

The proclamation also lists a variety of specific events that the people should express gratitude for God's "Providential" care. That a committee comprised of Sherman; Witherspoon, a Presbyterian minister from Scotland; and Joseph Montgomery, a Presbyterian minister from Pennsylvania, should write such a theologically rich proclamation is not surprising. The document leaves no doubt that the authors understood God to be active in the affairs of men and nations. However, there is no presumption that Americans had merited His favor. Indeed, the text calls on them to "confess our manifold sins." That this proclamation is similar to the other calls for prayer, fasting, and thanksgiving issued by Congress only reinforces the argument that Calvinism influenced many founders. The doctrines referenced in these calls are not uniquely Reformed, and such proclamations were issued in other states, but they were most clearly a part of the political culture of Calvinist New England.[15]

The Continental and Confederations Congresses issued more than a dozen explicitly Christian calls for prayer, fasting, and thanksgiving. This figure does not include texts such as the May 1778 "Address of Congress to the Inhabitants of the United States of America" which was "recommended to ministers of the gospel of all denomination to read or cause to be read, immediately after divine services . . . in their respective churches and chapels, and other places of divine worship." This document proclaims that America is relying on God's providential care, incorporates scripture into the text without citation (e.g., "the time will soon arrive when every many shall sit under his own vine and under his own fig-tree, and there shall be none to make him afraid" [Micah 4:4]), and encourages Americans to "assiduously cultivate" the "assistance of Heaven."[16]

Sherman also supported having congressional and military chaplains, and in 1784 he made a motion to "advance" congressional chaplain Daniel Jones one hundred and fifty dollars. He also agreed to military regulations that "earnestly recommended to all officers and soldiers, diligently to attend Divine Service," and he voted in favor a resolution stating:

> Whereas true religion and good morals are the only solid foundations of public liberty and happiness:
>
> Resolved, That it be, and it is hereby earnestly recommended to the several states, to take the most effectual measures for the encouragement thereof, and for the suppressing of theatrical entertainments, horse racing, gaming, and such other diversions as are productive of idleness, dissipation, and a general depravity of principles and manners.
>
> Resolved, That all officers in the army of the Unites States, be, and hereby are strictly enjoined to see that the good and wholesome rules provided for the discountenancing of prophaness and vice, and the preservation of morals among the soldiers, are duly and punctually observed.

Congress overwhelmingly approved these resolutions, with no dissenting votes from any New England delegate (some of the southern delegates were less than sanguine about condemning horse racing).[17]

In spite of Congress's limited powers, the body regularly encouraged Christian practices and morality. In September 1777, it approved the importation of twenty thousand Bibles at Congress's expense, although this motion was ultimately tabled. Four years later, Robert Aitken (1734–1802), a Presbyterian elder and congressional printer, asked Congress to authorize him to publish the first American edition of the holy scriptures in the English language. Congress provided an endorsement but no subsidy. Sherman was not a member of Congress when these votes were taken, but not a single delegate from New England dissented from the first proposal, and the endorsement was apparently approved without objection, so there is no reason to think Sherman would have objected to either.[18]

Sherman and his colleagues saw no contradiction between promoting Christianity and respecting the liberty of conscience. They primarily conceived of religious liberty as permitting men and women to worship God according to the dictates of their consciences. Congress never required individuals to worship God or to engage in religious practices against their wills. This commitment to religious liberty is evident in a famous text written by a committee consisting of Sherman, John Adams, and George Wythe. These delegates were charged with penning instructions for commissioners being sent to Canada to convince colonists there (particularly French Roman Catholics) to join the fight for independence. Among other things, Sherman, Adams, and Wythe wrote that the commissioners should

> declare, that we hold sacred the rights of conscience, and may promise to the whole people, solemnly in our name, the free and undisturbed exercise of their religion; and, to the clergy, the full, perfect, and peaceable possession and enjoyment of all their estates; that the government of every thing relating to their religion and clergy, shall be left entirely in the hands of the good people of that province, and such legislature as they shall constitute; Provided, however, that all other denominations of Christians be equally entitled to hold offices, and enjoy civil privileges, and the free exercise of their religion, and be totally exempt from the payment of any tythes or taxes for the support of any religion.[19]

These instructions were adopted by Congress on March 20, 1776, and this and other messages were duly relayed to Canada. Unfortunately, from the American perspective, they did not have the desired effect. One must be careful not to read too much into this highly political letter, yet the sentiments expressed in it are consistent with Sherman's views as reflected over the course of his political career.

Articles of Confederation

Students of the American founding rarely treat the Articles of Confederation as anything other than a failed constitution.[20] Yet its drafters did not presume it would fail, so they approached their work quite seriously. As well, there were important debates at the state level about whether the Articles should be ratified, and essays were published attacking and defending the document. Sherman was heavily involved in creating and defending America's first national constitution.

On June 11, 1776, Congress appointed Sherman, Benjamin Franklin, John Adams, Thomas Jefferson, and Robert Livingston to a committee to write the Declaration of Independence. The next day, it selected one delegate from each state to be on a committee charged with preparing the "form of a confederation to be entered into between these colonies." Sherman was placed on this committee, along with Josiah Bartlett, Samuel Adams, Stephen Hopkins, Robert Livingston, John Dickinson, Thomas McKean, Thomas Stone, Thomas Nelson, Joseph Hewes, Edward Rutledge, and Button Gwinnett. The following day, Sherman, John Adams, Benjamin Harrison, James Wilson, and Edward Rutledge were elected to the Board of War and Ordinance—one of the busiest of all congressional committees.[21]

John Dickinson wrote the first major draft of the Articles of Confederation. Merrill Jensen proposed that he was chosen for this task because he was the "outstanding man on the committee."[22] Certainly he was respected, but another reason for choosing him might have been that other prominent delegates were serving on multiple committees and so could not spend as much time on any one task. With respect to the committees mentioned earlier, John Adams, James Wilson, Edward Rutledge, and Robert Livingston were each on two, while only Roger Sherman served on all three. Thomas Jefferson and John Dickinson—authors of drafts of the major documents produced by these committees—served on only one each.

Dickinson did not compose the Articles in a vacuum, but, unfortunately, few records of the committee's deliberations exist. We do know that the debates were serious, indicated by Josiah Bartlett's letter noting that "[a]s it is a very important business, and some difficulties have arisen, I fear it will take some time before it will be finally settled."[23] The committee eventually came to a consensus, and on July 12 a draft of the Articles of Confederation in Dickinson's handwriting was submitted to Congress. This was printed and debated, amended significantly, and then reprinted on August 20. Because of the war, Congress did not address the Articles again until April 8, 1777. They were debated sporadically throughout the spring and summer, but it was not until the fall that Congress returned to the document in earnest. In November, one last committee consisting of Richard Henry Lee, James Duane, and James Lovell was appointed to put the text into its final form.

The primary objection to Dickinson's initial draft was that it gave the new national government too much power. This is particularly evident in its "guarantee" that each state would maintain "as much of its present Laws, Rights and Customs, as it may think fit, and reserves to itself the sole and exclusive Regulation and Government of its internal policy, *in all matters that shall not interfere with the Articles of Confederation*" [emphasis added]. Advocates of states' rights feared that if Congress determined what did or did not interfere with the Articles, that the national government's power would be essentially unlimited. Even the Dickinson draft's stipulation that "the United States assembled shall never impose or levy any Taxes or Duties, except in managing the Post-Office" did not placate them. Moreover, many opponents worried that the draft's provision for an executive, or "Council of State," consisting of one delegate from each colony that would govern when Congress was not in session would lead to tyranny.[24]

Sherman, like many of his New England colleagues, was simultaneously an advocate of democracy, states' rights, and a stronger national government. He was protective of Connecticut's political order, where decisions most immediately impacting citizens were made in town and society meetings or by elected representatives in the General Assembly. He was not about to turn over the ability of Connecticut citizens to govern themselves to others—even to his fellow Americans. Yet he recognized the need to form a stronger national government, if for no other reason than to protect fellow citizens from external aggression. Accordingly, he supported the Articles as they made their way through Congress but always insisted that the powers of the new national government be limited.[25]

Both Dickinson's draft of the Articles and the final version provided for one-state-one-vote. As in 1787, this issue was hotly debated, with some delegates arguing for representation based on population. Not surprisingly, this view was generally held by delegates from large states, who appealed to democratic principles to support their position. Delegates from smaller states insisted on equality of representation, contending that the confederation was one of equal, sovereign states. Sherman suggested a compromise. According to John Adams, he

> thinks we ought not to vote according to numbers. We are representatives of States, not individuals. States of Holland. The consent of every one is necessary. Three Colonies would govern the whole, but would not have a majority of strength to carry those votes into execution. The vote should be taken two ways; call the Colonies, and call the individuals, and have a majority of both.[26]

Sherman's proposal is notable for remaining faithful to his democratic principles *and* his commitment to state sovereignty. Moreover, it exhibits a sound recognition that the new national government would need the support of both small and large states if it was to be successful. The small states won the debate, and the Articles retained one-state-one-vote; a victory that eventually contributed to the collapse of the confederation. However, Sherman's proposal resurfaced at the Constitutional Convention and eventually was adopted as the Connecticut Compromise.

On November 17, 1777, after extensive debates about sovereignty, western lands, and taxes, Congress approved the final version of the Articles of Confederation and sent it to the states for ratification. Dickinson's draft had been amended to protect state sovereignty, the executive council had been weakened, and the right of states with western land claims to govern their territory had been protected. This latter provision encouraged Maryland to refuse to ratify the Articles until all of the states with western claims agreed to cede them to Congress. After Virginia finally abandoned its rights to land northwest of the Ohio River, Maryland agreed to ratify the Articles. They went into effect on March 1, 1781.[27]

Debating the Articles of Confederation

One of the most important attacks on the Articles of Confederation was made by Pelatiah Webster in his pamphlet "A Dissertation on the Political Union and Constitution of the Thirteen United States, of North-America" published under the pseudonym of "A Citizen of Philadelphia" in 1783. Webster (1725–1795) was born in Connecticut, graduated from Yale, and served as a minister for several years before moving to Philadelphia in 1755 to engage in business. He wrote regularly on politics and economics, and he has been credited with being the "brain" behind the federal Constitution. In a series of articles published in the early twentieth century, Hannis Taylor contended that Webster was the "architect of our federal constitution" and that he should be ranked behind only George Washington in terms of importance. This claim goes much too far, as Edward S. Corwin and others effectively demonstrated, but the pamphlet remains a significant yet over-looked piece of constitutional commentary—as does Sherman's reply.[28]

Webster's fundamental complaint against the Articles of Confederation was that they did not give the national government sufficient power. Notably, Congress must have the power to raise its own revenues—ideally by being empowered to lay a tariff on imported luxury goods. Webster also argued that it was foolish to prohibit delegates from serving more than three years in a six-year period because the restriction would remove good men from office. He desired to reopen the debate about how to apportion revenue bur-dens among the states, contending that land values are difficult to measure and that it would be more just to use population (both free and slave).

Webster acknowledged that strengthening the national government would be dangerous because of "the imperfect state of human nature," so he proposed requiring all debates to be public and dividing the legislative assembly into two branches. However, members of each chamber would still be appointed by the states, and each state would still have one vote. Because these delegates would have "strong local attachments," he advo-cated appointing ministers of finance, state, war, and foreign affairs who would be experts in their fields and to whom Congress would submit pro-posed legislation. These ministers would have no veto power, but would provide objective feedback on bills from the perspective of the good of the nation rather than particular states. Similarly, Webster wanted a "chamber of commerce" that would represent merchants and advise Congress.[29]

Webster conceded that having a bicameral legislature would make it easier to defeat bills, but suggested it is "much better in the main, to lose a good bill than suffer a bad one to pass into a law." In case of an emergency, he suggested that, as in ancient Rome, the legislature might choose a tem-porary dictator to rule until the crisis passed. He also advocated placing the executive departments under a council of state, consisting of the ministers of finance, state, war, foreign affairs, and three others (one each from the north, middle states, and south). This body would run executive agencies, appoint executive officers, and have the power (along with Congress) to remove officers "for just cause." Like many opponents of the Articles of

Confederation, Webster thought it ridiculous that a single state could prevent amendments to the document, so he sought to abolish this require-ment. Yet he also suggested that a majority of states should be able to repeal any national law. Finally, he hinted at the creation of a more robust federal judiciary, a suggestion Hannis Taylor transformed into a full-scale proposal for a "Supreme Court, with jurisdiction both original and appellate" that would definitively interpret the supreme law of the land.[30]

Webster pointed out weaknesses inherent in the Articles of Confederation and suggested creative ways they might be remedied. Sherman was not convinced by his arguments; at least not in 1784. That year, writing under the pseudonym of "A Connecticut Farmer," he offered a scathing critique of Webster's pamphlet in "Remarks on a Pamphlet Entitled 'A Dissertation on the Political Union and Constitution of the Thirteen United States of North America by a Citizen of Philadelphia'..." Surprisingly, scholars writing about Sherman have never attributed this pamphlet to him, even though Joseph Sabin and Charles Evans agree that he wrote it.[31]

Sherman's fundamental concern was that Webster's proposals would lead to a tyrannical national government that would undermine state sov-ereignty. Notably, he claimed the new national "*offices* and *officers*," would rapidly become as corrupt as court offices and officials in England. To Sherman, a large, complicated national government was contrary to "the true spirit and genius of *republican* government," which should be small and simple:

The fewer the laws—the more simple the form of government the better.—The whole code of laws which related to the civil polity of the *Jews* might be comprised in less compass than any one of the five books of *Moses*, although *they were as the stars of heaven for mul-titude, and as the sand on the sea shore innumerable.*—Their Judges were the elders of their cites, who held their sessions in their gates, and in their causes determined without long, tedious and expensive processes.

To ensure that states maintain their "*sovereignty, freedom* and *independence*" they must "carefully and rigorously instruct their representatives to pay the strictest regard to the articles of our federal union."[32]

Sherman proceeded to explain how Webster's proposals would signifi-cantly expand the size of the national government and why this would be dangerous. He especially objected to the idea that Congress be given the power to raise revenue—a prerogative, he pointed out, that went beyond the powers claimed by George III. Although he agreed that a national impost on luxury goods would be useful, he professed to be agnostic about whether the tax should be collected by national or state officials. However, giving Congress a generic power to raise revenue would remove the critical safeguard of states being able to refuse to fund bad policies favored by the national government. Between the power to tax and the power to appoint national officers, the national government would embark on a path to tyranny, one Sherman believed would lead to Congress appointing a temporary dictator who would soon become a permanent ruler who would "reduce us to an ABSOLUTE MONARCHY." He did not share Webster's confidence that open legislative proceedings and bicameralism would prevent this outcome.[33]

In the middle of his pamphlet, Sherman made a brief digression where he criticized the recent decision by a commission created under the Articles of Confederation that sided with Pennsylvania over Connecticut in the Wyoming Valley dispute. He offered a stirring argument about the right of the "original natives" to sell their land to whomever they wished; in this case the Susquehannah Company. The argument seems out of place because Webster did not mention the controversy in his pamphlet, but Webster had written about the issue elsewhere, and he and Sherman had corresponded about it. The digression is significant as it prompted Webster to write a friend noting that "Mr. Sherman of Connecticut has replied to my pamphlet, being displeased with my views concerning the western lands. I enclose you a copy of his pamphlet." This letter is a critical piece of evidence identifying Sherman as "A Connecticut Farmer."[34]

At times Sherman went too far in his criticism of Webster, such as when he inaccurately accused him of wanting to give Congress the power to appoint state officials. As well, he unfairly neglects Webster's suggestion that a majority of states should be able to overrule the national government. By 1787, Sherman must have come to accept Webster's basic point that the national government needed to be strengthened, as demonstrated by his arguments and actions at the Federal Convention. Nevertheless, Sherman's essay helps demonstrate his commitment to local government. Like many founders, he was suspicious of concentrated power and favored small commonwealths where "electors [are] personally acquainted with public characters." He was dedicated to preserving the sovereignty of states, and while he eventually came to accept a stronger national government, he did so only after insisting on constitutional provisions designed to protect their independence.[35]

Revision of Connecticut's Laws

In spite of his active service at the national level, Sherman often returned to Connecticut to serve as an assistant during the spring and fall meetings of the General Assembly. As one might expect, many of the issues addressed by the legislature during these years concerned the War for Independence. The Assembly routinely debated and passed laws such as "An Act to Secure to the Officers and Soldiers of the Connecticut Line of the Continental Army" and "An Act for Filling up the Connecticut Battalions in the Continental Army."[36] Of course, many states passed similar laws; what is notable in Connecticut's case is that they were implemented. No state did a better job meeting Congress's requests, a fact recognized by General Washington who singled out Connecticut for filling its quotas and referred to it as "the provisions state."[37]

Sherman was appointed to Connecticut's Council of Safety in 1777, 1778, 1779, and 1782. This fourteen-person council consisted of the governor, deputy governor, and twelve other members, almost inevitably prominent statesmen. When the Assembly was not sitting, the Council of Safety had the

> full power and authority to order and direct the militia and navy of this State and the marches and stations of the troops that have been or shall be inlisted and assembled for the special defence of this or the neighbouring States…and to give all necessary orders from time to time for furnishing and supplying said militia, troops, and navy.

Business with the national Congress often kept him from these meetings, but when he was in Connecticut he was usually in attendance.[38]

After the war, one of Sherman's most significant accomplishments was his revision of Connecticut statutes. He had been involved in a similar project in 1768, but since that time many new statutes had been passed, some had been repealed, and independence had made others obsolete. The legislature asked Sherman and Richard Law to revise existing statutes "and make such Alterations Additions exclusions and Amendments as they shall Judge Proper and expedient." It was an enormous task. To divide it, Sherman took statutes beginning with the letters A–L and Law took the rest. Sherman and Law worked on their project throughout the summer and fall of 1783. The two men corresponded about changes in each other's sections. Sherman participated in debates over them as an assistant when the Assembly reviewed their work, accepting, rejecting, and amending their proposals, and approving the new one-volume state code (still organized alphabetically) in January of 1784.[39]

Connecticut's revisions of 1784 are particularly important because it was the first systematic revision of the state's laws to be made without the oversight of Great Britain. The first statute in the 1769 code was "An Act for Securing the General Privileges of His Majesty's Subjects in This Colony." It clearly acknowledges the Crown's sovereignty, yet it still stipulates that citizens have "such Liberties and Privileges as Humanity, Civility, and Christianity call for, as due to every Man in his place and proportion" and asserts the necessity of the rule of law.[40] The first statute proposed by Sherman in his revisions was entitled "An Act Containing an Abstract and Declaration of the Rights and Privileges of the People of this State, and Securing the Same." It incorporated provisions from statutes adopted in Connecticut from 1650–1776 and begins:

> The people of this State, being by the Providence of God, free and independent, have the sole and exclusive Right of governing themselves as a free, sovereign, and independent State and as such to exercise and enjoy every power, jurisdiction and right not expressly delegated to the Unites States in Congress assembled. And having from the ancestors derived a free and excellent constitution of government, whereby the Legislature depends on the free and annual election of the people, they have the best Security for the preservation of their civil and religious rights and liberties. And forasmuch as the free fruition of such liberties and privileges as humanity, civility, and christianity call for, as is due every man in his place and proportion, without impeachment and infringement, hath ever been, and will be the tranquility and stability of churches and commonwealths, and the denial thereof, the disturbance, if not the ruin of both.

The remainder of the law included a provision from a 1776 law affirming the "form of civil government, contained in the charter from Charles the Second, King of England, and adopted by the people of this State" as the state's "Civil Constitution." Sherman also included a list of rights drawn originally from articles 1, 2, and 18 of the Massachusetts Body of Liberties (1641) that had been adopted by the General Court as Connecticut's "Declaration of Rights" in 1650. These provisions prohibited a man's life, liberty, or property from being taken "unless it be by virtue or equity of some express law of this State warranting the same established by the general court, and sufficiently published; or in case of defect of such law in any particular case, by some clear and plain rule warranted by the word of God." They also required equal justice for all free persons and that individuals charged with most crimes be permitted to post bail.[41]

The first law in Connecticut's 1784 revisions is sometimes referred to as Connecticut's "Declaration of Rights" or "Bill of Rights." It is often erroneously presented as having been approved by the Connecticut Assembly in 1776, but the only part adopted by the legislature that year was the provision declaring the charter issued by Charles II to be the state's civil constitution. Scholars dispute whether this document is technically a bill of rights, and it is clearly statutory law, not part of the state's constitution. Sherman did not author this list of rights, but that he included them in the first statute of his revisions shows that he considered them to be important. With a few minor exceptions, the General Assembly approved the list of rights that he compiled.[42]

In light of my argument for the influence of Reformed theology on Sherman and his colleagues, it is noteworthy that when the Assembly revised Sherman's prefatory statute they replaced "unless it be by virtue or equity of some express law of this State warranting the same established by the general court, and sufficiently published; or in case of defect of such law in any particular case, by some clear and plain rule warranted by the word of God" with "unless clearly warranted by the Laws of this State."[43] Prohibiting judges from finding someone guilty for violating the "word of God" may suggest a drift toward secularization in Connecticut jurisprudence. However, the revised preface is also significantly shorter, so the change may have been driven by editorial considerations. Of course, over time, Connecticut law did become increasingly secular, but this did not begin in earnest until the early nineteenth century. Most likely, the alteration reflects the incipient movement toward the codification of law and a desire to limit the discretion of judges. This possibility gains support against a "secularization" interpretation from the numerous statutes passed by the General Assembly the same year clearly informed by or aimed at protecting and promoting Protestantism and Christian morality (discussed later in the chapter).

The General Assembly made an additional change in Sherman's prefatory statute—one that reflects several other alterations to his draft. He began the statute by proclaiming:

> The people of this State, being by the providence of God, free and independent, have the sole and exclusive Right of governing themselves as a free, sovereign, and independent State *and as such to exercise and enjoy every power, jurisdiction and right not expressly delegated to the Unites States in Congress assembled* [italics added].

Sherman's fellow legislators apparently thought the italicized phrase was too deferential to the new national government, so they removed it. His colleagues also negated a provision suggested by Sherman requiring all treaties made by Congress "with any foreign nation agreeable to the powers with which they are invested by the Confederation shall be duly observed." Sherman was firmly committed to the ideal of local government, but his years of national service made him more willing to cede limited power to the national government than many of his colleagues.[44]

In his revision of other statutes, Sherman proposed several institutional reforms, including strengthening the executive power by vesting "the Governor and Council of this State... the power to Superintend the prudential affairs" of the state, particularly with respect to the collection of revenue. He also wanted these men to have the ability to remove state officials for "neglect of duty or Malconduct in office," with the exception of judges acting in their judicial capacity. Sherman's proposed act would have reduced the legislature's work, and may have provided for a more effective execution of state business. However, it also reduced the power of the lower house—which, not surprisingly, negated the proposal. Similarly, Sherman offered a variety of minor reforms aimed at simplifying the judiciary and limiting the appellate jurisdiction of the General Assembly. He also proposed the creation of a court of chancery. Most of these proposals were initially rejected by the lower house but were adopted by the state in subsequent years.[45]

Slavery

One of the General Assembly's most important acts was to amend Connecticut's statute on slavery to manumit children born to slaves after March 1, 1784, when they reached the age of twenty-five. Because the subject of the law begins with *S*, the statute fell under Richard Law's purview. He did not suggest this change, but it was added when the legislature debated the proposed statute in early 1784. There is no reason to believe that Sherman, a lifelong opponent of slavery, did not support the alteration. He consistently opposed slavery because he believed all humans were made in the image of God and must be treated with dignity. In the same year the revisions were adopted, he wrote in his defense of the Articles of Confederation: "*That God hath made of one blood, all nations of the earth, and hath determined the bounds of their habitation,*"—a paraphrase of Acts 17:26. In the pamphlet, Sherman was addressing the rights of Native Americans, not African Americans, but his career provides numerous examples of his opposition to slavery. Thomas S. Kidd has observed that Acts 17:26 was the "the most commonly cited text used to demonstrate human equality by creation."[46]

As an assistant, Sherman was involved in passing several acts aimed at restricting and eventually eliminating slavery in Connecticut. For instance, he was serving in the General Assembly when it enacted an "Act for Prohibiting the Importation on Indian, Negro or Molatto Slaves" in 1774. As the title makes clear, the law made it illegal to bring slaves into Connecticut— although the stated reason for the statute, "[w]hereas the increase of slaves in this Colony is injurious to the poor and inconvenient," is less than inspiring. As well, in 1779, the Assembly declared that a slave seized from the estate of a Loyalist ought not be "continued in slavery by an act of government" or "sold for the benefit of the State" and so emancipated him.[47]

Connecticut had long permitted owners to manumit slaves, but unscrupulous masters sometimes freed elderly or injured slaves so that they would not be responsible for them. To prevent this, Connecticut passed a law in 1702 requiring slave owners to provide for manumitted slaves if they became destitute. Although well-intentioned, the act had the perverse effect of discouraging owners from freeing slaves. To address the problem, in 1777 the General Assembly permitted selectmen to certify the physical and moral character of slaves. If they concluded manumission "is likely to be consistent with the real advantage of such servant or slave, and that it is probable that the servant or slave will be able to support his or her own person" then he/she could be manumitted without future liability. Again, Sherman was an assistant when this law was passed, and there is no reason to believe he did not support it.[48]

Connecticut's gradual emancipation act of 1784 did not immediately free any slaves, yet it sped the decline of slavery in the state. Between 1790 and 1800 the number of slaves dropped from 2,764 to 951. Some slaves may have been shipped out of state; a practice the legislature prohibited in 1788 with respect to children entitled to freedom at age twenty-five and for all slaves in 1792. Sherman was not in the legislature when these acts were passed, but they illustrate the significant opposition to slavery that had developed in the state. By 1820, there were fewer than one hundred slaves in Connecticut, and when the state abolished slavery altogether in 1848 the number had dropped to seventeen.[49]

As a judge, Sherman ruled on several cases involving slavery. The most interesting one involved a slave named Jack Arabas, who had enlisted in the Continental army in 1777 as a substitute for his owner's son. After Arabas was honorably discharged the owner, Thomas Ivers of New York, sought to reclaim his property. Arabas was jailed in New Haven, where he appealed to the Superior Court for a writ of habeas corpus. Jesse Root, in his famous reports, noted that the Court granted the writ and proclaimed Arabas to be "a freeman, absolutely manumitted from his master by enlisting and serving in the army." Yet it is not clear from the *Reports* which judges participated in the case or why Arabas was freed. One of the best students of the case notes that "the full opinion of the court in Arabas has not survived," but he suggests several reasons the court ruled as it did, including the possibility that Arabas was freed as a "reward" for "service to the cause of American independence."[50]

In the summer of 2010, I was able to find Superior Court records that reveal that Samuel Huntington, Eliphalet Dyer, Roger Sherman, and William Pitkin presided over *Arabas v. Ivers*. More significantly, I located the original decision (a transcript of which is reprinted at the end of this chapter, along with Root's version of the case). The opinion, recorded by the court's clerk, George Pitkin, shows the court reasoned because "none but freemen Could by the Regulations of Congress be Enlisted in the Continental army," and because Ivers clearly consented to allow Arabas to enlist (he received the bounty for the enlistment), that it must be presumed that Ivers manumitted his slave.[51]

The logic in *Arabas v. Ivers* is straightforward, but it is not clear that the legal analysis is accurate. The relevant order by General Washington, which was affirmed by Congress, held that "the free negroes who have served faithfully in the army at Cambridge, may be re-inlisted there, but no others." Arabas did not serve in the army at Cambridge, so it would appear that he was ineligible to serve in the Continental army under this order. Yet slaves definitely served in the army, including in units from

Connecticut. After the war, courts and legislatures often declared these slaves to be free, but they did not always do so. Thus the Superior Court's decision in *Arabas v. Ivers* is not as obvious as it appears at first glance. Sherman and his colleagues must have been familiar with the complications noted in this paragraph, which suggests that they consciously pushed the boundaries of the law in order to reach a just decision.[52]

In seventeenth- and eighteenth-century Connecticut, Native Americans captured in war or in a few other circumstances could be enslaved. In the Superior Court case of *Hinkley v. Willson* (1787), judges Sherman, Pitkin, Ellsworth, Law, and Dyer, in an opinion written in Sherman's hand, addressed a case involving the widow of a Native American who had been held as a "servant and slave" to Joseph Hovey. The judges ruled that because Timothy Cutler was "born of a free woman, a native of the land," he was not a slave and thus was able to establish residency in the town of Coventry (which made the town liable for the support of his widow and children). This case played an important role in establishing the principle that anyone born to a free person is free.[53]

Sherman opposed slavery in Connecticut, and he criticized it at the national level. In the Constitutional Convention of 1787, he attacked the slave trade and labeled it "iniquitous." He also argued that there should not be a tax on imported slaves because "it implied they were *property*." He ultimately compromised with slave states in the Federal Convention in order to keep them in the union, but this was only because he was convinced that slavery was a dying institution. One of his first acts as a congressman was, almost certainly, to vote to reauthorize the Northwest Ordinance, which, among other things, banned slavery in the new territories.[54]

Religious Liberty Statute

Scholars have often appealed to Virginia's Statute for Religious Liberty (1786) as evidence that the authors of the First Amendment embraced the separation of church and state. Almost always neglected in this sort of argument is that all states passed statutes dealing with religious liberty and church-state relations between 1775 and 1790. In many cases, these laws expanded the scope of religious liberty, but they often perpetuated state and/or local support for Christianity. Moreover, unlike the author of the Virginia Statute for Religious Liberty, the authors of many of these other statutes actually helped draft and/or ratify the First Amendment. Such is the case with Roger Sherman and Connecticut's "An Act for

Securing the Rights of Conscience in Matters of Religion, to Christians of Every Denomination in This State," which he wrote in 1783.

Connecticut was founded by Congregationalists who believed that church and state were separate institutions that should nevertheless be mutually supportive. Internally, churches were largely self-governing, first following the almost purely congregational form of government under the Cambridge Platform (1649) and then under the presbyterian-leaning Saybrook Platform, which was written by Connecticut clergy and adopted by the Connecticut General Assembly in 1708. Under both models, colonial law provided for the creation of "societies," or precincts, where all adults were taxed to support the established Congregational church. Initially, unruly dissenters such as "Quakers, Ranters, and Adamites" were banned from the colony. In 1705, and again in 1706, the Privy Council disallowed this law. The General Court never formally recognized that it was voided, but it repealed the statute on its own authority in 1706 (presumably to avoid a confrontation with the Crown). The 1708 statute approving the Saybrook Platform specifically protected the ability of "sober" dissenters to exercise "worship and discipline in their own way, according to their consciences." However, they were not exempted from compulsory church attendance statutes, taxes that supported Congregational churches, Sabbath legislation, and other potentially offensive laws.[55]

Connecticut's restrictions sound onerous, but few complained in the seventeenth century, in part because there were few dissenters. However, as the eighteenth century progressed, the number of dissenters increased. In some cases, growth came by immigration, but in others it was a result of conversion—the most famous instance of which was when a rector of Yale College and several ministers became Anglicans in 1722. Anglicans and Quakers were particularly effective at bringing British pressure to bear by appealing to the Toleration Act of 1689 and hinting that Connecticut's charter might be revoked if state leaders were too intolerant. Largely as a result of this pressure, Anglicans were permitted to direct their ecclesiastical taxes to Anglican societies in 1727. Two years later, Quakers and Baptists were excused from ecclesiastical taxes altogether if they could "produce a certificate from [Baptist or Quaker] societies of their having joyned themselves to them." Yet other dissenting sects, and atheists or adherents to non-Christian faiths in the state (if any), received no relief.[56]

In the 1740s, New England was shaken by the Great Awakening. New Lights supported the revivals and promoted a vibrant, personal faith. They generally rejected the Half-Way Covenant and the Saybrook Platform, and they attacked what they perceived to be the spiritual laxness of the Old Lights. New Lights who wanted to form churches outside of the consociations (associations of Congregational churches) were called "separatists," but many New Lights chose to work within the existing ecclesiastical structures. The General Assembly initially opposed the New Lights, as evidenced by "An Act for Regulating Abuses and Correcting Disorders in Ecclesiastical Affairs" (1742), which prohibited itinerate preaching and other manifestations of revivalism. These measures were abandoned in the 1750 revision of the laws, a testimony to the growth of New Light political power. The New Light advance became even more evident when President Clap of Yale College joined the movement in the early 1750s. In 1770, Connecticut passed a law excusing Protestants who "soberly and conscientiously" dissent from laws requiring them to worship in established churches, provided they worshiped God in their own congregations. That year the Assembly also exempted dissenting "ministers of the gospel," like Standing Order ministers, from civil taxes.[57]

In 1756, New Lights in New Milford sent a petition to the General Assembly declaring that they

> do Soberly Dissent from the way of worship and method of support-
> ing the Gospel Ministry Established by the Law of this Colony and
> do maintain and attend the Public Worship of God among them-
> selves in a way which they think most agreeable to the word of God
> contained in the Scriptures of the Old and New Testament which
> your memorialists believe to be a perfect Rule of Faith and Practice.
> Your memorialists also believe that those who Preach the Gospel
> ought to be maintained (not by a Rate or Tax nor by Constraint; but)
> by a Free-will offering.

Accordingly, the dissenters requested an exemption from ecclesiastical taxes. Their petition was accompanied by a document from the established society written by "Roger Sherman Society Clerk," stating that "this Society are willing and desirous" that the exemption be granted "so long as they shall Continue Soberly to Dissent from the Established Constitution." Sherman noted that the society "voted in the affirmative by a great Majority without Computing any of the persons making said Request," but he did not record the names of supporters or opponents. Given that there were few negative votes and that Sherman joined a New Light congregation a few years later, it is almost certain that he supported the dissenters. The lower house approved the petition, but it was negated by the council. Unfortunately for dissenters, this was a common occurrence until the General Assembly exempted all separatists from such taxes in 1777.[58]

Sherman's "Act for Securing the Rights of Conscience" did not radically reconfigure church-state relations in Connecticut. As noted earlier, the scope of religious liberty protected in Connecticut often expanded in the eighteenth century because of actions, or the threat of action, by Parliament and the Crown. Obviously this was not an issue in 1783, but Sherman and his fellow legislators resisted the temptation to restore restrictions on religious minorities or to tax them to support the established Congregational church. Indeed, Sherman's act, in conjunction with a separate law regulating church societies, permitted "Christians of every Denomination" to form their own societies or to support themselves through voluntary contributions. Congregationalism was still favored insofar as individuals "who do not attend and help Support, any other public Worship" would be taxed to support the established church. Finally, it is noteworthy that the 1783 revisions dropped all reference to the Saybrook Platform which, according to William McLoughlin, meant that the "state no longer gave its civil support to actions of various Congregational associations and consociations nor any endorsement to the Savoy Confession of Faith which was imbedded in the Platform."[59]

One significant element of Sherman's statute was his preamble arguing for the importance of religion and the *duty* of civil authorities to promote the Christian faith. The preamble was approved with no substantial changes by the General Assembly, so it may reasonably be taken as reflecting both Sherman's and his colleagues' views:

> As the happiness of a People, and the good Order of Civil Society, essentially depend upon Piety, Religion and Morality, it is the Duty of the Civil Authority to provide for the Support and Encouragement thereof; so as that Christians of every Denomination, demeaning themselves peaceably, and as good Subjects of the State, may be equally under the Protection of the Laws: And as the People of this State have in general, been of one Profession in Matters of Faith, religious Worship, and the mode of settling and supporting the Ministers of the Gospel, they have by Law been formed into Ecclesiastical Societies, for the more convenient Support of their Worship and Ministry: And to the End that other Denominations of

Christians who differ from the Worship and Ministry so established and supported, may enjoy free Liberty of Conscience in the Matters aforesaid.[60]

Sherman's preamble illustrates the very common view among America's founders that Christianity was necessary for public happiness and political prosperity. This view was so widespread that James H. Hutson has called it "the founders' syllogism."[61] As such, it followed logically for Sherman and most founders that the civil authority had a duty to support Christianity. Toward the end of his life, in the midst of the controversy over Jonathan Edwards Jr., Sherman wrote to his son-in-law Simeon Baldwin:

> I hope the Society will with a good degree of unanimity agree to grant a sufficient tax to defray the Society expenses for the ensuing year. I shall chearfully pay my proportion of it. We have made a solemn contract with Doct. Edwards which we are under indispensible obligations to fulfil so long as he shall perform it on his part. What is expended for the support of religion is applied to advance the best interest of a people—and if they do it willingly it will have the most likely tendency to promote their temporal as well as spiritual good. I think we may rest assured of this if we believe a Special Divine Providence, and that what was written (aforetime) in the holy Scriptures was written for our learning. Such as Prov. 3.9, 10. Haggai 1.3, to 11, verses & Chapter 2.15, to 19 inclusive. Mal.3.6, to 12. Rom.15.4.[62]

Although Sherman thought that religious dissenters should be tolerated, he did not believe that this required neutrality by the state between religion and irreligion. This is crystal clear from Connecticut's revised statutes of 1784, which, among other things,

1. required all citizens "on the Lord's-Day carefully to apply themselves to duties of Religion and Piety, publicly and privately";
2. required all citizens to attend church each Sunday;
3. provided tax money to support churches and ministers;
4. punished Sabbath breakers;
5. required each family to possess a Bible and instructed town leaders to "supply" Bibles and "a suitable Number of Orthodox Catechisms, and other good Books of practical Godliness" to families in need;

6. required civil office holders and voters to take explicitly Christian oaths witnessed "by the Everlasting GOD" (although Quakers were permitted to "solemnly, sincerely, and truly affirm");
7. required families who adopted "an Indian Child" to instruct him or her in "the principles of the Christian Religion";
8. passed numerous statutes reflecting Christian morality as understood at the time on issues such as adultery, divorce, drunkenness, fornication, gaming, and horse racing—to name vices covered only in Sherman's half of the revisions;
9. provided that persons who:

presume willfully to blaspheme the Name of God the Father, Son, or Holy Ghost, either by denying, cursing, or reproaching the true God or his Government of the World; every Person so offending, shall be punished by whipping on the naked Body not exceeding forty Stripes, and sitting in the Pillory one Hour...

if any Person within this State, having been educated in, or having made Profession of the Christian Religion, shall by writing, printing, teaching, or advised speaking, deny the Being of a God; or any One of the Persons in the Holy Trinity to be God; or shall assert and maintain that there are more Gods than One; or shall deny the *Christian* Religion to be true, or the Holy Scriptures of the Old and New-Testament to be of Divine Authority, and be thereof lawfully convicted before any of the Superior Courts of this State, shall for the first Offense, be incapable to have or enjoy any Offices or Employments, ecclesiastical, civil or military.

Some of these provisions were rarely enforced, but it should, nevertheless, be clear that in 1784 Connecticut leaders generally thought it proper for the state to promote and protect Christianity. To be sure, leaders like Isaac Backus and John Leland were making powerful arguments that Christianity would flourish best if the state were to become less involved in promoting the faith, but their arguments did not win the day in late eighteenth-century New England.[63]

Sherman's religious freedom statute provided extensive protection for "Christians of every Denomination," but what about Roman Catholics? Nothing in the act suggests that they would not be tolerated, but in the final paragraph, the ability of dissenting Christians to "use and exercise the same Powers and Privileges for maintaining and supporting their respective

Ministers" is specifically limited to "Protestant Churches." Intriguingly, "Protestant" is not in the original draft, but it is careted into the text. Perhaps omitting the word was simply an oversight on Sherman's part, but it was clearly added when the General Assembly discussed the proposed legislation (which made minor changes to many draft laws penned by Sherman or Law). Certainly, Reformed Christians had little patience with Papists, and there is little reason to doubt Sherman was any different. In 1776, he was recorded in Congress as opposing "employing in our [military] Service Foreign Papists."[64] On the other hand, a few months later he co-authored a letter to French Roman Catholics encouraging them to join America's fight for independence and promising to respect their "free and undisturbed exercise of their religion." Similarly, in 1778 Ezra Stiles wrote in his diary that Sherman had no objection to Yale hiring a professor from France who was a Roman Catholic. It is probably most accurate to say that Sherman thought Catholics were dangerous and that they should not be supported by the state, but that they should be tolerated if they behaved peacefully.[65]

Sherman never specified how he thought adherents to non-Christian religions should be treated. His religious freedom statute literally protected only "Christians of every Denomination," although it arguably embraced a broader principle of toleration. Technically, state oaths required for freemen and officeholders could be honestly taken by anyone who believed in the "Everliving God," although the General Assembly almost certainly did not contemplate the possibility of Jews or Muslims taking them. The revised statutes of 1784 contained Sabbath legislation requiring worship and prohibiting work on "the Lord's Day," with no exception for those who desired to worship on other days. Simply put, Sherman and his colleagues did not seriously consider the possibility that Connecticut would be anything other than a Christian society. Within the context of such a society, it made tremendous sense to these men for the civil government to support Christianity as an end in itself and because of the tremendous private and public goods associated with it.[66]

In the spring of 1791, Sherman's religious freedom act was amended to require dissenters to obtain a certificate "signed by two of the Civil Authority living in the Town where such Dissenter dwells."[67] This requirement was more difficult to meet than the one in Sherman's act, which required dissenters to obtain a certificate from ministers or officers of their own dissenting church. Dissenters feared that because civil officials tended to belong to the established churches, they would be unwilling to issue certificates. Among the vigorous responses to this innovation was

John Leland's famous pamphlet "The Rights of Conscience Inalienable, and, Therefore, Religious Opinions Not Cognizable by Law: Or, the High-flying Churchman, Stripped of his Legal Robe, Appears a Yaho."[68] The controversy became so great that in its fall session the General Assembly repealed both Sherman's act and the new certification requirement, providing instead that a dissenter simply file a certificate written "under his Hand lodged in the Office of the Clerk of the Society to which he belongs." Moreover, the new statute made it clear that dissenters had the same right as members of established churches for "maintaining and supporting their respective ministers." Thus, by late 1791, Connecticut had adopted a robust system of plural or multiple establishments.[69] Sherman was not in the General Assembly when these changes were made, but he must have approved of them because the result was effectively the same as that provided by his 1784 religious liberty statute.

Sherman's approach to religious liberty and church-state relations may seem parochial today. However, his views reflect well the political culture of Connecticut in the late eighteenth century, and the views held by many Reformed Christians throughout the United States. Of particular note, they were well represented among the men who drafted and approved the First Amendment. But, before the Constitution could be amended, it had to be drafted, and it is to that process that we now turn.

Arabas v. Ivers. 1 Root 92 (1784)

THE case was—Jack was a slave to Ivers, and enlisted into the continental army with his master's consent—served during the war, and was discharged. Ivers claimed him as his servant; Jack fled from him to the eastward, Ivers pursued him, and took him and brought him to New Haven on his return to New York, where he belonged, and for safe-keeping while he stayed at New Haven, he got the gaoler to commit Jack to prison; and upon Jack's application to the court, complaining of his being unlawfully and unjustly holden in prison, the court issued a habeas corpus, to bring Jack before the court; also ordering the gaoler to certify wherefore he held Jack in prison; which being done, Ivers was cited before the court; and upon a summary hearing, Jack was discharged from his imprisonment, upon the ground that he was a freeman, absolutely manumitted from his master by enlisting and serving in the army as aforesaid.

Manuscript of the case:

Arabas v. Ivers

A Superior Court holden at New Haven in the County of New Haven in the State of Connecticut by adjournment on the Fifth Tuesday of December being the 7th Day, Anno Domini 1784

One Jack Arabass a Negro Man Confined in the Gaol in this place being brot Before this Court by Writ of Habeas Corpuss Directed to the Sheriff of Said County Commanding him to bring his Said Prisoner together with the Time, Cause and Reason of his Commitment And the Sheriff having Returned that said Jack was Commited by Thomas Ivers of the City and State of New York as a Runaway Slave and by said Ivers Claimed as a Slave for life. Whereupon this Court having fully Examined into the State of the facts Relative hereto and fully heared the Said parties with their proofs, pleas and allegations therein And it Appearing to this Court that Said Negro Jack Sometime in the Year 1777 being then a slave for life of the Said Ivers was by his Said Masters Leave and Consent Duly Enlisted as a Soldier into the Continental Army for and during the War—And that at said time of Enlistment his said Master Received the Bounty for Said Enlistment and that he the Said Jack faithfully performed the Duties of a Soldier during the Warr. and at the Close thereof was Honorourably discharged...Upon which facts this Court Are of Opinion that as none but freeman Could by the Regulations of Congress be Enlisted into the Continental Army, the Consent of Said Master to such Enlistment in judgment of Law Amounts to a Manumission and that Said Negro Jack cannot be any longer held as a Slave for life and therefore Order and Decree that he be no longer held in Custody but Set at Liberty. past and Allow'd in Court Test. Geo. Pitkin Clerk—[70]

5

"An Eel by the Tail"

IN 1784, ROGER Sherman defended the Articles of Confederation against Pelatiah Webster's wide-ranging attacks. By 1787, the failure of states to provide funds requested by Congress, problems with trade and currency, and events like Shays' Rebellion had convinced him that the Articles needed to be strengthened. As an advocate of local government, Sherman arrived in Philadelphia presuming that the Articles simply needed to be amended. Shocked by Madison's radical Virginia Plan, he joined whole-heartedly into the spirited debate. By the Convention's end, he had spoken more times than all but three delegates. Had he not missed the delibera-tions of July 20–26 because of a quick trip to Connecticut, he probably would have been the most loquacious of all the delegates.[1]

In this chapter, I explore Sherman's major contributions to the creation of the U.S. Constitution.[2] My central argument is that he was an effective advocate for limited government, states' rights, and legislative superiority. Of course he did not win every battle, but even when he lost, he often forced compromises that made the Constitution palatable to most Americans. In Jack Rakove's felicitous words, "America has had more Shermans in its politics than Madisons, and arguably too few of either, but it was the rivalry between their competing goals and political styles that jointly gave the Great Convention much of its drama and fascination— and also permitted its achievement."[3]

National Power and Representation

Connecticut had been almost completely self-governing since its incep-tion. The state never had a royal governor, and Christopher Collier notes that "the King's veto of the General Assembly's anti-Quaker law in 1705 and 1706" is a "rare, perhaps unique exception" to the colony's freedom from royal disallowance. In 1692, George Bulkeley complained that Connecticut citizens "have assumed and exercised all supreme power ... in all matters ecclesiatic, civil and military, capital, criminal, and common." Virtually all political decisions were made at the town or state level. Sherman, like most statesmen from Connecticut, greatly valued this autonomy, referring to it as "our darling liberty." Yet his long service in the national government—no delegate at the Federal Convention had more experience at this level of government than Sherman—convinced him that the country needed a reliable source of revenue and that it should have the power to regulate commerce and currency. Other state leaders were coming to the same conclusion. Thus, although Connecticut sent no delegates to the Annapolis Convention, on May 12, 1787, the General Assembly appointed William Samuel Johnson, Oliver Ellsworth, and Erastus Wolcott to represent the state at a convention to be held in Philadelphia.[4]

Fortunately for the fledgling nation, Wolcott refused to attend the Convention citing "the Small Pox" to which "he would be greatly exposed in the City." At the council's insistence, Sherman was chosen to replace him, and the full slate of delegates was formally approved on May 16, 1787. Unlike every state except Maryland, Connecticut's General Assembly permitted any of the delegates to act on behalf of the state (most states required a minimum of two or three delegates, with Pennsylvania requiring four). Like several other states, the legislature specified that the trio was appointed "for the Sole and express Purpose of revising the Articles of Confederation."[5]

Although the delegates were supposed to arrive on May 14, a quorum was not present until May 27, and Sherman did not arrive in Philadelphia until May 30. He was appalled by Madison's Virginia Plan, which had been introduced the previous day. Madison, and a few other leading lights—notably James Wilson and Alexander Hamilton—had become convinced that the United States needed a powerful national government that could act independently of the states. Madison's plan included a legislature where members of the lower house would be elected by the people from proportionately sized districts. There would be an upper house, but its members would be chosen by the lower house from candidates nominated by state legislatures. An executive and judges would be appointed by the legislature, and acting together they might negate legislation. The national legislature would have a general grant of power and the ability to veto state laws.[6]

Madison's plan would have created a national government with effectively unlimited power and where states-qua-states would be completely unrepresented. Of course, smaller states would have significantly less power under Madison's proposal than they did under the Articles of Confederation, and *all* state governments would be at the mercy of the new national government's ability to pass laws and veto state legislation. Madison, Wilson, Hamilton, and other extreme nationalists thought that a powerful national government was necessary for prosperity and the protection of liberty, and that the state governments and local attachments were detrimental to these ends. For many Americans, particularly Reformed Americans, such concentrated power was a threat to liberty. However, Madison, Wilson, and Hamilton (two of whom were born and raised outside of the United States), argued that liberty and power were compatible under properly constituted political structures.[7]

Throughout his career, Sherman had consistently urged Connecticut's General Assembly to meet its obligations to the national government, yet the state's nationalists correctly feared that he would not support radically increasing the strength of the government. Jeremiah Wadsworth wrote to Massachusetts delegate Rufus King:

> I am satisfied with the appointment—except Sherman who, I am told, is disposed to patch up the old scheme of Government. This was not my opinion of him, when we chose him: he is as cunning as the Devil, and if you attack him, you ought to know him well; he is not easily managed, but if he suspects you are trying to take him in, you may as well catch an Eel by the tail.[8]

Wadsworth was correct in his assessment of Sherman, both with respect to his view of national power and his ability as a legislator.

Sherman may have been tempted to dismiss Madison's proposals as utopian speculation if not for the convention's May 31 votes for electing members of the first branch by the people (rather than appointment by the state legislatures, as preferred by Sherman), and, more significantly, the 9-0-1 vote to grant the new national legislature the power to legislate "in cases to which the States are not competent." Indeed, Sherman cast the *only* recorded vote dissenting from this general grant of power, which led to Connecticut's delegation being split (Johnson was not yet present).[9]

Sherman favored strengthening the national government, but only for a few limited ends. He enumerated these a week later:

The objects of the Union, he thought were few. 1. defence agst. foreign danger. 2. agst. internal disputes & a resort to force. 3. Treaties with foreign nations 4. regulating foreign commerce, & drawing revenue from it...All other matters civil & criminal would be much better in the hands of the States.

Madison responded directly to Sherman, contending that the national government should go well beyond these "important and necessary objects" to do things like secure "private rights, and the steady dispensation of Justice." Madison also made it clear that he thought state governments were among the greatest abusers of these rights.[10]

Sherman argued that the national government's proper ends could be achieved by a confederation acting on and through the states. As such, he opposed election of the lower house of the national legislature "by the people, insisting that it ought to be by the <State> Legislatures. The people he said, <immediately> should have as little to do as may be about the Government. They want information and are constantly liable to be misled." This quote has been used to show that the founders were undemocratic, but this makes little sense in Sherman's case. He was from one of the most democratic states in the nation, and he fully supported Connecticut's political arrangements. However, he believed some civic offices requiring specialized knowledge were best filled by appointment. State legislatures would be more likely than the people at large to select qualified representatives to a national government that would focus on a few, limited matters, such as economic regulation and international relations.[11]

Sherman understood that Wilson and Madison intended to significantly increase the power of the national government by grounding it immediately on the authority of the people. Wilson, for instance, openly

> contended strenuously for drawing the most numerous branch of the Legislature immediately from the people. He was for raising the federal pyramid to a considerable altitude, and for that reason wished to give it as broad a basis as possible.

Because Sherman wanted to keep the "federal pyramid" as shallow as possible, and because of his commitment to states' rights, he vigorously opposed Wilson's proposal. A week later, he responded to a similar argument by Wilson by noting that "[i]f it were in view to abolish the State

Govts. the elections ought to be by the people." Two years later, he elaborated on the significance of having state legislatures select members of Congress when he wrote to John Adams that "senators being eligible by the legislatures of the several states, and dependent on them for reelection, will be vigilant in supporting their rights against infringement by the legislature or executive of the United States."[12]

Sherman was far less visionary than Madison, Wilson, or Hamilton with respect to shifting power from the state governments to the new national government. He admitted as much a few weeks later when he noted that he was "not fond of speculation. I would rather proceed on experimental ground." Accordingly, he advocated strengthening the power of the national government under the Articles of Confederation and keeping the government firmly under the control of the state legislatures.[13]

If the Federal Convention had been an academic seminar, the powerful minds of Madison, Wilson, and Hamilton might have won the day. However, as a political convention, delegates from smaller states could not be expected to give up the disproportionate power they possessed under the Articles in the name of abstract pyramids. On June 6, John Dickinson, George Read, and other small-state delegates insisted that states be represented equally in at least one house of the legislature. The next day, Dickinson proposed and Sherman seconded a motion requiring senators to be chosen by state legislatures.[14] Discussion about the composition and power of the Senate led to Sherman's most significant contribution to the Constitution.

On June 11, Sherman proposed

> that the proportion of suffrage in the 1st branch should be according to the respective numbers of free inhabitants; and that in the second branch or Senate, each State should have one vote and no more. He said as the States would remain possessed of certain individual rights, each State ought to be able to protect itself: otherwise a few large States will rule the rest.

Sherman's motion was defeated at the time, but his observation that the "smaller States would never agree to the plan on any other principle" would eventually convince a majority of delegates to support his compromise. Sherman's plea was reinforced a few days later by Paterson's New Jersey Plan, to which Max Farrand believed Sherman made significant contributions. Certainly, the plan contained many of Sherman's ideals, notably a strengthened national government dependent immediately on the states and the state legislatures. At a minimum, the New Jersey Plan helped delegates from the larger states to see that delegates from smaller ones would not simply surrender the power they possessed under the Articles. In a similar fashion, Hamilton's hyper-nationalist speech on June 18 may have helped small-state delegates understand that retaining the Articles of Confederation was not an option. On June 20, Sherman reiterated his compromise, and it was debated intermittently over the next week. By the end of June, the nationalists were running out of patience, as suggested by Wilson's identifying supporters of equality in the Senate with advocates of rotten boroughs in England. Sherman calmly responded by noting that the "question was not what rights naturally belong to men; but how they may be most equally & effectively guarded in Society."[15]

After weeks of debate and a multitude of proposals (including one for a legislature consisting of three branches), the delegates agreed to form a committee consisting of one member per state to "devise & report some compromise" on the issue of representation. Ellsworth was appointed to represent Connecticut, but he was unable to serve and was replaced by Sherman. On July 5, the committee proposed that "in the 1st branch of the Legislature each of the States now in the Union shall be allowed 1 member for every 40,000 inhabitants" and "that in the 2d branch each State shall have an equal vote." Delegates spent significant time debating this proposal and a variety of sub-issues, such as whether it was meaningful to require revenue bills to originate in the House, the number of representatives each state would have in this body, how and when representatives would be reapportioned, and how western states would be treated. On these matters, Sherman's most notable comments were his inaccurate prediction that "there was no probability that the number of future States would exceed that of Existing states" coupled with his insistence that new states should be treated equally because we "are providing for our posterity, for our children & our grand Children, who would be as likely to be citizens of new Western States, as of the old States."[16]

While these issues were important, the critical divide remained representation in the Senate. Sherman never wavered in his insistence that states must be represented equally in this body. This was important to him, not because Connecticut was a small state (according to the 1790 census it had the sixth-largest white population), but because equal representation was necessary to protect states-qua-states.[17] A week after the committee issued its report, Sherman urged

the equality of votes not so much as a security for the small States;
as for the State Govts. which could not be preserved unless they
were represented & had a negative in the Genl. Government. He
had no objection to the members in the 2d b. voting per capita, as
had been suggested by [Mr. Gerry].

On July 16, the Convention considered the final report of "the Grand
committee," which proposed that states be represented proportionally
in the House with Connecticut having 5 of 65 votes (or 7.69231% of the
total, giving it the exact same weight it had in the Confederation
Congress where it had 1 of 13 votes, or 7.69231% of the total), and equal
representation in the Senate. The Convention agreed to the report by a
vote of 5-4-1.[18]

Sherman had proposed something akin to the Connecticut Compromise
in the Continental Congress, and by any measure he and Ellsworth were
its primary advocates in the Convention. The compromise provided the
small states and all state governments with an important measure of
protection. Extreme nationalists like Madison, Wilson, and Hamilton
remained displeased with it, but they should have recognized that without
this compromise the Constitution would not have been ratified by more
than a handful of states. Nevertheless, they continued to advocate measures aimed at restraining states and expanding national power. Sherman,
in turn, continued to oppose them.

On July 17, the day after they agreed to the Connecticut Compromise,
delegates returned to Madison's proposal that the national legislature be
able to negate state laws that violate the Constitution or treaties. Sherman
objected that such a provision was "unnecessary, as the Courts of the
States would not consider as valid any law contravening the Authority of
the Union, and which the legislature would wish to be negativated."
Madison responded that he "considered the negative on the laws of the
States as essential to the efficacy & security of the Genl. Govt." The proposed veto failed by a vote of 7-3.[19] Sherman may have been unduly optimistic about the willingness of state courts to support the new national
government, but it is unlikely the experienced politician and judge was
not aware of the possibility. However, when Sherman had a chance to err
on the side of the state governments, he generally did.[20]

The Virginia Plan gave the national legislature the ability to legislate
"in all cases to which the separate states are incompetent." Because
Congress would judge for itself what this entailed, the provision

amounted to a general grant of power. Sherman preferred instead a limited grant, and he and his allies consistently fought for an enumeration of powers. Sherman had offered a general enumeration of powers on June 6, and he read a more detailed list of powers on July 17, less than a week before the issue was sent to the Committee of Detail.[21] Although Sherman was regularly appointed to important committees, he did not serve on this one because he and William Samuel Johnson left for New Haven before its members were appointed. Sherman was particularly anxious to return to his hometown so that he could attend the July 29 wedding of his daughter, Rebecca, to Simeon Baldwin. Nevertheless, his views were well represented on the committee by his protégé Ellsworth, who had written to his wife that "Mr. Sherman and Doctor Johnson are both run home for a short family visit. As I am a third younger than they are I calculate to hold out a third longer, which will carry me to about the last of August." The committee's draft constitution, submitted to the Convention on August 6, contained an early version of what became Article I, Section 8.[22]

The committee's proposed list of powers were debated over the next month, and the final version of Article I, Section 8 largely limits the national government's powers to those suggested by Sherman on June 6. In considering the extensive debates over these powers, it is noteworthy that delegates adopted the "necessary and proper" clause with little comment or opposition. Savvy delegates like Sherman and Ellsworth could not have construed this clause as granting virtually unlimited power to Congress as some later politicians and jurists would claim.[23]

Sherman would have preferred retaining the Articles of Confederation and simply strengthening the power of the Confederation Congress, but the delegates' early votes on the Virginia Plan made it clear that this was not a realistic possibility. However, by winning equal representation in the Senate and the election of senators by state legislatures, he was able to effectively protect states against the national government. This protection was reinforced by his insistence that Congress's powers be enumerated and that it not have the ability to negate state laws. Moreover, in the final days of the Convention, he proposed adding a provision to Article V stipulating that "no State should be affected in its internal police, or deprived of its equality in the Senate." When this proposal was defeated, he moved to eliminate the article altogether, which was rejected as well. However, the latter proposal encouraged delegates to approve a variation of his original proposal to require "that no State, without its consent shall be deprived of its equal suffrage in the Senate." Sherman thus secured one of his critical goals—equal representation of the states in the Senate.[24]

Sherman was an effective advocate for a stronger but limited national government that would not interfere with states' rights. Partially as a result of the Fourteenth, Sixteenth, and Seventeenth amendments, but primarily because of Congress's assertion of power and the federal courts' acquiescence, the national government today acts as if it has a general grant of powers and the notion of states' rights has been consigned to the dustbin of history. It is impossible to know exactly what Sherman would have thought of these changes, but it is clear that those who argue that the founders *intended* the national government to have a general grant of power are wrong in the case of Roger Sherman and his allies.

Presidential Power

Throughout the Convention, James Wilson advocated a single, powerful executive independent of the legislature. Because he was so concerned about the dangers of concentrated power, Sherman opposed him at every step. For instance, on June 1, Wilson and John Rutledge proposed a single executive with the power of "war and peace" who could give the "most energy[,] dispatch[,] and responsibility to the office," Sherman countered that

> he considered the Executive magistracy as nothing more than an institution for carrying the will of the Legislature into effect, that the person or persons ought to be appointed by and accountable to the Legislature only, which was the depository of the supreme will of the Society. As they were the best judges of the business which ought to be done by the Executive department, and consequently of the number necessary from time to time for doing it, he wished the number might <not> be fixed, but that the legislature should be at liberty to appoint one or more as experience might dictate.

When Wilson argued on the same day that the executive should "at least in theory" be elected "by the people," Sherman reiterated his support for "the appointment by the Legislature, and for making him absolutely dependent on that body, as it was the will of that which was to be executed. An independence of the Executive on the supreme Legislative, was in his opinion the very essence of tyranny if there was any such thing."[25]

Several days later, Wilson suggested that because most states had a single executive, the national government should have one as well. It was a poor argument to make in Sherman's presence, for he was well aware that in "all the states there was a Council of advice, without which the first magistrate could not act. A Council he thought necessary to make the establishment acceptable to the people." Indeed, he had served on such a council longer than any other member of the Convention. Nevertheless, Sherman lost this battle, as he did many others involving the executive. On June 4, the states voted 7-3 to approve a single executive, with Sherman unable to convince even his colleagues from Connecticut to support his position.[26]

Nationalists wanted the president to have a wide range of executive powers, including an absolute veto of congressional legislation. Sherman objected that he "was agst. enabling any one man to stop the will of the whole. No one could be found so far above all the rest in wisdom." Late in the Convention, when the issue arose again, he repeated this sentiment, asking if "one man [can] be trusted better than all the others if they all agree?" On this issue he was initially successful—the state delegations rejected giving the executive an absolute veto 10-0. He eventually failed to keep the veto power from the president altogether, but in the waning days of the Convention, he seconded and argued for Williamson's motion to reduce the percentage of each branch necessary to override a veto from three-quarters to two-thirds; a battle they won 6-4-1.[27]

Debates over the executive virtually disappeared after June 4 as delegates focused on the issue of representation. After Madison's plan for a national legislature based solely on the people was significantly limited and its ability to veto state laws was defeated, he and his allies began advocating for a stronger chief executive who could vigorously promote nationalist goals. On July 17, Morris and Wilson returned to the "chimerical" proposal that the executive be elected directly by the people. In doing so, they raised the specters of "cabal" and "faction" if the executive was chosen like "a pope by a conclave of cardinals." Sherman rejected this analogy, contending that "the sense of the Nation would be better expressed by the Legislature, than by the people at large. The latter will never be sufficiently informed of characters, and besides will never give a majority of votes to any one man." Less concerned about democracy than quality, Mason supported Sherman's position, arguing that "it would be as unnatural to refer the choice of a proper character for chief Magistrate to the people, as it would, to refer a trial of colours to a blind man." Morris's motion to have the people elect the president failed 9 states to 1.[28]

Sherman was content to have the executive completely dependent on the legislature, and he even argued that the president should be eligible for reelection and be able to serve multiple terms if he pleased Congress. However, enough delegates had been convinced by Montesquieu, whom Madison paraphrased as contending that it is "essential to the preservation of liberty that the Legisl: Execut: & Judiciary powers be separate." Accordingly, the Convention moved haltingly toward the eventual compromise of having the president chosen by electors selected in a manner determined by state legislatures. Of course, the presumption was that electors would seldom give a majority of their votes to a candidate, and so the election would be thrown into, initially, the Senate. Sherman was on the committee that proposed this solution, and he was highly supportive of it because of the influence state legislatures had in this body. Nationalists were eventually able to shift election to the House, but Sherman salvaged a partial victory by convincing delegates to have members of the House vote by state delegations, with each state having a single vote.[29]

Sherman opposed or tried to limit virtually every power his fellow delegates attempted to give to the executive. For instance, he was against allowing the president to appoint many officers, such as "general officers in the Army in times of peace &c." because "[h]erein lay the corruption in G. Britain. If the Executive can model the army, he may set up an absolute Government." On a related matter, when Charles Pinckney and others wanted to give the president the ability to declare war, Sherman contended that the legislature should have the power to declare *and* make war. The only war power he conceded that the executive should have was the ability to repel an invasion. Sherman's proposal that presidential pardons be subject to Senate confirmation was defeated, but he successful offered an amendment clarifying that the executive is commander in chief of the state militias only when they are called into the actual service of the United States.[30]

The virtues of separating powers were not appreciated in late eighteenth-century Connecticut, and Sherman brought his pro-legislative convictions to the Federal Convention. His reasoning is encapsulated well in his argument against requiring a decennial census in the Constitution: "he was agst. Shackling the Legislature too much. We ought to choose wise & good men, and then confide in them." Such an approach may sound naïve, but it must be coupled with Sherman's commitment to frequent elections. Early in the Convention he proposed that members of the first branch should be elected annually, and he wanted senators elected every five years rather than the then-planned seven years. Sherman lost both battles, although he never gave up. When the delegates returned to the length of Senate terms on June 26, then set at six years, Sherman argued that

> Govt. is instituted for those who live under it. It ought therefore to be so constituted as not to be dangerous to their liberties. The more permanency it has the worse if it be a bad Govt. Frequent elections are necessary to preserve the good behavior of rulers. They also tend to give permanency to the Government, by preserving that good behavior, because it ensures their re-election. In Connecticut elections have been very frequent, yet great stability & uniformity both as to persons & measures have been experienced from its original establishmt. to the present time.[31]

Sherman eventually compromised on term lengths, and he supported the proposed Constitution in spite of the power concentrated in the executive. One of the major debates among students of American politics has been the proper extent of presidential powers. As with respect to the national government's powers, participants in these debates often refer to "the founders" without bothering to distinguish between different founders. Some founders, notably Wilson and Hamilton, wanted an independent and vigorous president, but others, like Sherman, wanted a carefully constrained chief executive. Article II is a compromise between these positions, although throughout the twentieth and into the twenty-first centuries the Supreme Court has allowed the president to assume powers more in accord with Wilson's and Hamilton's ideals than Sherman's.[32]

The Judiciary

Throughout the Convention, Sherman argued for a federal judiciary that would look much like the judiciary in Connecticut. His proposals often fell on deaf ears. Early in the debates, he seconded Rutledge's motion to strike the Virginia Plan's provision for "establishing *inferior* tribunals under the national authority." Both men contended that state courts could handle any cases lower federal courts might hear, and the thrifty Sherman emphasized the added cost of a new judicial system. Although their proposal initially succeeded, Wilson and Madison's counter proposal to "*empower*" the national legislature to establish such courts was approved

8-2-1. When the issue was debated again on July 18, Sherman had either changed his mind or understood the delegates would not accept his views. He noted that he "was willing to give the power to the Legislature but wished them to make use of the State Tribunals whenever it could be done. with safety to the general interest."[33]

In eighteenth-century Connecticut, jurists, from justices of the peace to Superior Court judges, were appointed by the legislature. Moreover, the General Assembly served as the court of final resort. Sherman, who had served as a Superior Court judge since 1766, supported the system. When delegates turned to the question of how federal judges should be selected, he and Charles Pinckney proposed that they be appointed by Congress. Madison responded that the Senate would be in a better position to appoint judges than the legislature as a whole, and Pinckney and Sherman acquiesced. The appointment of judges by the Senate was agreed to "nem. con." on June 13.[34]

After the Connecticut Compromise, some nationalists (but not Madison) had second thoughts about having Senators appoint federal judges. When delegates returned to the issue on July 18, Wilson proposed that presidents appoint judges. Sherman objected, offering the intriguing argument that the Senate "would be composed of men nearly equal to the Executive, and would of course have on the whole more wisdom. They would bring into their deliberations a more diffusive knowledge of characters. It would be less easy for candidates to intrigue with them, than with the Executive Magistrate." After some debate, Nathaniel Gorham proposed that judges be appointed by the executive with the advice and consent of the Senate. Sherman found this "less objectionable than an absolute appointment by the Executive, but disliked it as too fettering the Senate." Although Gorham's motion initially failed, it eventually won the day.[35]

Sherman's views on judicial review are not crystal clear, but he seems to have supported the practice. He was among the Connecticut Superior Court judges who declared an act of the General Assembly to be void in the *Symsbury Case* (1785)—one of the handful of such cases recorded in America prior to *Marbury v. Madison* (1803). More significantly, in the Federal Convention, he argued that the national legislature should not be given the power to veto state laws because "it was unnecessary, as the Courts of the States would not consider as valid any law contravening the Authority of the Union." This argument relies on the premises that state courts can refuse to enforce laws passed by state legislatures and that the future national Constitution and statutes passed under its authority would be the supreme law of the land. Sherman never clearly said federal courts could declare an act of Congress to be void, but given his commitment to the rule of law it is likely that he would support the practice in the case of unconstitutional or unjust laws.[36]

The Virginia Plan contained a proposed Council of Revision consisting of the executive and "a convenient number" of justices that would have the power to veto laws. A council was eventually rejected by the delegates, and Madison never records Sherman as participating in debates over the body (he was absent during the July 21 debates on the subject). On August 15, Madison, with Wilson's support, attempted to resurrect a version of this plan by proposing that laws be submitted to the executive and the judiciary for approval. If either branch disapproved, it could be overruled by a two-thirds vote of the legislature, but if both disapproved, an override would require a vote of three-quarters in each house. The motion was defeated 3-8, but as discussion continued, Sherman made it clear that he "disapproved of Judges meddling in politics and parties."[37] By this he may have meant that he did not think judges should rule on a law until there is a real case and controversy, a classic requirement of standing. Alternatively, he might have been articulating a version of the departmental theory of judicial review whereby legislatures determine the constitutionality of laws with respect to political matters and the judiciary with respect to judicial matters.

Connecticut was the only state never to have separate courts of law and equity, so it is perhaps no coincidence that it was a Connecticut delegate, William Samuel Johnson, who proposed that federal judicial power ought to extend to "equity as well as law," which was affirmed by a vote of 6-3. On the same day, Sherman moved to expand the Supreme Court's Article III original jurisdiction to include suits "between Citizens of the same State claiming lands under grants of different States," which was agreed to without objection. Although he may have had broader concerns, foremost in his mind must have been controversies involving Connecticut citizens in Wyoming Valley and the lingering issue of Vermont. Sherman's final contribution with respect to the role of the Supreme Court was to oppose Madison's proposal to try impeachments in the Supreme Court rather than the Senate because "Judges would be appointed by him [the president]."[38] This was certainly not the only reason Sherman opposed Madison on this point—he never hesitated to vest powers in the Senate—but his argument may have, nevertheless, helped convince delegates to defeat the proposal.

Sherman was not opposed to a federal Supreme Court, but he would have preferred to allow state courts to handle most cases involving the national Constitution, treaties, or laws. He wanted justices to be appointed by the Senate, and he did not want them to play any role in vetoing congressional laws before they took effect. He lost many of these battles, but in the final analysis, he was able to support the Constitution with respect to the judiciary because of the significant role played by the Senate in the confirmation of federal judges and exclusion of judges from the lawmaking process.

Slavery

Sherman was a longtime opponent of slavery, yet he did nothing to end slavery or the slave trade in the Convention. Other than calling the slave trade "iniquitous," he did not even engage in antislavery rhetoric, unlike Gouverneur Morris, who declared slavery to be "a nefarious institution...the curse of heaven on the States where it prevailed." Although he was not an active advocate of the three-fifths compromise, whereby five slaves were counted as three "persons" for the purposes of representation, he accepted it as necessary. He argued that the national government should not have the power to tax the importation of slaves "because it implied they were *property*," but this symbolic point rings hollow coming from a seasoned politician who understood the power of taxation to discourage undesirable activities.[39]

Richard Barry, in his popular biography of John Rutledge, recounted a dinner at which Sherman and Rutledge agreed that the South "would give up its claim to a two-thirds vote on the navigation clause if New England...would oppose any immediate effort to abolish the importation of slaves." Forrest McDonald, relying in part on Barry's account of the dinner, asserted that Sherman and Rutledge agreed that Connecticut would not oppose the slave trade if South Carolina would support Connecticut's claim to the Western Reserve.[40] However, Barry provided no evidence that Sherman and Rutledge discussed any of these issues.[41] That a deal was eventually made is suggested by the Committee of Eleven's report of August 24 recommending that Congress be prohibited from banning the slave trade before 1800 and from taxing exports, but that it have the power to pass navigation acts by a simple majority vote. Yet Rutledge and Sherman were not on that committee, and there is no evidence that Sherman was immediately involved in crafting this compromise.[42]

Sherman was a dealmaker, and compromises likely played a role in his relative silence on this issue. But the central reason that Sherman did not push the abolition of slavery or the slave trade at the Federal Convention is that he understood doing so would result in a constitution that would not be ratified by states in the Deep South and perhaps in the upper South as well. This is evident from the remarkable debate on August 20 concerning taxing the importation of slaves. Luther Martin, himself a slave owner, proposed allowing Congress to prohibit or tax the importation of slaves because the institution was "inconsistent with the principles of the revolution and dishonorable to the American character." Rutledge responded by proclaiming that "Religion & humanity had nothing to do with this question—Interest alone is the governing principle with Nations—The true question at present is whether the Southn. States shall or shall not be parties to the Union." Sherman's protégé Ellsworth was unwilling to concede Rutledge's relativistic premise, but he was prepared to reject Martin's proposal because the "morality or wisdom of slavery are considerations belonging to the States themselves." Finally, Charles Pinckney concluded the brief exchange by restating Rutledge's point from the perspective of his state: "South Carolina can never receive the plan if it prohibits the slave trade."[43]

Pinckney's comment ended the debate on August 21. The next day, Sherman opened the Convention by making an argument

> for leaving the clause as it stands. He disapproved of the slave trade: yet as the States were now possessed of the right to import slaves, as the public good did not require it to be taken from them, & as it was expedient to have as few objections as possible to the proposed scheme of Government, he thought it best to leave the matter as we find it. He observed that the abolition of slavery seemed to be going on in the U.S. & that the good sense of the several States would probably be degrees compleat it.

The issue was not resolved that day, but eventually the delegates agreed to let Congress tax imported slaves up to ten dollars per person and ban the trade as early as 1808. Congress would eventually take both actions.[44]

Sherman detested slavery, but he calculated that proposing a constitution that would not be ratified by southern states would do little to end the institution. His comment that "the public good did not require" banning the importation of slaves cannot be taken as tacit approval of the institution. It must be understood in light of the reality that only three states, North Carolina, South Carolina, and Georgia, allowed the importation of slaves, and his conviction that *all* states were moving toward the abolition of slavery. Sherman, it must be recalled, had recently served in a state legislature that passed a gradual manumission act. Moreover, five other states had approved similar statutes or ended slavery through judicial decisions, and a total of eight would do so by 1804.[45] Opposition to the institution was even developing in southern states, and in the Convention itself current and former slave owners including George Mason, Luther Martin, Rufus King, James Madison, Gouverneur Morris, and John Dickinson spoke against the institution.[46] Finally, the Northwest Ordinance enacted by the Confederation Congress on July 13, 1787, banned the expansion of slavery into the territory "northwest of the river Ohio." Sherman may have concluded along with Wilson and other opponents of slavery that as the nation expanded and new states were admitted on equal terms with existing states, that the power of the slave states would be diminished.[47]

Religion and the Constitution

In the polemical literature on the founders and religion, no event at the Federal Convention receives more attention than Franklin's suggestion on June 28 that the delegates should seek divine assistance. In the midst of divisive debates over representation, he asked why "we have not hitherto once thought of humbly applying to the Father of lights to illuminate our understandings?" As the oldest member of the Convention, he went on to state "the longer I live, the more convincing proofs I see of this truth—*that God governs in the affairs of men.*" Accordingly, he proposed that a minister from the city be requested to officiate at prayer services at the assembly every morning. In light of Franklin's appeal to his age, it is perhaps fitting that the second-oldest man at the Convention, Roger Sherman, seconded his motion. Hamilton and several others objected that bringing in clergy "might at this late day, 1. bring on it some disagreeable animadversions. & 2. lead the public to believe that the embarrassments and dissentions within the convention, had suggested this measure." After further discussion the delegates adjourned without voting on Franklin's proposal.[48]

Advocates of a "Christian founding" often point to Franklin's proposal as a turning point in the Convention.[49] Proponents of a "secular founding" contend that lack of enthusiasm for prayer is evidence that America's founders wanted a "godless constitution."[50] However, when serving in other offices—at both the state and the national level—virtually every delegate to the Federal Convention supported paid chaplains, calls for prayer and fasting, and the use of religious rhetoric in public addresses. It is therefore reasonable to conclude that they rejected Franklin's proposal for the reasons offered by Hamilton, not because they were committed to the separation of church and state.[51]

The Constitution contains four provisions that touch on religion or religious issues, and three of them were adopted without debate. First, the Committee of Detail initially gave the president seven days to veto legislation, but on August 15 this period was extended to "*Ten* days (Sundays excepted)." The latter clause presumes civic business would not normally be conducted on the Christian Sabbath. Second, the Constitution contains three oath provisions that permit an oath taker to "affirm" rather than to "swear." The first instance of an oath requirement in Farrand's *Records* is found in the Virginia Plan's requirement for state officeholders to swear to uphold the national Constitution. It did not contain an exemption. The first exemption appears in the Committee of Detail's draft of what became Article II, and exemptions were eventually added to all oath requirements without debate or dissent. Although a nonreligious person might choose to affirm rather than swear an oath, in the context of late eighteenth-century America there is little doubt that the exemption was added to benefit Quakers and other religious minorities who had religious objections to taking oaths. Third, and of least significance, Article VII contains a pro forma reference to "the Year of our Lord."[52]

The most interesting and substantial constitutional provision concerning religion is Article VI's prohibition on religious tests for office. On August 30, Charles Cotesworth Pinckney proposed that "no religious test shall ever be required as a qualification to any office or public trust under the authority of the U. States." Sherman immediately objected that such a prohibition was "unnecessary, the prevailing liberality being a sufficient security agst. such tests." Gouverneur Morris and General Pinckney voiced their support for the motion, and it was approved with only North Carolina voting "no" and with Maryland's and Connecticut's delegations being divided.[53] Oliver Ellsworth had departed Philadelphia by that time, so presumably William Samuel Johnson, an Anglican from a Congregationalist state, voted for the proposal and Sherman voted against it.

In light of the disagreement between Morris and Sherman on the necessity of prohibiting religious tests in the Constitution, it is noteworthy that Sherman argued against Morris's nomination to be minister to France in 1792. He began his speech by noting that "I bear Mr. Morris no ill will," acknowledging his "superior talents," and conceding that "I never heard that he betrayed a Trust." Nevertheless:

> With regard to his moral character, I consider him an irreligious and profane man—he is no hypocrite and never pretended to have any religion. He makes religion the subject of ridicule and is profane in his conversation. I do not think the public have as much security from such men as from godly and honest men—It is a bad example to promote such characters; and although they may never have betrayed a trust, or exhibited proofs of a want of integrity, and although they may be called men of honor—yet I would not put my trust in them—I am unwilling that the country should put their Trust in them, and because they have not already done wrong, I feel no security they will not do wrong in the future. General Arnold was an irreligious and profane character—he was called a man of honor, but I never had any confidence in him, nor did I ever join in promoting him.

Many of Sherman's fellow senators apparently did not share his concerns, evidenced by their 16-11 vote to confirm Morris.[54]

Sherman came from a state that required officeholders to swear or affirm explicitly theistic oaths of office, and there is no indication he ever opposed them. Although he argued at the Constitutional Convention against the necessity of banning religious tests, he *was* opposing and presumably voting against their prohibition. Sherman clearly favored electing and appointing godly men to public office. Still, his opposition to religious tests at the Federal Convention may have been genuine if he thought them to be ineffective. It is difficult to imagine Morris's appointment being prevented by any religious test likely to be included in the Constitution. Sherman probably would not have objected to a religious test for federal offices that did not discriminate among Christians. In this respect, the old Puritan differed from many of his fellow delegates who, at a minimum, thought a religious test at the national level was imprudent. Yet Sherman was not so far out of step with some participants in the ratification debates, and the lack of a religious test for office became a major issue in several ratification conventions—including Connecticut's.[55]

On September 7, Jonas Phillips, "one of the people called Jews of the City of Philadelphia," sent the only known petition to the Federal Convention. In it, he noted that Pennsylvania's constitution requires officeholders to swear: "I do believe in one God the Creature [sic] and governor of the universe the Rewarder of the good and the punisher of the wicked—and I do acknowledge the scriptures of the old and New testement to be given by a devine inspiration" and asked that the Convention remove the latter part of the oath so that Jews, as well as Christians, might hold civic office. He apparently thought the Federal Convention could alter the Pennsylvania oath, which obviously it could not. It is tempting to think that his petition influenced Article VI's ban on religious tests, but this provision had already been approved. Nevertheless, Phillips must have been pleased when he read Article VI, and it is noteworthy that when Pennsylvania revised its constitution in 1790, it altered its religious test exactly along the lines suggested by Mr. Phillips.[56]

According to Isaac Kramnick and R. Laurence Moore, the Constitution is "Godless." This observation would have come as quite a shock to Roger Sherman, Nathaniel Gorham, Caleb Strong, John Langdon, Nicholas Gilman, Abraham Baldwin, James Wilson, Gunning Bedford, James McHenry, William Livingston, William Paterson, Hugh Williamson, Jared Ingersoll, Oliver Ellsworth, John Lansing Jr., Robert Yates, James McClurg, William Blount, William Houston, William Davie, and Alexander Martin—delegates to the Federal Convention who were raised in the Reformed tradition. It is true that the Constitution says little about religion and morality, but this is because most founders believed that *to the extent to which* governments should promote these perceived goods, that it should be done at the state and local level. Indeed, the very notion of federalism, some scholars have argued, was itself modeled after Reformed approaches to church governance (especially Presbyterianism) and New England civic arrangements which, as we have seen, were themselves heavily influenced by Calvinist political ideas. It is noteworthy that the authors of the Connecticut Compromise, Roger Sherman and Oliver Ellsworth, were both solid, serious Reformed Christians who were leaders in their Congregationalist churches. Enlightenment thinkers, who had a far more optimistic view of human nature and faith in experts, generally embraced unicameralism and the centralization of power in a national government.[57]

By the end of the Federal Convention, even nationalists recognized that they had created a government with limited powers. Of course, the exact parameters of these powers had to be worked out. Few thought the national government could create a national church or ban particular religious beliefs, but the propriety of hiring chaplains, issuing calls for prayer and fasting, providing funds to religious schools in federal territories, and using religious rhetoric in public addresses would be determined by future congresses, presidents, and, eventually, the courts. Some delegates were not convinced that Congress's powers were sufficiently delineated and so proposed adding a bill of rights to the Constitution. Sherman and most of his colleagues were convinced one was not necessary, and various proposals were rejected. However, the issue would rise again in the ratification debates, and eventually lead to the addition of a bill of rights aimed at keeping the national government's powers well within the boundaries set up by the Constitution.[58]

Ratification

Sherman initially opposed popular ratification of the Constitution, noting that "the articles of Confederation provid[e] for changes and alterations with the assent of Congs. and ratification of State Legislatures." After ratification by state conventions was approved, he contended that because the states were "now confederated by articles which require unanimity in changes, he thought the ratification in this case of ten States at least ought to be made necessary." Sherman lost both battles, although the delegates did eventually agree that the Constitution should be ratified by a supermajority of nine out of thirteen states. After the Constitution was signed on September 17, Sherman returned to Connecticut to argue for its approval.[59]

On September 26, Sherman and Ellsworth sent a printed copy of the proposed Constitution to Governor Samuel Huntington, "to be laid before the legislature of the state." They included with the Constitution a letter which was submitted to the General Assembly and printed in eight Connecticut newspapers and, eventually, in fifteen newspapers in other states. In it, Sherman and Ellsworth explained that although Congress was differently organized, Connecticut's "proportion of suffrage" remained the same. They also pointed out that equal representation in the Senate "will secure the rights of the lesser as well as the greater states." As well, Congress had been given additional power, but only as it concerned "the common interests of the Union and are specially defined, so that the particular states retain their *Sovereignty* in all other matters." The former

delegates concluded by emphasizing that the Convention "endeavored to
provide for the energy of government on the one hand and suitable checks
on the other hand to secure the rights of the particular states, and the liberties and properties of the citizens."[60]

After discussing the proposed Constitution and related documents,
the General Assembly adopted a resolution requiring towns to hold meetings on November 12 to elect delegates to a state ratification convention.
Each town could elect the same number of delegates as it had members
in the lower house of the legislature. Sherman, Ellsworth, and Johnson
(who had already begun to serve as president of Columbia College) were
all elected—thus making Connecticut one of only two states to send all
of their Federal Convention delegates to the state ratifying convention
(New York was the other). The delegates were to convene in Hartford on
January 3, 1789.[61]

As in many states, newspapers were filled with essays on the proposed
Constitution. Unlike most states, Connecticut had virtually no anti-
Federalist essayists, and the newspapers were so dominated by Federalists
that few out-of-state anti-Federalist pieces were printed. The presses did
reprint Federalists' essays from other states, notably those by Tench Cox,
James Wilson, and John Hancock. Oliver Ellsworth led the Federalist
defense of the Constitution in Connecticut with his thirteen "Letters of a
Landholder" essays. In a few rare instances, out-of-state anti-Federalist
essays were published so they could be answered. For instance, Landholder
requested that Elbridge Gerry's letter to the Massachusetts General Court
be published so he could respond to it.[62]

Sherman's contribution to the flood of Federalist literature included
five essays published from November 15 to December 20 under the pseudonym of "Countryman." He also wrote an essay as "A Citizen of New
Haven" during the midst of Connecticut's ratification convention.[63]
Unlike the better known *Federalist Papers*, Sherman's essays are not filled
with theoretical arguments or fine rhetoric. Indeed, his temperament is
reflected well in his fifth Countryman essay, where he warns readers,
"Philosophy may mislead you. Ask experience." This conservative dispo-
sition is evident in his first essay, where he encourages his readers to
carefully examine the proposed Constitution to determine if it will bring
about more good than harm. He immediately addressed the perceived
threat to the state's "darling liberty" by asserting that there is no reason to
suspect that a larger government over a bigger area will be tyrannical.
After all, he asked, does "any person suppose that the people would be

more safe, more happy, or more respectable, if every town in this State was independent, and had no State government?"[64]

Sherman began his second essay by contending that it was not necessary to respond to attempts by the anti-Federalist "the Centinel" to dismiss Washington's, Franklin's, and Wilson's support of the Constitution because the first is a soldier, the second is too old, and the third is too haughty (as the second-oldest member of the Convention, Sherman must have bristled at Centinel's comment about Franklin). Substantively, Sherman's primary consideration in this essay was the criticism that the proposed Constitution lacked a bill of rights. He began by asserting that rights such as *"the liberty of the press, the rights of conscience"* etc. were "much too important to depend on mere paper protections.... The only real security that you can have for all your important rights must be in the nature of your government." Specifically, rulers must be "interested" in protecting rights. At the most practical level, this is accomplished by making them accountable to the people through elections. Sherman strengthened his argument by pointing to Connecticut's experience. Citizens of Connecticut enjoyed a number of civic rights, but these could be abolished or amended by the General Assembly at any moment. Legislators did not do so because if they did they would be voted out of office.[65]

Sherman began his third essay by noting: "The same thing once more—I am a plain man, of few words; for this reason perhaps it is, that when I have said a thing I love to repeat it." And he did. After asserting again that a bill of rights was unnecessary, he added that one might also be dangerous. For instance, "a provision that [Congress] should never raise troops in time of peace, might at some period embarrass the public concerns and endanger the liberties of the people." In his fourth essay, he reminded his readers that Connecticut's General Assembly already has *"all the powers of society"* and that voters cannot *"possibly* grant anything new." On a practical level, the security of Connecticut citizens depended on their ability to hold legislators accountable through popular elections. In his final Countryman essay, Sherman tied his arguments together by showing that just as citizens of Connecticut were safe because of their ability to hold legislators accountable, so too would citizens under the Constitution be safe because of the ability of the people to elect members of the House and the state legislatures to appoint senators.[66]

"Observations on the new Federal CONSTITUTION" by "A Citizen of New Haven" appeared on January 7, 1788, during the middle of Connecticut's ratification convention. Sherman's first five essays focused on one major issue, the lack of a bill of rights, and were short, wooden, and repetitive. By contrast, "Observations" laid out the major purposes of the proposed Constitution and addressed all of the political institutions created by it. One of Sherman's major themes was the limited nature of the new government:

> The immediate security of the civil and domestic rights of the people will be in the governments of the particular states. And as the different states have different local interest and customs which can be best regulated by their own laws, it would not be expedient to admit the federal government to interfere with them any further than may be necessary for the good of the whole. The great end of the federal government is to protect the several states in the enjoyment of those rights against foreign invasion, and to preserve peace and a beneficial intercourse among themselves, and to regulate and protect their commerce with foreign nations.

The national government's new powers, Sherman emphasized, "are particularly defined, so that each state still retains its sovereignty."[67]

Sherman contended that it was necessary to "make some alteration in the organization of government" so that the new government could effectively, and safely, execute these new powers. As he discussed these institutions, he highlighted safeguards built into each. With respect to Congress, for instance, the "rights of the people will be secured by a representation in proportion to their numbers in one branch of the legislature, and the rights of the particular states by their equal representation in the other branch." The president, vice president, and all members of Congress would serve fixed terms and were eligible for reelection, "which will be a great security for their fidelity in office." He said little about the judicial branch other than to note that the Constitution did not require the creation of inferior courts and that state courts could serve in that capacity.[68]

Regarding separation of powers, Sherman noted that it "is by some objected that the executive is blended with the legislature, and that these powers ought to be entirely distinct and unconnected, but is not this a gross *error* in politics? The united wisdom and various interests of a nation should be combined in framing the laws." He also responded to other criticisms, assuring his thrifty brethren that the new government would not be expensive, that most revenue would be raised through imposts and the sale of western lands, and that "the liberty of the press can be in no danger, because that is not put under the direction of the new government."[69]

Sherman's concluding paragraph reflects well his major political concerns and highlights his prudential approach to politics:

> Upon the whole, the Constitution appears to be well framed to secure the rights and liberties of the people and for preserving the governments of the individual states, and, if well administered, to restore and secure public and private credit, and give respectability to the states both abroad and at home. Perhaps a more perfect one could not be formed on mere speculation; and if upon experience it shall be found deficient, it provides an easy and peaceable mode to make amendments. Is it not much better to adopt it than to continue in present circumstances? Its being agreed to by all the states that were present in Convention is a circumstance in its favor, so far as any respect is due to their opinions.[70]

Sherman's fellow delegates to the state's ratifying convention largely agreed with his assessment. They convened at the State House in Hartford on January 3, 1788. After approving election certificates they moved to the North Meeting House where, after a prayer by the Reverend Nathan Strong, they unanimously agreed to examine the Constitution passage by passage but to vote only on the entire document. Unfortunately for scholars, no official record of the debates was kept, and newspapers only reported a few speeches in support of the Constitution (and none by Sherman). Sherman did participate in the debates, however, as indicated by a *Connecticut Courant* article noting that "all the objects to the Constitution vanished before the learning and eloquence of a Johnson, the genuine good sense and discernment of a Sherman, and the Demosthenian energy of an Ellsworth." The reporter was obviously biased, but the sense of Federalist domination conveyed in this account was accurate as evidenced by the January 9 vote of 128-40 to ratify the Constitution. Connecticut thus became the fifth state to approve the document.[71]

Sherman's ratification essays only indirectly reflect his commitment to Reformed political theory, but they in no way contradict it. However, the influence of this tradition is more evident in his allies' comments on issues such as the nature of rights, the scope of liberty, sovereignty, and religious tests. For instance, in Landholder III, Ellsworth contended:

Liberty is a word which, according as it is used, comprehends the most good and the most evil of any in the world. Justly understood, it is sacred next to those which we appropriate in divine adoration; but in the mouths of some, it means anything which will enervate a necessary government, excite a jealousy of the rulers who are our own choice, and keep society in confusion for want of a power sufficiently concentered to promote its good. It is not strange that the licentious should tell us a government of energy is inconsistent with liberty.

Throughout his Landholder essays, Ellsworth argued that liberty is a gift of God, that governments must protect it, and that it is not equivalent to licentiousness. Similarly, in one of the few recorded speeches in the convention, Governor Samuel Huntington contended that "the people themselves must be the chief supporter of liberty. While the great body of the freeholders are acquainted with the duties which they owe to their God, to themselves, and to me, they will remain free." With regards to sovereignty, the essayist "Philanthrop" asked rhetorically "are not the people at large forever to remain the sole governors (under God) of the land we live in?"[72]

Puritans and their successors assumed that magistrates should be godly men, and it was inconceivable to many Reformed citizens that non-Christians could be rulers in Christian societies. Accordingly, the Constitution's ban on religious tests for federal office was particularly controversial in Connecticut. William Williams was the most articulate critic of the Article VI test ban, and he raised objections before, during, and after the ratification convention. Ellsworth offered a thorough response in Landholder VII, where he made a variety of prudential arguments about the feasibility and usefulness of such tests. Critically, he contended that "the sole purpose and effect of it is to exclude persecution and to secure to you the important right of religious liberty." Somewhat uncharacteristically, he argued at one point that civil government "has no business to meddle with the private opinions of the people," a sentiment that may be defended on Calvinist grounds but which also has a libertarian flavor. That Ellsworth was more influenced by Calvinism than a liberalism is suggested by his quick qualification that he "heartily approve[s] of our laws against drunkenness, profane swearing, blasphemy, and professed atheism. But in this state we have never thought it expedient to adopt a test law and yet I sincerely believe we have as great a proportion of religion and morality as they have in England, where every person who holds a public office must be either a saint by law or a hypocrite by practice."[73]

Reporters for the *Connecticut Courant* did not see fit to record Williams's speech objecting to the test ban in the ratification convention, but they did print Oliver Wolcott's argument that the Constitution actually *did* provide a religious test for federal offices:

> I do not see the necessity of such a test as some gentlemen wish for. The Constitution enjoins an oath upon all the officers of the Unites States. This is a direct appeal to that God who is the Avenger of Perjury. Such an appeal to Him is a full acknowledgement of His being and providence.

The seriousness with which the issue was taken is indicated by post-convention debates over religious tests among Ellsworth, Williams, and others.[74]

The day before Sherman and Ellsworth submitted their September 26 letter to the General Assembly, the New Haven County Congregational Clergy held their annual meeting. A brief item in the *New Haven Gazette* noted that "the subject of the Constitution proposed by the convention was discussed in conversation; and we [the editors] are assured that every gentleman expressed his approbation of it." The meeting almost certainly included Sherman's pastor, Jonathan Edwards Jr., and his good friend and Yale President Ezra Stiles. Stiles routinely commented on the constitution-making process in his famous diary. For instance, he noted in the summer that the Federal Convention "embosoms some of the most sensible and great characters in America," and in December that he thought the Constitution should be ratified even though he feared it gave the national government too much power. The day after New Haven's clergy voted to approve the Constitution, Sherman wrote in a letter to William Floyd, "I hope that Kind Providence, that guarded these states thro a dangerous and distressing war to peace and liberty, will still watch over them and guide them in the way of safety." The ratification convention in Connecticut was held in a church, and a Congregationalist minister opened the proceedings with prayer. Of the delegates whose religious affiliation is known, 92% of the Federalists and 95% of the anti-Federalists were Congregationalists. Newspaper and ratification debates drew from ideas and rhetoric similar to that used by participants' Puritan ancestors. To be sure, in some cases the rhetoric hid modern ideas of young Connecticut Turks such as Joel Barlow (who would later negotiate the famous Treaty of Tripoli). However, this is a difficult argument to make with respect to Roger Sherman, his protégé Ellsworth, and most of his colleagues.[75]

It might be argued that the presence of Calvinists on both sides of the question of ratification undercuts my thesis that many of America's founders were influenced by the Reformed political tradition. This would be the case if an argument for intellectual influence requires that everyone influenced by a thinker or tradition has to agree on every specific policy, law, constitutional provision, etc. Yet individuals with similar values often apply them differently in particular contexts. My position is that founders influenced by Calvinist political thought shared a commitment to, and a similar understanding of, basic political ideas such as the importance of individual rights, government by the consent of the governed, the rule of law, limited government, and the right to resist tyrannical rulers. With respect to the ratification of the Constitution, they differed primarily on questions such as the potential of the national government to become tyrannical, the significance of the lack of references to the deity, and the usefulness of explicit religious tests.

It is true that Calvinist opinions on the Constitution were more fractured than they were on, say, support for the War for Independence. Indeed, some Calvinists objected so vehemently to the lack of acknowledgement of God in the Constitution that they continued to oppose the Constitution until well into the nineteenth century. But although sincere Calvinists like Roger Sherman, Oliver Ellsworth, William Williams, Timothy Dwight, Alexander M'Leod, and James R. Willson differed on this issue, they agreed on many political ideas and policies. This is not to deny that Calvinists were influenced, to one degree or another, by secular ideologies, personal and state interests, practical political considerations, and personal likes and dislikes. The argument is not that the Reformed political tradition explains everything about the American founding (or even Calvinist founders), simply that it is an important part of the picture—and one too often neglected by students of the era.[76]

Assessment

At the end of his wonderful book *1787: The Grand Convention*, Clinton Rossiter assessed the contributions made by the fifty-five delegates to the Federal Convention. He concluded that only four of the delegates were "Principals": James Madison, James Wilson, George Washington, and Gouverneur Morris. Rossiter relegated Sherman to the second rank of delegates, the "Influentials," with Rutledge, Franklin, King, Ellsworth, Gorham, Mason, Randolph, and the two Pinkneys. Like most commentators on the Convention, Rossiter recognized Sherman's contributions to Connecticut Compromise, but he considered him outshone by nationalists such as Madison and Wilson.[77]

Appreciation for Sherman's role in Philadelphia has increased in recent years, as indicated by historian Jack N. Rakove's Pulitzer Prize–winning book *Original Meanings*, political scientist David Brian Robertson's article "Madison's Opponents and Constitutional Design," and his book *The Constitution and America's Destiny*. Indeed, Robertson contends that in many respects Sherman was a more effective delegate than Madison, and he suggests that the "political synergy between Madison and Sherman... very well may have been necessary for the Constitution's adoption."[78]

Intriguingly, Christopher Collier presents an accurate and appreciative account of Sherman's contributions at the Constitutional Convention and the ratification debates in *Roger Sherman's Connecticut* and *All Politics Is Local*, but in the latter book he disparages Sherman as being "deluded" and "confused." Specifically, he criticizes him for not detecting the Constitution's "nationalist booby traps," even though he concedes: "No one in 1787 could foresee the expansive uses to which the three explosive clauses would be put; but the supremacy, commerce, and necessary and proper clauses lay in wait to blow the states'-rights defenders off the constitutional battlefield."[79]

Collier's critique is unfair insofar as it ignores the impact of the Fourteenth, Sixteenth, and Seventeenth amendments on the constitutional order designed by America's founders. States' rights advocates lost ground during and immediately after the Civil War, but this ground was not lost because of "nationalist booby traps," and Sherman would hardly have been troubled by constitutional amendments banning slavery and protecting (at least in theory) the rights of the newly freed slaves. More significantly from the perspective of federalism, Sherman specifically warned that having the people rather than state legislatures select U.S. senators would effectively "abolish State Govts." Of course, the Seventeenth Amendment did not literally have this effect, but it helped lay the groundwork for the tremendous expansion of the national government's power that began in the 1930s.[80]

Sherman helped to create a constitution that kept the national government largely within the bounds of its enumerated powers for a century-and-a-half. He undoubtedly would have been shocked to see how the supremacy, commerce, and necessary and proper clauses were used to expand the power of the national government in the twentieth century, but that hardly means he was "deluded" or "confused." Of course, there were serious debates about the exact scope of the national government's power from the earliest days of the republic, but by most accounts, defenders of states' rights were not "blown off the battlefield" until the mid-1930s. Even that outcome does not necessarily mean that Madison, Wilson, and Hamilton won the day because of clever traps, as twentieth-century crises may have led to the expansion of the national government's power irrespective of constitutional limitations. This is not an argument for historical inevitability, but it is a caution for those who would hold Sherman accountable for the arguably unconstitutional actions of his great-great-great-great-grandchildren.

By any reasonable measure, Sherman was one of the most influential and effective delegates at the constitutional and ratification conventions. A chief rival for this title is undoubtedly Madison—largely because he set the agenda with his Virginia Plan and so eloquently and powerfully defended the Constitution in the *Federalist Papers*. Yet we must remember that there are significant differences between Madison's initial proposals and what he supported in his *Federalist Papers*. In a number of instances, Madison praised as virtues elements in the proposed Constitution that he opposed and Sherman had supported in the Federal Convention.[81]

Of course, Sherman hardly won every battle. If he had, the Federal Convention would have proposed something akin to the New Jersey Plan. The forceful advocacy of Madison and other nationalists, as well as the political realities of the day, made this outcome highly implausible. The point is not that Sherman should be awarded Madison's title of "Father of the Constitution," but that his support for limited government, states' rights, and legislative superiority helped create a constitution that was ratified by the states and that has served America well for more than two hundred years.

6

Roger Sherman and the New National Government

CONNECTICUT WAS THE only state to send each of its Federal Convention delegates to serve in the legislature created by the new Constitution. Johnson and Ellsworth, Sherman's legal mentor and his protégé, were selected by the General Assembly to be Connecticut's first United States senators. The state elected members of the House of Representatives as it elected delegates to the Confederation Congress; freemen nominated candidates in November, and in December they cast ballots for five of the top-twelve nominees. Sherman was fourth on the list of nominations, and second in the general, at-large election. His election was bittersweet because it forced him to choose between serving in the House of Representatives or as a judge on Connecticut's Superior Court. He petitioned the General Assembly for an exception to the 1784 statute prohibiting holding both offices, but his plea was rejected. Thus in February of 1789, after twenty-three years on the bench, he resigned from the Superior Court.

Sherman arrived at the nation's temporary capital of New York City on March 5, 1789. At sixty-nine years of age, he was the oldest member of the Congress. No representative or senator had more experience in the Continental and Confederation Congresses than "father Sherman." In spite of his age, he jumped into the business of putting flesh on the skeleton of the new national government. Indeed, in the first Congress, he spoke more often than any other member of the House of Representatives except for James Madison. He made particularly important and interesting contributions to debates over representation, executive power, revenue, debt, the proper scope of the national government, and, especially, the Bill of Rights.[1]

The Role of the National Legislator

Sherman lived in one of the most republican states in the nation. For virtually all of his political life every significant legislative, executive, and judicial office in the state was held by elected officials, and many of the policies most directly affecting citizens were made in society and town meetings or by local officials who were elected biannually.[2] Separation of powers was in its infancy and the legislature was supreme. The system was not perfect—no Calvinist would ever make such a claim—but overall, Sherman thought it helped maintain a good and godly society. He had fought in the Constitutional Convention to balance the need to strengthen the national government with the virtues of local autonomy, and he regularly supported legislative supremacy. He brought these values to the House of Representatives.

Sherman did not support democracy for its own sake. Fundamentally, civic authorities are responsible for doing what is right. He remarked in a speech on May 9, 1789, that members of Congress

> have had recourse to popular opinion in support of their arguments. Popular opinion is founded in justice, and the only way to know if the popular opinion is in favor of a measure, is to examine whether the measure is just and right in itself. I think whatever is proper and right the people will judge of and comply with. The people wish that the government may derive respect from the justice of its measures; and they have given it their support on this account.[3]

Democracy and democratic institutions are valuable because they are most likely to create legislation that promotes the common good.

Sherman believed many civic decisions, such as education and care for the poor, are best decided by citizens at the local level. Some issues, such as defense, international commerce, and currency policy, must be addressed at the national level by representatives who are well informed on these complicated issues. Because most voters are uninformed, legislators cannot simply reflect the views of their constituents. As such, Sherman opposed the practice of constituents instructing their national representatives. Instead, he argued that it "is the duty of a good representative to enquire what measures are most likely to promote the general welfare, and after he has discovered them, to give them his support; should his instructions therefore coincide with his ideas on any measure, they would be unnecessary; if they were contrary to the conviction of his own mind, he must be bound by every principle of justice to disregard them."[4]

Within its delegated powers, the national government is obligated to pursue "the common good," the "general welfare of society," and the "principle of justice." Sherman had been in politics too long to deny that self-interest often informed the actions of civic leaders, but like all Reformed political thinkers he continually argued that the common good is the end of government. As Alan Heimert remarked with respect to evangelical ministers of the era (with whom Sherman had much in common), "In their thought, the purposes of society and of government were one, and their very terms of discussion evinced the urgency with which all their thinking drove to the question of the 'general good.' "[5] He believed the legislature was the institution best suited to this task.

Executive Power

In the Constitutional Convention, Sherman had suggested that executive functions might be fulfilled by an executive committee composed of an unspecified number of appointed officials serving at the will of the national legislature. He never reconciled himself to a single executive independent of the legislature, an executive veto, or executive prerogatives. Sherman continued to fight the growth and concentration of executive power while in Congress. The first significant battle on this issue was sparked on May 19, 1789, when representatives began discussing the organization of the executive branch. Madison proposed a "department of foreign affairs; at the head of which there should be an officer, to be called, the secretary to the department of foreign affairs, who shall be appointed by the president, by and with the advice and consent of the senate; and to be removable by the president." No one doubted that there would be such an officer, or that he would be appointed by the president with the advice and consent of the Senate. The critical issue, as William Smith immediately pointed out, is whether the president could unilaterally remove the secretary. The Constitution does not address the removal of executive branch officials by the president, and the issue remained hotly contested in American constitutional law well into the twentieth century.[6]

Sherman tenaciously argued against giving the president the power to remove members of the executive branch. He contended that the president's power to appoint and the Senate's power to confirm are "mutual checks, each having a negative upon the other." The alternative, he suggested, would result in institutions like the courts in England, where the "king had the power of appointing judges...and they might be removed when the monarch thought proper." Sherman often referred to the Crown when opposing executive power; indeed, on the following day, he noted that "the crown of Great Britain, by having that prerogative, has been enabled to swallow up the whole administration; the influence of the crown upon the legislature subjects both houses to its will and pleasure." However, this rhetoric was not as powerful as it once was—as indicated by the defeat of his motion to strike the words "to be removable by the president" from the bill by a vote of 34–20.[7]

A similar battle was fought in the Senate, where a tie vote on the issue was broken in favor of presidential power by Vice President John Adams on July 16. The following day, Adams wrote Sherman a letter politely criticizing portions of his January 7, 1788, essay, "Observations on the New Federal Government," that addressed presidential power and republican government.[8] Adams began by questioning Sherman's claim that the Crown's ability to veto laws is "an extreme that ought not to be imitated by a republic." He suggested, on the contrary, that if a republic is "[a] *government whose sovereignty is vested in more than one person,*" then Great Britain is a monarchical republic as sovereignty is vested in more than one person; "it is equally divided, indeed, between the one, the few, and the many." He went on to argue that "the regal negative upon the laws is essential to that republic" in order to "preserve the balance of power between the executive and legislative."[9]

Turning to America's constitutional system, Adams launched into a forceful defense of "prerogatives and dignities" given to the chief executive so that he can execute laws and protect "the lives, liberties, properties and characters of the citizens." In America's case, the danger is not from the executive power but from the legislative, for it "is greater than the executive; it will, therefore, encroach." The remedy, Adams suggested, is to amend the Constitution to provide the president with an absolute rather than a partial veto. He also listed seven reasons why having the Senate confirm executive appointments was problematic—although he did not propose to amend the Constitution on this score.[10]

Sherman responded to Adams's letters with two of his own written on July 18 and July 27. He began by stating that he understood a republic to be

a government under the authority of the people, consisting of legislative, executive, and judicial powers; the legislative powers vested in an assembly, consisting of one or more branches, who, together with the executive, are appointed by the people, and dependent on them for continuance, by periodical elections, agreeably to an established constitution; and that what especially denominates it a *republic* is its dependence on the *public* or *people at large*, without any hereditary powers.

He conceded that the people could divide power between the one, the few, and the many in a variety of different ways within this framework, but he also made it clear that he thought the legislature should be supreme. In Great Britain it might be necessary for the monarch to have an absolute veto to protect himself against the nobility, "but in a republic like ours, wherein is no higher rank than that of common citizens, unless distinguished by appointments to office, what occasion can there be for such a balance?" Ironically, especially given his opposition to even a partial veto in the Constitutional Convention, Sherman suggested that the president would be more likely to use a partial veto than an absolute veto to force Congress to revise a piece of legislation. Not surprisingly, he had no patience for Adams's suggestion that the president should be able to appoint officers without the Senate's consent, arguing that the practice had led to significant corruption in England.[11]

It is tempting to view Adams as promoting a traditional British concept of republicanism and Sherman as articulating a new, egalitarian version. As Christopher Collier points out, however, Sherman was defending "a form of government established for Connecticut in the mid-seventeenth century."[12] This is a helpful reminder for those seeking to trace the origins of American egalitarianism, democracy, or fear of concentrated power to modern thinkers such as Locke or Rousseau. Sherman's conclusion to his essay reinforces his pragmatic conservatism: "I have said enough upon these speculative points, which nothing but experience can reduce to a certainty."[13]

In January 1790, the House turned to a fairly benign bill permitting the president to draw "a sum not exceeding forty thousand dollars annually to compensate the salaries of such officers as shall be sent abroad." Representative Richard Bland Lee suggested that it was the Senate's responsibility to give advice and consent to each salary. This engendered a lengthy debate concerning the freedom of the president in foreign affairs, wherein Sherman argued:

> The establishment of every treaty requires the voice of the senate, as does the appointment of every officer for conducting the business; these two objects are expressly provided for in the constitution, and they lead me to believe, that *the two bodies ought to act jointly in every transaction which respects the business of negociation with foreign powers.* But the bill provides for the president to do it alone, which is evidently a deviation from the apparent principle of the constitution.

And what do gentlemen urge as an argument to induce the committee to adopt their idea? Why, that the singleness of the officer, who appropriates and disburses the public money, will insure a higher degree of responsibility than the mode recommended (at least by inference) by the constitution. This argument would extend to prove, that a single person ought to exercise the powers of this house, consequently it goes too far. There is something more required than responsibility in conducting treaties. The constitution contemplates the united wisdom of the president and the senate, in order to make treaties for the benefit of the United States. The more wisdom there is employed, the greater security there is that the public business will be well done [emphasis added].[14]

Throughout American history, but particularly since World War I, presidents have claimed almost unlimited power in the realm of international relations. They have argued that the need for energy and secrecy may require them to act without the advice and consent of Congress, even with respect to using military force against other countries (a power that would seem to belong to Congress). A few founders supported giving the president relatively free reign in such matters, but Sherman was certainly not one of them.[15]

Revenue and the Common Good

Sherman's conviction that the national government should promote the common good is illustrated well by his contributions to debates over national revenue. In 1776, he served on the first congressional committee to address this issue, and he repeatedly urged the Continental and Confederation Congresses to adopt a national impost to raise funds. In Congress he supported duties because they promote domestic industries and because the taxes are voluntary. Some representatives complained that they discriminated against merchants, but Sherman contended that "the consumer pays them eventually, and they pay no more than they chuse, because they have it in their power to determine the quantity of taxable articles they will use. A tax left to be paid at discretion must be more agreeable than any other."[16]

Of course, Sherman-the-merchant and Sherman-the-politician understood that duties often reduce merchants' profit margins. As well, he recognized that a national impost that superseded state imposts would shift the benefits of the tax from states with deep water harbors to the nation as a whole (thus benefiting states like Connecticut, which had no deepwater harbor). These practical considerations cannot be ignored, but a critical reason Sherman supported them was because they could be used to discourage vice.

Throughout his career, Sherman regularly promoted sumptuary laws because he thought they advanced the common good. In 1752, he had argued that it would benefit the "Publick Good" to "Lay a large Excise upon all Rum imported into this Colony, or distilled therein, thereby effectually to restrain the excessive use thereof, which is such a growing Evil among us and is leading to almost all other Vices." Sherman was not a teetotaler, but he believed that excessive drinking was harmful and that hard liquor was particularly damaging. Accordingly, he was willing to use the power of the state to address this evil. More broadly, in his 1784 "Remarks on a Pamphlet," he declared that luxury was a chief cause of the downfall of Rome and Great Britain and argued that the Continental Congress should place impost taxes upon luxuries. His votes at both the state and the national level reflected these convictions.[17]

With this record, it should come as no surprise that as a member of the new federal Congress, Sherman supported a duty on distilled spirits because it would contribute to the "general welfare of the community" and "in itself is reasonable and just." One year later, he advocated an excise tax on domestically produced spirits, arguing that it was necessary "to make the tax operate equally." Without a tax on spirits distilled in the United States, the government would lose money and there would be a "bounty of home-made spirits." This was not an object "that deserved the particular encouragement of the government." The tax finally passed along regional lines, but it proved widely unpopular and eventually led to the Whiskey Rebellion.[18]

Given his willingness to use the power of taxation to promote moral ends, it is notable that Sherman objected to a proposal to place a ten dollar tax on the importation of slaves. As in the Constitutional Convention, he contended that Africans should not be treated like consumer products. Sherman noted that he "approved of the object of the motion," but that

he did not think this bill was proper to embrace the subject. He could not reconcile himself to the insertion of human beings, as an article of duty, among goods, wares and merchandize. He hoped it would be withdrawn for the present, and taken up hereafter as an independent subject.[19]

Nine months later, Congress received a petition from Quakers in New York urging the abolition of slavery. Sherman recommended that the petition be sent to a committee consisting of a member from each state. This committee eventually received several other petitions from Quakers and one from the Pennsylvania Society for Promoting the Abolition of Slavery that was signed by its president, Benjamin Franklin. In March 1790, it issued a report concluding that Congress had no power to ban the importation of slaves prior to 1808, free the slaves, or interfere with internal regulations of particular states. However, it encouraged the states to "revise their laws from time to time, when necessary, and promote the objects mentioned in the memorials, and every other measure that may tend to the happiness of slaves." The report also recommended informing the authors and signers of the memorials that "in all cases, to which the authority of Congress extends, they will exercise it for the humane objects of the memorialists, so far as they can be promoted on the principles of justice, humanity, and good policy." When William Smith of South Carolina moved to have the report recommitted to the committee, Sherman "opposed this motion; he said that this report was agreeable to his ideas, it was prudent, humane and judicious." Smith's motion lost, and the report was eventually included in the House Journal.[20]

It is worth noting in this context that the Connecticut Society for the Promotion of Freedom, and for the Relief of Persons Unlawfully Holden in Bondage was founded in 1790. Its president was Sherman's old friend Ezra Stiles, and its secretary was his son-in-law Simeon Baldwin. On January 7, 1791, the newly formed society submitted an antislavery petition to Congress, but it was "referred to a special committee and never more heard of." Later that year, Sherman's pastor, Jonathan Edwards Jr., preached a sermon at the society's annual meeting roundly condemning the slave trade and slavery per se. There is no evidence that Sherman joined this society, but on March 7, 1792, he wrote to Governor Huntington about the "distressed situation" in Haiti and commented: "This shews the bad effects of slavery and I hope it will tend to its abolition."[21]

Sherman opposed slavery in word and deed, but he recognized that Congress had virtually no power to interfere with the institution in existing states. The First Congress did reauthorize the Northwest Ordinance, which prohibited slavery in the federal territory around the Great Lakes, but it could not ban the importation of slaves until 1808. Sherman resisted placing a token tax of ten dollars on slaves because it implied that they were commodities, not humans. He was willing to debate the morality of the institution in Congress, and thought it proper for Congress to urge states to pass just and humane laws regulating slaves. Ideally, states would ban the institution altogether, but doing so was an issue the Constitution left to the states.

Public Credit and the Assumption of State Debts

Sherman valued the secondary effects imposts might have on discouraging vice, but he believed that their primary value was raising revenue to pay the national debt. Paying the debt was a moral obligation. His position on the matter is reflected well by his response to Representative Thomas Scott's proposal to lower interest payments on public debt. Sherman contended that

> every legislature acts in a threefold capacity: They have a power to make laws for the good government of the people, and a right to repeal, and alter those laws as public good requires; in another capacity, they have a right to make contracts; but here I must contend, that they have no right to violate, alter, or abolish; but they have a right to fulfil them.

He emphasized the latter point, noting, "I don't see but what the public are bound by that contract, as much as an individual, and that they cannot reduce it down in either principal or interest, unless by an arbitrary power, and in that case there never will be any security in the public promises." There are solid prudential reasons for states to pay their debts, and Sherman the pragmatist agreed with them. Perhaps even more critical for him, however, was the moral obligation to do so and his abhorrence of arbitrary power.[22]

In 1780, Sherman wrote a report urging the Continental Congress to assume state war debts, so it surprised no one when he supported Hamilton's plan for the new national government to do the same. On April 21, 1790, Sherman made a motion providing that all "the debts contracted by the several states for the common defence and benefit of the union" be "considered as a part of the domestic debt of the United States." He then offered a specific proposal for the amount of debt to be assumed from each state. Sherman's motion did not succeed at this time, but when Congress finally agreed to assume state debts, the amounts were virtually identical to those proposed by Sherman.[23]

On May 25, 1790, Sherman gave a lengthy speech supporting the assumption of state debts. He began by contending that state "debts were contracted on behalf and for the benefit of United States, and therefore justice requires that they should be assumed." He offered six major arguments in favor of assumption, culminating with the prudential point that assumption is "founded in good policy, as well as justice, as it will produce harmony among the various classes of creditors, and among the several states, and attach them to the [national] government." He also responded to thirteen objections to Hamilton's plan. A few days after the speech, Abigail Adams wrote to Cotton Tuffs that: "For the Assumption of the debts you will see in the papers a wise and judicious speach of Father Sherman, as he is call'd, and a very able & lengthy one of Mr. Ames's. all has been said upon the subject that reason justice, good policy could dictate."[24]

Sherman agreed with Hamilton that the national government should not discriminate between original creditors and speculators who purchased discounted notes. He claimed to have investigated the matter in Connecticut and found that there was relatively little speculation. More significantly, he argued that distinguishing between the two classes of bondholders would be impractical. Sherman, it should be noted, owned between $6,000 and $7,000 in state notes, some of which he purchased in 1790. However, given his long support for the assumption of state debts, there is little reason to believe these notes influenced his position on this issue.[25]

There are no records of Sherman participating in the famous dinner where Jefferson, Madison, and Hamilton struck the bargain to have the national government assume state debts in exchange for locating the nation's capital temporarily in Philadelphia and permanently on the banks of the Potomac River. Sherman consistently opposed placing the capital in the South, arguing for a more central location. His preference was "somewhere in the state of Pennsylvania," but he supported both Baltimore and Wilmington as alternatives to the Potomac location. Nevertheless, he was pleased that Congress finally agreed to assume debts incurred in America's War for Independence.[26]

The National Bank and National Power

In the Constitutional Convention, Sherman tenaciously opposed giving the national government a general grant of power, preferring instead that its powers be enumerated. Madison, on the other hand, had contended for

a general grant of power. When Congress turned to the creation of a
national bank, Sherman and Madison again found themselves on opposite
sides of the issue—but with Sherman supporting the bank and Madison
opposing it! Madison's constitutional objections, including his arguments
based on original understanding, are recorded in newspaper accounts of
House debates. Sherman was relatively silent on the subject, although on
February 3, 1791, he remarked that he supported the "plan of a National
bank" because it "had not been thought of for the benefit of individuals. It
was intended to be of public benefit." The next day, Sherman slipped
Madison a note addressing the constitutional arguments. It read:

> You will admit that Congress have power to provide by law for
> raising, depositing & applying money for the purposes enumerated
> in the Constitution and generally of regulating the Finances.
>   That they have power so far as no particular rules are pointed
> out in the constitution to make such rules & regulations as they
> may judge necessary & proper for effecting these purposes. The
> only question that remains is—Is a Bank a proper measure for
> effecting these purposes?
>   And is not this a question of expediency rather than of right?

Madison responded by returning the note with the words "a necessary
and" careted in before "proper measure," thus rephrasing Sherman's
question to emphasize the necessity of a bank. In this brief exchange,
Sherman and Madison foreshadowed the long, contentious debate over
the constitutionality of the bank.[27]
    Sherman was usually an advocate of states' rights and of keeping the
national government within its enumerated powers. The major exception
to this rule involved finances and currency. In the Constitutional
Convention, he had supported the Article I, Section 10 prohibition on
states issuing bills of credit or paper money. During his congressional
career, he faithfully promoted Hamilton's plans to establish public credit
and assume state debts. Similarly, he favored a national bank because he
believed it necessary to bring order to America's chaotic financial system
and help provide for a system of sound currency. This is not to say that
Sherman abandoned his commitment to the enumerated powers. Unless
one takes the "necessary" of "necessary and proper" absolutely literally, it
is not unreasonable to view a national bank as a necessary and proper
means to accomplish powers clearly given to Congress.

A good example of Sherman's commitment to keeping the national government within the bounds of its enumerated powers is his reaction to a House committee report proposing that the secretary of treasury be authorized to loan John F. Amelung up to $8,000 to support his "glass manufactory." Sherman objected that he did not think Congress was "authorized by the Constitution to advance money for this purpose. Particularly can't advance money for encouragement of useful arts." When Daniel Carroll responded that the general welfare clause authorized such legislation, Sherman argued that the "general welfare extended to every-thing. I look on it [as a] restrictive clause because they have the powers only herein granted. Though the power given to congress to raise armies yet they will not do unless for the general welfare." It is noteworthy that Sherman remarked that states are free to subsidize such endeavors. He did not oppose government aid to industry per se, but he believed the national government did not have the power to subsidize private industries.[28]

By the same token, when Congress moved toward considering the creation of a national university, Sherman informed his colleagues "that a proposition to vest Congress with power to establish a National University was made in the General Convention—but it was negativated—It was thought sufficient that this power should be exercised by the States in their separate capacity." Sherman believed in higher education, as demonstrated by his long-time support of Yale College. He had served as treasurer of the college, made donations to it, and as a member of the upper-house of the legislature almost certainly approved state subsidies for the institution. His opposition to a national university was simply a matter of federalism.[29]

Bill of Rights

When George Mason proposed the addition of a bill of rights to the Constitution in the waning days of the Constitutional Convention, Sherman said that he "was for securing the rights of the people where requisite. The State Declaration of Rights are not repealed by this Constitution; and being in force are sufficient." Mason's proposal was rejected 10-0, but the vote reflects the delegates' weariness more than a lack of support for a bill of rights. During the ratification debates, the anti-Federalists continued to agitate for an enumeration of rights, and, in many states, proponents of the Constitution promised to pursue one. Sherman did not join their ranks.[30]

During the ratification controversy, four of Sherman's six essays defending the Constitution addressed anti-Federalist criticisms concerning the lack of a bill of rights. He argued that "rights are too important to depend on mere paper protections" and that the only real security for them "must be in the nature of your government." Frequent elections, much more than parchment barriers, will protect the people. Most significantly, because the national government has strictly enumerated powers, it does not have the power to pass laws interfering with individual rights and liberties.[31]

On December 4, 1788, Sherman, writing as "A Citizen of New Haven," published an essay entitled "Observations on the Alterations Proposed as Amendments to the New Federal Constitution." He began by noting with approval that six states "have adopted the new constitution without proposing any alteration." However, he was well aware that five state conventions had proposed a host of constitutional amendments.[32] Sherman addressed seven of the proposed amendments, but only one of them touched on something eventually incorporated into the Bill of Rights. For instance, Sherman objected to proposals to require supermajorities for "certain acts" and "to make the president and senators ineligible after certain periods" because they were undemocratic. The first, he wrote, allowed the minority to control the majority, and the second "would abridge the privilege of the people, and remove one great motive to fidelity in office." In response to an amendment that would transfer the pardon power from the president to Congress, Sherman contended that no "great mischief" would result from leaving this power with the president, but he could not resist adding parenthetically that "(perhaps it might have been lodged in congress)."[33]

With respect to the future Bill of Rights, the most relevant proposed amendment addressed by Sherman was South Carolina's suggestion to "insert the word *other*, between the words *no* and *religious* in that article." The reference is to Article VI's prohibition on religious tests for federal offices; one of the most contentious issues in both Connecticut's and South Carolina's ratification debates. Sherman remarked that the addition is "an ingenious thought, and had that word been inserted, it would probably have prevented any objection on that head. But it may be considered as a clerical omission and be inserted without calling a convention; as it now stands the effect will be the same." Sherman, like many delegates to the Federal Convention, simply could not conceive of an oath as anything other than a religious test. In Connecticut, oaths were regularly taken "in the Name of the Everliving GOD," and it was God who was the primary witness to and enforcer of the oaths. Few, if any, New Englanders were troubled by *this* sort of religious test.[34]

Sherman was as committed to protecting rights as any founder, but he simply did not think a bill of rights was necessary. Moreover, he

> hoped that all the states will consent to make a fair trial of the constitution before they attempt to alter it; experience will best show whether it is deficient or not, on trial it may appear that the alterations that have been proposed are not necessary, or that others not yet thought of may be necessary; everything that tends to disunion ought to be avoided. Instability in government and laws tends to weaken a state and render the rights of the people precarious.[35]

The following week, Sherman published a slightly revised version of his original "A Citizen of New Haven" essay, which also denied that a bill of rights was needed.

On June 8, 1789, Madison encouraged his colleagues to take "into consideration the subject of amendments to the constitution," noting that he considered himself "bound in honor and in duty to do what I have done on this subject." Sherman responded that he understood that some of his colleagues thought it their duty to discuss a bill of rights, but he had "strong objections to being interrupted in completing the more important business." Madison, nevertheless, went ahead and made his famous speech proposing a bill of rights. The House declined to move forward at that time, and the issue was tabled. Sherman wanted to make sure it remained tabled, so he arranged to have his essays against adding bill of rights republished in the *New York Packet* and several New England papers during the summer of 1789.[36]

Undeterred by Sherman's literary efforts, on July 21, Madison "[b]egged the house to indulge him in the further consideration of amendments to the constitution." Sherman again objected, pointing out that eleven states had ratified the Constitution and that a majority of them did not propose amendments. Madison was again put off; although this time the House approved a motion by Fisher Ames to form a select committee composed of one member from each state to consider amendments. Sherman was appointed to represent Connecticut. There are no records of the committee's deliberations, but the committee did produce a draft bill of rights in

Sherman's handwriting. The draft, reprinted in the appendix, is the only handwritten draft of the Bill of Rights known to exist.[37]

James H. Hutson has argued that the draft shows Sherman "to have been more a collaborator than an adversary of Madison in his efforts to induce Congress to adopt a bill of rights." Scott D. Gerber challenged this assertion in a research note entitled "Roger Sherman and the Bill of Rights." He relied heavily on Sherman's initial opposition to a bill of rights and his later arguments against provisions contained in the draft to make his case. It is true that Sherman would have preferred to have avoided the subject altogether, but the draft and subsequent debates make it clear that Sherman was an active participant in the creation of the Bill of Rights.[38]

Madison's first draft of the Bill of Rights contained nine proposed amendments that would have been interspersed throughout the Constitution. It began by prefixing "to the constitution a declaration— That all power is originally vested in, and consequently derived from the people." Other amendments would have affected the number of representatives and their compensation, protected a variety of individual and procedural rights, and would have prevented *states* from violating "the equal rights of conscience, or the freedom of the press, or the trial by jury in criminal cases." In response to James Wilson's argument in the ratification debates that an enumeration of rights might be dangerous because rights not protected might be considered unprotected, he included a version of what became the Ninth Amendment. To assuage anti-Federalist fears regarding the scope of the national government's power, Madison proposed an early formulation of the Tenth Amendment.[39]

The select committee's draft in Sherman's hand follows Madison's draft, but there are important differences. First, with respect to religion, Madison proposed that "[t]he civil rights of none shall be abridged on account of religious belief or worship, nor shall any national religion be established," whereas the select committee's draft reads "[t]he people have certain natural rights which are retained in Society, Such are the rights of Conscience in matters of religion." Denoting religious liberty to be a "natural right" rather than a "civil right" is a stronger claim, and it is notable that the draft in Sherman's hand does not contain an embryonic establishment clause. This proposed amendment also listed several other "natural rights," many of which ended up being included in the First Amendment.[40]

A second major difference is that virtually all of the criminal procedural provisions contained in what became amendments four through six were present in Madison's draft but are missing from Sherman's. As well, Madison's proposal to add what became the Ninth Amendment was not included in this draft nor were his restrictions on states retained. Finally, it is noteworthy that the draft in Sherman's hand contained a provision that is not in Madison's speech or the final version of the Bill of Rights—an amendment stipulating that "Congress Shall not have power to grant any monopoly or exclusive advantages of commerce to any person or Company."[41]

The draft of the select committee's report in Sherman's hand includes some proposals that Sherman later opposed in the ensuing debates. For instance, it contains a version of what became the Third Amendment. When the House of Representatives debated the measure later in the summer, Sherman was the only member to object, noting that "it was absolutely necessary that marching troops should have quarters, whether in time of peace or war, and that it ought not to be put in the power of an individual to obstruct the public service." It is therefore misleading to refer to provisions in the draft as being "Sherman's proposals," as scholars have done on occasion.[42]

On July 28, the select committee issued a printed report proposing nineteen changes to the Constitution. The report differs significantly from the draft in Sherman's hand. On August 13, the House began debating the proposals amendment by amendment. The first proposal was to insert before the words "Government being intended for the benefit of the people, and the rightful establishment thereof being derived from their authority alone" before the words "We the people" in the Constitution's preamble. Sherman immediately rose to object both to the wording of the amendment and its placement. He argued that

we cannot incorporate these amendments in the body of the Constitution. It would be mixing brass, iron, and clay...I conceive that we have no right to do this, as the Constitution is an act of the people, and ought to remain entire—whereas the amendments will be the act of the several legislatures.

With respect to the substance of the amendment, Sherman remarked that he agreed with the basic sentiment, but because "if the constitution had been a grant from another power, it would be proper to express this principle; but as the right expressed in the amendment was natural and inherent in the people, it is unnecessary to give any reasons or ground on which they made their constitution. It was an act of their own sovereign will." Sherman's objections were overruled by the House on the 14th, but he eventually won on both points as the proposed amendment was rejected and the amendments that were adopted were annexed to the Constitution rather than interspersed throughout it as desired by Madison.[43]

The second amendment considered by the representatives would have required the House to consist of between 100 and 175 members. Sherman made a motion to strike 175 in favor of a smaller number. He did so because he believed that "the rights of the people are less secure in a large, than in a small assembly: The great object is information; and this may be acquired by a small number, and to better purpose than by a large." He also argued that the "objects of the federal government were fewer than those of the state governments; they did not require an equal degree of local knowledge."[44]

In the course of debating the proper size of the House of Representatives, Sherman suggested increasing the current ratio of representatives to population from 1:30,000 to 1:40,000. He noted that "in the convention that framed the constitution, there was a majority in favor of 40,000, and though there were some in favour of 30,000 yet that proposition did not obtain until after the constitution was agreed to, when the president [Washington] had expressed a wish that 30,000 should be inserted." Madison responded to this claim by noting that he "[h]oped gentlemen would not be influenced by what had been related to have passed in the convention; he expected the committee would determine upon their own sense of propriety." Madison won this argument, and a version of the amendment was presented to the states for ratification. It was ratified by every state that approved the Bill of Rights except Delaware, which calculated that a larger House would dilute the weight of its single delegate. The amendment thus became the only one of the twelve proposed amendments never to be adopted.[45]

On August 15, the House turned to Madison's proposal to insert the phrase "no religion shall be established by law, nor shall the equal rights of conscience be infringed" into Article I, Section 9. Sherman objected immediately that he "[t]hought the amendment altogether unnecessary, insomuch as congress has no authority whatever delegated to them by the constitution, to make religious establishments, he would therefore move to have it struck out." After a short discussion, the House agreed to Livermore's substitute, "congress shall make no laws touching religion, or infringing the rights of conscience," by a vote of 31–20.[46]

Sherman did not join the brief debate over the remainder of what became the First Amendment. He did contribute to discussions over the second provision concerning religion to come before the House; Madison's proposal attached to what is now the Second Amendment providing that "no person religiously scrupulous, shall be compelled to bear arms." Although largely forgotten today, this provision provoked almost as much recorded debate as the First Amendment's religion provisions. Sherman's most significant objection was to James Jackson's proposal that persons exempted from military service should be forced to pay for a substitute. Sherman contended:

> It is well-known that those who are religiously scrupulous of bearing arms, are equally scrupulous of getting substitutes or paying an equivalent; many of them would rather die than do either one or the other—but he did not see an absolute necessity for a clause of this kind. We do not live under an arbitrary government, said he, and the states respectively will have the government of the militia, unless when called into actual service.

Sherman was sympathetic to the plight of pacifists, but he preferred to rely on state and federal legislatures to protect them. Madison's proposal was eventually rejected by the Senate, but, as we shall see, Madison and Sherman were able to include a similar provision in the nation's first militia bill.[47]

Unlike Sherman, Madison did not trust states to protect rights, so he offered an amendment stipulating that "no state shall infringe the equal rights of conscience, nor the freedom of speech, or of the press, nor of the right to trial by jury in criminal cases." This restriction on the states, which Madison conceived "to be the most valuable amendment on the whole list," occasioned little debate and with minor revisions was passed by the House on August 17. However, the Senate rejected the proposed amendment on September 7, and Madison was unable to save it.[48]

It is ironic that Sherman, the great advocate of states' rights and proponent of limited, enumerated powers at the national level, opposed many of the proposed limitations that eventually made their way into the Bill of Rights. Perhaps most surprising is his resistance to attempts to fortify what became the Tenth Amendment. On August 18, he joined Madison in opposing a proposal by Thomas Tucker to alter this amendment to make it clear that Congress had no implied powers. Sherman argued that "all corporations are supposed to possess all the powers incidental to their corporate capacity: It is not in human wisdom to provide for every possible contingency." Three days later, he objected to Gerry's motion to add "expressly" to this amendment. Instead, Sherman moved and the House adopted the wording "the powers not delegated to the United States, by the Constitution, nor prohibited by it to the states, are reserved to the states respectively, or to the people." The motion was adopted without debate.[49]

To understand Sherman's approach to the Bill of Rights, it is necessary to recognize that he really believed that Congress was limited to the powers enumerated in Article I, Section 8 of the Constitution. Because of these constraints, amendments prohibiting Congress from doing things it did not have the power to do, like establishing a religion or restricting the press, were unnecessary. However, Sherman did think Congress possessed powers reasonably implied by those enumerated in the Constitution. Accordingly, he could in good conscience support the creation of a national bank, and he opposed versions of what became the Tenth Amendment that might have made it more difficult for Congress to act on these implied powers.[50]

Many proposed amendments engendered little discussion, and Sherman made few additional comments that shine light on his political ideas. On August 21, he again referred to the views of delegates at the Constitutional Convention to oppose an amendment that would prohibit Congress from regulating federal elections "except when any state shall refuse or neglect, or be unable, by invasion or rebellion, to make such election." He supported without comment a motion to eliminate the prohibition on double jeopardy and opposed an amendment concerning the separation of powers as "unnecessary." He also argued against a cumbersome amendment proposed by Thomas Tucker respecting when and how Congress could levy direct taxes.[51]

On August 22, the House appointed Egbert Benson, Theodore Sedgwick, and Sherman to "prepare an introduction to and arrangement of Articles of Amendment."[52] Their report of August 24 consisted of sixteen articles and was sent to the Senate, which amended and returned them to the House on September 14. The House Journal notes that the changes were debated on September 19, but there are no records of these debates. On September 21, the House agreed to some of the Senate's amendments, disagreed to others, and appointed Madison, Sherman, and John Vining to a conference committee to reconcile the differences. The Senate appointed Sherman's protégé Oliver Ellsworth to head the Senate delegation, and he was joined by Charles Carroll and William Paterson. On September 24, the committee reported twelve proposed amendments, which the House approved with a few minor changes. There was no role call vote, so it is impossible to know if Sherman supported the amendments, but it is unlikely that he would have been appointed to the conference committee if he still opposed them. The next day, the Senate approved the twelve amendments passed by the House, and they were sent to the states where the ten that we now know as the Bill of Rights were quickly ratified.[53]

Original Intent and the Bill of Rights: The Case of Church and State

America's founders differed with respect to whether and/or how civic authorities should support Christianity. On balance, Reformed Christians were more sympathetic to significant state support for religion, as suggested by the survival of establishments in Vermont (1807), Connecticut (1819), New Hampshire (1819), Maine (1820), and Massachusetts (1833). Yet when Supreme Court justices have turned to founding era history to shine light on the meaning of the religion clauses, they have overwhelmingly relied on the views of two southern Anglicans—Thomas Jefferson and James Madison. This approach is particularly ahistorical because Jefferson was not even involved in crafting or ratifying the First Amendment.[54]

In the 1947 establishment clause case of *Everson v. Board of Education,* Justice Wiley Rutledge observed that "no provision of the Constitution is more closely tied to or given content by its generating history than the religious clause of the First Amendment. It is at once the refined product and the terse summation of that history." In his opinion, Rutledge made sixty-two distinct historical references, including eleven to Thomas Jefferson and twenty-eight to James Madison, to support his conclusion that the First Amendment requires the strict separation of church and state. He made no reference to Roger Sherman.[55]

James Madison is often called the father of the Bill of Rights, and there is no doubt that he deserves much credit for the final product. He initially proposed it, he pushed for it, and he was heavily involved in debates and committee work surrounding it. However, even the brief treatment provided here makes it evident that he did not dominate the process. Sherman was on the important committee of eleven that reported amendments to the House (a committee chaired by John Vining, not

Madison), and the draft Bill of Rights in Sherman's hand shows that he was an active participant. The text of every amendment put forward by Madison was ultimately changed, and some of his suggestions were rejected altogether. Notably, his proposal to prohibit states from restricting certain rights, which he considered "the most valuable amendment on the whole list," was not adopted. It was not a critical committee, yet it is worth noting that Sherman, not Madison, sat on the three-person House committee charged with arranging the amendments proposed by the House. While Madison may have chaired the conference committee, if this study has shown anything, it is that "father Sherman" hardly deferred to the young Madison. Moreover, the House delegation had to negotiate with a formidable delegation from the Senate—a delegation headed by Sherman's protégé Ellsworth. The committee's conference report, it is worth noting, was penned by Ellsworth.[56]

It is understandable that scholars and jurists favoring the strict separation of church and state are drawn to Madison and Jefferson. Although even those founders did not consistently act on this principle; Madison's *Memorial and Remonstrance* (1785) and his "Detached Memoranda" (c. 1817), and Jefferson's *Bill for Establishing Religious Liberty* (1779) and his letter to the Danbury Baptists (1802) offer support for this position. Yet Jefferson was in France when the Bill of Rights was drafted, and if Madison was a driving force behind the First Amendment, the document was ultimately a product of a community—a community that included the following members of Reformed churches: Roger Sherman, Oliver Ellsworth, John Langdon, Caleb Strong, Paine Wingate, Philip Schuyler, Abraham Baldwin, Elias Boudinot, Jonathan Elmer, William Paterson, Fisher Ames, Abiel Foster, Benjamin Huntington, James Jackson, Jeremiah Wadsworth, Nicholas Gilman, Egbert Benson, James Schureman, Henry Wynkoop, Daniel Hiester Jr., Daniel Huger, Benjamin Bourne, William Smith, and Hugh Williamson. Certainly these men were not all equally influential, but at least Sherman, Ellsworth, Huntington, Baldwin, Boudinot, Paterson, and Ames played important roles in key committees and/or debates. None of these seven men advocated anything like a wall of separation between church and state, and there is little reason to believe that many of their colleagues did either.[57]

One way to illustrate this point is to look at other actions of the First Congress that concern religion. Notably, *on the day after* the House approved the final wording of the Bill of Rights, Elias Boudinot proposed that the president recommend a public day of thanksgiving and prayer.

In response to objections by Aedenus Burke and Thomas Tucker that those practices mimicked European customs and that such calls were properly issued by states, Sherman:

> Justified the practice of thanksgiving, on any signal event, not only as a laudable one in itself, but as warranted by a number of precedents in holy writ: For instance, the solemn thanksgivings and rejoicings which took place in the time of Solomon, after the building of the temple, was a case in point. This example he thought, worthy of christian imitation on the present occasion; and he would agree with the gentleman who moved the resolution.

The House approved the motion and appointed Boudinot, Sherman, and Sylvester to a committee to meet with senators on the matter. The Senate concurred with the House's motion, and Congress requested that President Washington issue what became his famous 1789 Thanksgiving Day Proclamation.[58] The proclamation reads in part:

> Whereas it is the duty of all Nations to acknowledge the providence of Almighty God, to obey his will, to be grateful for his benefits, and humbly to implore His protection and favor...
> I do recommend and assign Thursday the 26th day of November next to be devoted by the People of these States to the service of that great and glorious Being, who is the beneficent Author of all the good that was, that is, or that will be....
> And also that we may then unite in most humbly offering our prayers and supplications to the great Lord and Ruler of Nations and beseech Him to pardon our national and other transgressions, to enable us all, whether in public or private stations, to perform our several and relative duties properly and punctually, to render our national government a blessing to all the People.[59]

It is noteworthy that both Burke and Tucker worked *against* the Bill of Rights and that Boudinot and Sherman almost certainly supported it. There is no record of the House vote in favor of asking the president to declare a day of public prayer and thanksgiving, but the September 26 *New York Daily Advertiser* noted that it passed by "a great majority."[60]

Similarly, among the very first actions of the House of Representatives was to appoint a committee consisting of Boudinot, Sherman, Tucker,

Madison, and Bland to communicate with a Senate committee about appointing chaplains. The two committees recommended that each house appoint a chaplain, that they be of different denominations, and that each week they alternate the chamber in which they would serve. On April 27, Sherman made the motion that the House "proceed to the nomination and choice of a Chaplain." The House eventually selected the Presbyterian William Linn and the Senate chose the Episcopalian Samuel Provost. After George Washington and John Adams took their oaths of office on April 30, they joined representatives and senators for "divine services" led by Reverend Provost at St. Paul's Chapel. Congress, including Madison, voted to pay the chaplains and other congressional officers a few months later.[61]

The Northwest Ordinance was passed by the Confederation Congress in 1787, and it was reauthorized by the First Congress. The act protected religious liberty by requiring, "No person demeaning himself in a peaceable and orderly manner shall ever be molested on account of his mode of worship or religious sentiments." It also declared that "Religion, Morality, *and knowledge being necessary to good government and the happiness of mankind,* Schools and the means of education shall forever be encouraged." Although the ordinance did not specifically provide for the funding of religious schools or churches, the early Congresses engaged in both of these activities.[62]

Two months after approving what became the First Amendment, representatives debated a bill regulating the militia when called into national service. Madison offered an amendment to exempt from militia service

> persons conscientiously scrupulous of bearing arms. It is the glory of our country, said he, that a more sacred regard to the rights of mankind is preserved, than has heretofore been known. The Quaker merits some attention on this delicate point, liberty of conscience: they had it in their own power to establish their religion by law, they did not. He was disposed to make the exception gratuitous, but supposed it impracticable.

Sherman immediately supported Madison's amendment, arguing that he believed

> the exemption of persons conscientiously scrupulous of bearing arms to be necessary and proper. He was well convinced that there was no possibility of making such persons bear arms, they would

rather suffer death than commit what appeared to them a moral evil—though it might happen that the thing itself was not a moral evil; yet their opinion served them as proof. As to their being obliged to pay an equivalent, gentlemen might see that this was as disagreeable to their consciences as the other, he therefore thought it adviseable to exempt them as to both at present.

The amended bill eventually passed, but with the requirement that conscientious objectors must hire a substitute.[63]

Records of the debates over the Bill of Rights are notoriously incomplete, but when the religion clauses are considered in light of other actions of the First Congress—as well as the arguments and actions of its authors and supporters elsewhere—a clear pattern emerges. Because of its limited powers, Congress could neither create an established church nor restrict religious liberty. The First Amendment restated these limitations, but there is little evidence to suggest that its authors intended it to create a "wall of separation between Church & State." For instance, Sherman and his colleagues clearly thought that the national government could encourage and fund religious practices. As well, there is no reason to conclude that these men understood the free exercise clause to require a religious exemption from generally applicable laws or that the establishment clause prohibited legislatures from making such exemptions.[64]

Sherman, like Thomas Jefferson, authored a significant state law concerning religious liberty, and, unlike Jefferson, he participated in debates on the First Amendment. It is therefore striking that when Supreme Court justices have used history to interpret the First Amendment's religion clauses, they have made 112 distinct references to Jefferson but have mentioned Sherman only three times. Indeed, excluding James Madison (referenced 189 times), justices have made only twenty-one references to all of the other members of the First Congress combined! If jurists or scholars are truly interested in the original intent of those who drafted the First Amendment, it makes little sense to ignore the views and actions of Sherman and most of his colleagues.[65]

The End

Connecticut elected its five members of the House of Representatives at large, so there were no one-on-one contests that regularly occurred in single-member districts. Nevertheless, Pierpont Edwards, youngest son of

Jonathan Edwards Sr. and brother of Sherman's pastor Jonathan Edwards
Jr., calculated that because both he and Sherman were from New Haven,
that Sherman had to be defeated in the fall of 1790 if Edwards were to be
elected to the House of Representatives. Accordingly, he wrote a series of
anonymous essays falsely accusing Sherman of lying about his support
for a controversial bill to raise congressional pay to six dollars per day
(Sherman, prudently, missed that vote). Once authorship of the letters
became known, the old Puritan wrote a public letter to Edwards denying
his involvement and lecturing the younger man:

> I am as sensible as you of the importance of having persons of irre-
> proachable characters to fill public offices; for promoting persons
> of bad moral character would be a dishonor to government, and
> tend to introduce a general dissolution of manners. The Psalmist
> says, *The Wicked walk on every side, when wise men are exalted.*
>
> That you may better know and pursue your own true interest to
> *love your neighbor as yourself* and *avoid vain jangling* is the desire of
> your sincere well wisher.[66]

Edwards, it turned out, had miscalculated the willingness of Connecticut
voters to elect multiple representatives from the same town. After the fall
1790 elections, three of Connecticut's five representatives were citizens
of New Haven: Sherman, Edwards, and James Hillhouse. Edwards,
remarkably, resigned his seat in the Connecticut legislature *and* in the
House of Representatives for personal reasons. He later served as a U.S.
attorney and was appointed a federal district court judge by Thomas
Jefferson in 1806.

After the election, Sherman returned to the House of Representatives
and participated in debates over the national bank. When Congress
moved from New York to Philadelphia, William Samuel Johnson resigned
from the Senate in order to remain president of Columbia College.
Sherman was appointed to his seat, and he served in the Senate from
June 13, 1791, until his death on July 23, 1793. Because Senate debates
were secret at that time, it is difficult to say much about his Senate service. He apparently continued his campaign to keep the House of
Representatives small and helped investigate General St. Clair's disas-
trous defeat by Native Americans. He regularly corresponded with his
son-in-law Simeon Baldwin about the creation of the federal judiciary,
but most of their letters center on the possibility of Baldwin being

appointed to the bench. He resided in Philadelphia, until illness finally necessitated his return to New Haven in April of 1793.[67]

From a political perspective, the last years of Sherman's life must have been a cause for great satisfaction. He was an influential member of Congress, serving a country whose freedom he had helped earn under a constitution he had helped write. But on the home front all was not well. His first son failed at business, became an alcoholic, and was divorced by his wife. His second son ran Roger Sherman's New Haven store into bankruptcy, abandoned his post as paymaster in the War for Independence, was divorced from his wife, and was dead by 1789. The third son succeeded only in contrast to his brothers; he served with honor in the War for Independence and as a surveyor, managing to fail only at business.[68]

Fortunately, Roger's daughters fared far better, and although Sherman could not know it, they helped create a legacy of which he could be proud. This is most evident in a short letter he received from his son-in-law on January 28, 1793:

> Mrs. Baldwin is getting well fast—We have taken the Liberty to give the child the name of Roger Sherman & I hope he will be no disgrace to the person whose name he bears.
> I am with much esteem your dutiful son
> Simeon Baldwin

Roger Sherman Baldwin grew up to have a long career in Connecticut state politics, culminating in service as a U.S. senator and governor. However, he is best remembered for his spirited defense of captured Africans in the *Amistad* case. Sherman, the opponent of slavery, would have been proud.[69]

Perhaps Sherman's familial difficulties are partially responsible for the burst of theological writings that occupied him in the late 1780s and early 1790s. Certainly there is a clear connection between his sons' divorces and his letters to Princeton President John Witherspoon on the conditions under which divorce is appropriate. Yet his 1789 sermon on qualifications for communion and his exchange of letters with Samuel Hopkins in the spring of 1790 do not seem immediately related to his personal problems. They are better understood as the product of a lifetime reflection on biblical theology. As discussed earlier, these texts are important primarily for helping to show that Sherman had a deep knowledge of the Bible, that he was theologically sophisticated, and that he was a committed Calvinist.

Sherman was ill throughout the spring of 1793, and on April 15 he participated in his final public act—laying the cornerstone for South College at Yale. He died on July 23, 1793, and was buried with New Haven's equivalent of a state funeral on July 25. Jonathan Edwards Jr. gave the eulogy, reflecting with some insight that Sherman

> could with reputation to himself and improvement to others con-verse on the most important subjects of theology. I confess myself to have been often entertained, and in the general course of my long and intimate acquaintance with him to have been much improved by his observations on the principal subjects of doctrinal and practical divinity.
>
> But his proper line was politics. For usefulness and excellence in this line, he was qualified not only by his acute discernment and sound judgment, but especially by his knowledge of human nature. He had a happy talent of judging what was feasible and what was not feasible, or what men would bear, and what they would not bear in government. And he had a rare talent of prudence, or of timing and adopting his measures to the attainment of his end.[70]

7

"Philosophy May Mislead You. Ask Experience"

WHEN MOST PEOPLE think about the founding era, only a handful of leaders come to mind. Although the list may vary from person to person, names like Franklin, Washington, Adams, Jefferson, Madison, and Hamilton inevitably surface. In some respects, this is not surprising because by any measure these statesmen are among the most important and influential men in American history. Yet a narrow focus on these great leaders does not tell the full story of the American founding, and it can be misleading in several ways:

1. It is tempting to generalize from those six men to all of the founders, but it is not self-evident that their views represent those held by all founders.

2. As with most history, the list is biased toward "winners." Even if they lost, some of the men and women who opposed the War for Independence or the U.S. Constitution nevertheless made important contributions to America's founding. Even with respect to those on the winning side, scholars may be inclined to emphasize founders with "progressive" views.

3. The list favors men who served prominently in the executive branch of government. It is noteworthy that four of the six most readily recognizable founders were presidents.

4. In an era when well over half of all white Americans identified with Calvinist denominations, it is noteworthy that only one of these men did so—and he was privately a Unitarian.

Daniel L. Dreisbach, in a wonderful essay entitled "Famous Founders and Forgotten Founders: What's the Difference, and Does the Difference Matter?" addresses the question why some founders are remembered and others are not. He argues that, in general, famous founders were recognized as great in their own day, came from power centers in the new nation, supported the Declaration of Independence and/or the new Constitution, left a voluminous paper trail, and, with one exception, played prominent roles in the new national government. He does not suggest that the famous founders were anything other than great men, but he does contend that there is "a much larger company of now 'forgotten founders' who made salient contributions in thought, word, and deed to the construction of the American constitutional republic and its institutions."[1]

Roger Sherman is one of those founders. Few members of the general public know who he is, and history, government, and law professors know little about him other than that he helped craft the Connecticut Compromise. One measure of his neglect is that unlike Elvis Presley, Bugs Bunny, and Sybil Ludington, Sherman has never been featured on an American postage stamp. By contrast, George Washington, John Adams, Thomas Jefferson, James Madison, Benjamin Franklin, and Alexander Hamilton have been individually portrayed on at least 112 stamps.[2] Likewise, Sherman is not featured on currency, there is no major national monument to him, he seldom plays more than a bit role in popular works on the founding era, and scholars have rarely turned their attention to him. Even if one concedes that the six famous founders were more important than Sherman, it is still reasonable to ask whether the disproportionate attention they receive is justified.[3]

As we have seen, Sherman was the only person to help draft and sign the Declaration and Resolves (1774), the Articles of Association (1774), the Declaration of Independence (1776), the Articles of Confederation (1777, 1778), and the Constitution (1787). He was an influential member of the Continental and Confederation Congresses, was on the five-person committee that wrote the Declaration of Independence, and played a critical role in the Federal Convention of 1787. As a representative and senator, he helped establish the nation's institutions and he had a significant impact on the Bill of Rights. Even as he served in the national government, he remained an active and influential member of Connecticut's General Assembly and Superior Court. Although not as prolific a writer as some founders, Sherman penned essays defending hard currency, supporting the Articles of Confederation, and urging the ratification of the U.S. Constitution.

Given this record, why is Sherman not better known today? One answer is simply age. With the exception of Franklin, all of the most famous founders lived long enough to serve prominently in the new national government. Because he died in 1793, he was unable to serve many years in the fledgling republic. As well, most famous founders were members of the executive branch where individuals may more readily distinguish themselves. Sherman labored in the legislature, where his contributions were always in the context of a larger group of men and for which records are sparse. Moreover, unlike the best-known founders, Sherman left relatively few papers with which scholars can work.[4]

It must be said as well that Sherman was not a profoundly original thinker or a provocative writer. By contrast, Franklin, Jefferson, Madison, and Hamilton were creative thinkers (at least on some issues) and excellent writers. If scholars are interested in founders who were ahead of their time, it makes sense to focus on these men. Compared with them, Sherman may even seem old-fashioned. However, if one is attempting to understand the ideas that motivated many of America's founders, particularly those in the Reformed tradition, Sherman is an ideal representative.

Sherman was a Calvinist at a time when the tradition still exercised significant influence in America. Like many of his colleagues, he took his faith seriously, and it had a significant impact on his political ideas and actions. Reformed political thought holds that humans are created in the image of God, are sinful, and possess God-given rights. Critically, it also teaches that legitimate governments are based on consent, that they should be limited, and that the people have a duty to resist tyrannical rulers. These ideas informed how Sherman and his colleagues responded to Great Britain, and it shaped their thinking when they crafted new political institutions.

As a matter of intellectual history, it is important to recognize that many founders were influenced by Calvinism. This volume demonstrates this point beyond a reasonable doubt with respect to Sherman, and it gives good reasons to believe a similar case can be made for many of his colleagues, including Samuel Adams, Fisher Ames, Abraham Baldwin, Isaac Backus, Elias Boudinot, Timothy Dwight, Eliphalet Dyer, Oliver Ellsworth, Matthew Griswold, John Hancock, Benjamin Huntington, Samuel Huntington, Richard Law, Joseph Montgomery, William Paterson, Tapping Reeve, Jesse Root, Ezra Stiles, Richard Stockton, John Treadwell, Jonathan Trumbull, Noah Webster, William Williams, John Witherspoon, and Oliver Wolcott. This list does not include founders outside the Reformed tradition who were, nevertheless, influenced by Christian ideas (e.g., John Jay); founders outside the tradition who may, nevertheless, have been influenced by it (e.g., James Madison); and founders who departed from their Calvinists roots but remained influenced by them (e.g., James Wilson).

Properly understanding the founders' political ideas and actions is important for its own sake, but it also has implications for contemporary law and politics. Legislators, jurists, and pundits routinely appeal to America's founders for guidance. If they extrapolate from the views of only a handful of founders, their generalizations may be profoundly misleading. As I have shown throughout the book, this is evidently the case with respect to the founders' views on church-state relations. Contemporary jurisprudence and scholarship has been distorted by Justice Wiley Rutledge's argument in *Everson v. Board of Education* that

1. the establishment clause must be understood in light of the founders' intent;
2. Jefferson and Madison represent the founders;
3. Jefferson and Madison favored the strict separation of church and state;
4. therefore, the establishment clause requires the strict separation of church and state.

This syllogism is problematic on numerous levels, but most relevant to the argument in this volume is the premise that Jefferson's and Madison's views on church-state relations reflect those held by most founders. This is demonstrably false, a reality that becomes evident if one expands the sample of founders beyond Jefferson and Madison to include the men mentioned in the preceding paragraph and other political thinkers and actors such as Abigail Adams, John Adams, Charles Carroll, Daniel Carroll, John Dickinson, Alexander Hamilton, Patrick Henry, Samuel Livermore, Luther Martin, Gouverneur Morris, Edmund Randolph, Benjamin Rush, John Vining, Mercy Otis Warren, and George Washington. The founders as a whole certainly supported religious liberty, and many were beginning to question the wisdom of established churches, but few supported anything approximating a modern conception of the strict separation of church and state.[5]

Sherman's ideas and actions also inform other hotly contested constitutional and political debates. Most significantly, although he was a Federalist who helped craft the Constitution, he was committed to the principle that the national government is limited to powers enumerated in Article I, Section 8 or *clearly* implied by these powers. He was absolutely opposed to giving the national government a general grant of power.

As well, he insisted that presidential powers be strictly limited. Although both views became passé in the twentieth century, if the founders' intentions are relevant to interpreting the Constitution, it may be necessary to revisit constitutional doctrines on these issues.

More broadly, Sherman's jurisprudence reflects the close connection that he and most founders saw between natural and human law. A good example of this is their insistence that there is a sharp distinction between liberty and licentiousness. This difference is critical if we hope to understand the scope of liberty proclaimed in the Declaration of Independence or protected by the Bill of Rights. Finally, Sherman serves as an important reminder that while some founders are legitimately criticized for proclaiming that "all men are created equal" and owning slaves (including many famous founders), others were actively opposing the institution.[6]

Roger Sherman was a principled and prudential statesman. His views and actions were informed by his deeply held faith, but he was a practical man with little interest in abstract theorizing. In the Constitutional Convention, Robert Yates recorded him as commenting, "I am not fond of speculation. I would rather proceed on experimental ground." Similarly, in an essay defending the proposed Constitution, Sherman wrote: "Philosophy may mislead you. Ask experience." His contributions to crafting the Declaration and Resolves, the Articles of Association, the Declaration of Independence, the Articles of Confederation, the Constitution, and the Bill of Rights all reflect this approach to politics. Sherman was not a radical thinker, a great author, or a stirring orator—realities that diminished his contemporary and future fame. Nevertheless, anyone who wishes to understand America's founding cannot afford to ignore the contributions this old Puritan made to the formation of a new nation.[7]

Notes

PRELIMS

1. Rhode Island, while technically in New England, was, as with many things, an outlier. When I refer to New England throughout this book, I do not include this colony/state.

CHAPTER I

1. Like Edmund S. Morgan, author of *The Gentle Puritan: A Life of Ezra Stiles, 1727–1795* (New Haven: Yale University Press, 1962), I use "Puritan" in a literary rather than a technical sense when referring to Sherman. David Brian Robertson, "Madison's Opponents and Constitutional Design," *American Political Science Review*, 99 (May 2005): 225–243, 242; Robertson, *The Constitution and America's Destiny* (Cambridge: Cambridge University Press, 2005).

2. William Williams to Jabez Huntington, September 30, 1776, in *The Founders on the Founders: Word Portraits from the American Revolutionary Era*, ed. John Kaminski (Charlottesville: University of Virginia Press, 2008), 466; Richard Henry Lee to Roger Sherman, January 22, 1780, Miscellaneous Bound Manuscripts, 1779–1784, Massachusetts Historical Society. In a 1789 letter, Lee complained to Samuel Adams about "our former respected, republican friend, old Mr. Ro-g-r-Sh-n," because he opposed adding a bill of rights to the Constitution. Sherman did initially oppose the Bill of Rights, but not because "it would make the people insolate" as Lee reported. James Curtis Ballagh, ed., *The Letters of Richard Henry Lee* (New York: Da Capo Press, 1970), 2: 173, 496. Unless otherwise noted, quotations are exact transcriptions of the original sources except that long *s*'s have been replaced with short *s*'s to conform to modern usage. As well, capitalization of words in titles has been standardized.

Of course Sherman had detractors as well. For instance, Silas Deane wrote to his wife that "of my Old Colleague, Sh—n suffice it to say, that if the order of Jesuits is extinct, their practices are not out of fashion, even among *modern New Light Saints*, or some of them, for I will never particularize any Sect." Silas Deane to Elizabeth Deane, January 21, 1776, in Kaminski, *The Founders on the Founders*, 466.

3. John Adams to Abigail Adams, March 16, 1777, in *Familiar Letters of John Adams and His Wife Abigail Adams, During the Revolution*, ed. Charles Francis Adams (New York: Hurd and Houghton, 1876), 251; John Adams to Roger Sherman, December 6, 1778, *The Adams Papers Digital Edition*, ed. C. James Taylor (Charlottesville: University of Virginia Press, Rotunda,), 2008, http://rotunda.upress.virginia.edu/founders/ADMS-06-07-02-0174 (accessed August 03, 2010); John Adams to John Sanderson, November 19, 1822, in *Biography of the Signers to the Declaration of Independence*, ed. Robert Waln and John Sanderson (Philadelphia: R. W. Pomeroy, 1822), 3: 298; Henry Howe, *Historical Collections of Virginia* (Charleston: WM. R. Babcock, 1852), 221.

4. Waln and Sanderson, *Biography of the Signers*, 3: 296; Timothy Pickering to Obadiah Gore, February 2, 1791, in *The Susquehanna Company Papers*, ed. Julian P. Boyd and Robert J. Taylor (Ithaca: Cornell University Press, 1936–1971), 10: 138.

5. Charles Francis Adams, ed., *The Works of John Adams* (Boston: Charles C. Little and James Brown, 1850), 2: 396 (hereafter *Works of John Adams*). Max Farrand, ed., *The Records of the Federal Convention of 1787* (New Haven: Yale University Press, 1911), 3: 88–89.

   Joseph Strong, a young physician from Connecticut, wrote to Sherman's son-in-law: "I much lament the death of Mr. Sherman.... He was kind to all, even to an enemy, for he forgave him. His wisdom has received and eulgium already from a thousand judicious mourners. May his character be held in view by all who would wish to establish an honorable and everlasting fame." Joseph Strong to Simeon Baldwin, March 16, 1794, in *Life and Letters of Simeon Baldwin*, ed. Simeon E. Baldwin (New Haven: Tuttle, Morehouse, and Taylor, 1919), 408.

6. Christopher Collier, *Roger Sherman's Connecticut: Yankee Politics and the American Revolution* (Middletown: Wesleyan University Press, 1971). Colliers's biography is superior to other accounts of Sherman's life: Lewis Boutell, *The Life of Roger Sherman* (Chicago: A. C. McClurg, 1896); Roger Sherman Boardman, *Roger Sherman: Signer and Statesman* (Philadelphia: University of Pennsylvania Press, 1938); and John G. Rommel, *Connecticut's Yankee Patriot: Roger Sherman* (Hartford: American Revolution Bicentennial Commission of Connecticut, 1979). See also Christopher Collier, *All Politics Is Local: Family, Friends, and Provincial Interests in the Creation of the Constitution* (Hanover: University Press of New England, 2003).

   Sherman is given a prominent place in William Edward Links, *Lives of Distinguished Shoemakers* (Portland: Davis and Southworth, 1849), 42–76.

7. Robertson, "Madison's Opponents and Constitutional Design"; Robertson, *The Constitution and America's Destiny*; Jack N. Rakove, *Original Meanings: Politics and Ideas in the Making of the Constitution* (New York: Knopf, 1996). Keith L. Dougherty and Jac C. Heckelman agree with Robertson and Rakove that "Sherman was an effective delegate that historians have traditionally

overlooked," but suggest that his "influence at the Convention was partly the result of the voting scheme and partly his position relative to others." "A Pivotal Voter from a Pivotal State: Roger Sherman at the Constitutional Convention," *American Political Science Review*, 100 (May 2006): 297–302, 302.

8. Scott Gerber, "Roger Sherman and the Bill of Rights," *Polity*, 28 (Summer 1996): 531. Sherman placed fifth in the survey, but there was negligible difference in the number of votes received by the third, fourth, and fifth place finishers (Gouverneur Morris, John Jay, and Sherman). James Wilson and George Mason were ranked first and second among the forgotten founders. Gary L. Gregg and Mark David Hall, eds., *America's Forgotten Founders*, 2nd ed. (Wilmington: ISI Books, 2012), xv.

9. See, for instance, Geoffrey Stone, "The World of the Framers: A Christian Nation?" *University of California Law Review*, 56 (October 2008): 1–26; David L. Holmes, *The Faiths of the Founding Fathers* (New York: Oxford University Press, 2006); James H. Hutson, *Forgotten Features of the Founding: The Recovery of Religious Themes in the Early American Republic* (Lanham: Lexington Books, 2003); Frank Lambert, *The Founding Fathers and the Place of Religion in America* (Princeton: Princeton University Press, 2003); and Michael Novak, *On Two Wings: Humble Faith and Common Sense at the American Founding* (San Francisco: Encounter Books, 2002).

10. Sydney E. Ahlstrom, *A Religious History of the American People* (Garden City: Doubleday, 1975), 1: 492; Mark Noll, Nathan Hatch, and George Marsden, *The Search For Christian America* (Westchester: Crossway Books, 1983), 74; James H. Hutson, ed., *The Founders on Religion: A Book of Quotations* (Princeton: Princeton University Press, 2005), xiv. A few Sherman scholars have addressed his faith, but they generally contend that it did not impact his political ideas and actions. Their analysis is discussed in chapter 2.

11. Prominent advocates of this position include Carl L. Becker, *The Declaration of Independence: A Study in the History of Political Ideas* (1922; New York: Vintage Books, 1942) and Louis Hartz, *The Liberal Tradition in America* (New York: Harcourt, Brace and World, 1955). More recent proponents of this position tend to make significantly more nuanced and careful arguments. They include Michael P. Zuckert, *The Natural Rights Republic: Studies in the Foundation of the American Political Tradition* (Notre Dame: University of Notre Dame Press, 1996); Jerome Huyler, *Locke in America: The Moral Philosophy of the Founding Era* (Lawrence: University Press of Kansas, 1995); Joyce Appleby, *Liberalism and Republicanism in the Historical Imagination* (Cambridge: Harvard University Press, 1992); Steven M. Dworetz, *The Unvarnished Doctrine: Locke, Liberalism, and the American Revolution* (Durham: Duke University Press, 1990); and Thomas Pangle, *The Spirit of Modern Republicanism: The Moral Vision of the American Founders and the Philosophy of Locke* (Chicago: University of Chicago Press, 1988).

A good example of this phenomenon by a scholar who takes religion seriously is John Fea, *Was America Founded as a Christian Nation?: A Historical Introduction* (Louisville: Westminster John Knox Press, 2011), 118–119, 231. Fea argues that Jonathan Mayhew was influenced by Locke because the Bible does not sanction resisting tyrannical authority. He briefly considers the possibility that the Reformed political tradition might teach something different but rejects this idea because John Calvin "taught that rebellion against civil government was never justified." As evidence, he relies on a secondary source and quotes a few lines from Calvin taken from the same source. This interpretation of Calvin is debatable, but, as we shall see, some of Calvin's contemporaries, such as John Knox, and later Reformed thinkers writing well before Locke penned the *Second Treatise*, contended that resistance to tyrants is justifiable in light of, or even required by, the Bible. Fea's neglect of other Reformers is particularly ironic in light of the name of the press that published his book.

12. As I make crystal clear in chapter 2, I am not arguing that founders *only* came to these conclusions because of the Reformed tradition. I recognize that even Calvinists were influenced by secular ideas, and I concede that self, class, and state interests played important roles in the era.

13. Alan Heimert, *Religion and the American Mind: From the Great Awakening to the Revolution* (Cambridge: Harvard University Press, 1966), 15. A useful overview of how Heimert's book was received is Philip Goff, "Revivals and Revolution: Historiographic Turns since Alan Heimert's *Religion and the American Mind*," *Church History* (December 1998): 695–721. Barry Alan Shain, *The Myth of American Individualism: The Protestant Origins of American Political Thought* (Princeton: Princeton University Press, 1994). Of course, Heimert was not the first to argue for a connection between the Reformed tradition and the development of American democracy. See most famously Alexis de Tocqueville, *Democracy in America* (Indianapolis: Liberty Fund Press, 2010), esp. 1: 54–70.

    Scholarly works that recognize the influence of Christianity on American political thought include Daniel J. Elazar, *Covenant & Constitutionalism: The Great Frontier and the Matrix of Federal Democracy* (New Brunswick: Transaction, 1998); John G. West, Jr., *The Politics of Revelation and Reason: Religion and Civic Life in the New Nation* (Lawrence: University Press of Kansas, 1996), 1–78; Ellis Sandoz, *A Government of Laws: Political Theory, Religion, and the American Founding* (Baton Rouge: Louisiana State University Press, 1990); Donald Lutz, *The Origins of American Constitutionalism* (Baton Rouge: Louisiana State University Press, 1988); Willmoore Kendall and George W. Carey, *The Basic Symbols of the American Political Tradition* (Baton Rouge: Louisiana State University Press, 1970); David W. Hall's *The Genevan Reformation and the American Founding* (Lanham: Lexington Books, 2003).

There are also a variety of popular polemical works that assert the significance of Christianity in the founding era. See, for instance, Peter Marshall and David Manuel, *The Light and the Glory* (Grand Rapids: Fleming H. Revell, 1977); John Eidsmoe, *Christianity and the Constitution: The Faith of Our Founding Fathers* (Grand Rapids: Baker Book House, 1987); Tim LaHaye, *Faith of Our Founding Fathers* (Brentwood: Wolgemuthand Hyatt, 1987); and Gary DeMar, *America's Christian Heritage* (Nashville: Broadman and Holman, 2003).

All of these works, and many listed in the following notes, recognize the influence of Christianity, generally, or even Protestantism, more specifically, in the founding era. However, they do not all agree with each other, and in many cases they attribute too much influence to a secularized Lockean liberalism or other intellectual traditions. I occasionally respond to particular works, but the focus of this book is to make an argument, not to engage every piece of literature that touches on the subject.

14. Alan Gibson, *Interpreting the Founding: Guide to the Enduring Debates Over the Origins and Foundations of the American Republic* (Lawrence: University Press of Kansas, 2006), 3.

15. See, for instance, Thomas Kidd, *God of Liberty: A Religious History of the American Revolution* (New York: Basic Books, 2010); Carl Bridenbaugh, *Mitre and Sceptre: Transatlantic Faiths, Ideas, Personalities, and Politics: 1689–1775* (New York: Oxford University Press, 1962); Patricia U. Bonomi, *Under the Cope of Heaven: Religion, Society, and Politics in Colonial America* (New York: Oxford University Press, 1986); Ruth H. Bloch, *Visionary Republic: Millennial Themes in American Thought* (Cambridge: Cambridge University Press, 1985); Charles Royster, *A Revolutionary People at War: The Continental Army and American Character, 1775–1783* (Chapel Hill: University of North Carolina Press, 1979); Nathan O. Hatch, *The Sacred Cause of Liberty: Republican Thought and the Millennium in Revolutionary New England* (New Haven: Yale University Press, 1977); Melvin B. Endy Jr. "Just War, Holy War, and Millennialism in Revolutionary America," *William and Mary Quarterly,* 3rd ser. 42 (1985): 3–25; Bernard Bailyn, "Religion and Revolution: Three Biographical Studies," *Perspectives in American History,* 4 (1970), 83–169; and Perry Miller, "From Covenant to the Revival" in Miller, *Nature's Nation* (Cambridge: Harvard University Press, 1966).

Of course these works differ as to the *nature* of religion's influence. For instance, Bailyn recognizes that Americans were religious, but treats religion primarily as a vehicle for a secular Whig ideology. He contends that "it is a gross simplification to believe that religion as such, or any of its doctrinaire elements, had a unique political role in the Revolutionary movement. The effective determinants of religion were political." "Religion and Revolution," 85.

16. For example, Mark A. Noll, *One Nation Under God?: Christian Faith and Political Action in America* (San Francisco: Harper and Row, 1988), 14–53, and *America's God: From Jonathan Edwards to Abraham Lincoln* (New York: Oxford University Press, 2002); James T. Kloppenberg, "The Virtues of Liberalism: Christianity, Republicanism, and Ethics in Early American Political Discourse," *Journal of American History* 74 (June 1987): 9–33; and Thomas S. Engeman and Michael Zuckert, eds., *Protestantism and the American Founding* (Notre Dame: University of Notre Dame Press, 2004).

17. See, for instance, Ira Stoll, *Samuel Adams: A Life* (New York: Free Press, 2008); Jeffry H. Morrison, *John Witherspoon and the Founding of the American Republic* (Notre Dame: University of Notre Dame Press, 2005); Garrett Ward Sheldon, *The Political Philosophy of James Madison* (Baltimore: Johns Hopkins University Press, 2001); William R. Casto, *Oliver Ellsworth and the Creation of the Federal Republic* (New York: Second Circuit Committee on History and Commemorative Events, 1997); and Mark David Hall, *The Political and Legal Philosophy of James Wilson: 1742–1798* (Columbia: University of Missouri Press, 1997).

18. For example, Alice M. Baldwin, *The New England Clergy and the American Revolution* (1928; reprint, New York: Frederick Ungar, 1965); Keith L. Griffin, *Revolution and Religion: American Revolutionary War and the Reformed Clergy* (New York: Paragon House, 1994); Mark Valeri, *Law and Providence in Joseph Bellamy's New England: The Origins of the New Divinity in Revolutionary America* (New York: Oxford University Press, 1994); and Dale Kuehne, *Massachusetts Congregational Political Thought, 1760–1790* (Columbia: University of Missouri Press, 1996).

19. Mark David Hall, "Faith and the Founders of the American Republic," *Faith and Politics: Religion in the Public Square* (Proceedings of the Maryville Symposium 2010, 2011), 55–79 (assessing evidence that these and other founders were deists). Washington's religious views are somewhat of an enigma, but he clearly thought it was appropriate for governments to support Christianity. See, for instance, Michael Novak and Jana Novak, *Religion, Liberty, and the Father of Our Country* (New York: Basic Books, 2006); and Tara Ross and Joseph C. Smith Jr., *Under God: George Washington and the Question of Church and State* (Dallas: Spence, 2008).

20. Edwin S. Gaustad, *Faith of Our Fathers: Religion and the New Nation* (San Francisco: Harper and Row, 1987). Similarly, Gary Kowalski writes that Franklin, Washington, Paine, Adams, Jefferson, and Madison are "representative" of the founders, although he concedes that "some who fought for independence were more orthodox in their opinions." Kowaski, *Revolutionary Spirits: The Enlightened Faith of America's Founding Fathers* (New York: BlueBridge, 2008), 5–7.

21. Steven Waldman, *Founding Faith: Providence, Politics, and the Birth of Religious Freedom in America* (New York: Random House, 2008), xiii. Waldman has individual chapters on these five men, and he discusses a variety of other founders. However, he often generalizes from Franklin, Adams, Washington, Jefferson, and Madison to all founders, such as when he addresses the

"Conservative Fallacy" that "Most Founding Fathers were serious Christians" by remarking that "if we use the definition of *Christianity* offered by those who make this claim—conservative Christians—the Founders studied in this book were not Christians" (193). This claim may be true for his "five main characters," but it is highly debatable with respect to founders such as Samuel Adams, Fisher Ames, Isaac Backus, Elias Boudinot, Charles and Daniel Carroll, Samuel Davies, Timothy Dwight, Oliver Ellsworth, Patrick Henry, John Jay, John Leland, Henry Muhlenberg, Roger Sherman, John Witherspoon, and many others who are mentioned (albeit often in passing) in his book.

22. David L. Holmes, *The Religion of the Founding Fathers* (Charlottesville: Ash Lawn-Highland; Ann Arbor: Clements Library, 2003); Daniel L. Dreisbach, review of *The Religion of the Founding Fathers*, by David L. Holmes, *Virginia Magazine of History and Biography* 112, no. 2 (2004): 192–193; Holmes, *The Faiths of the Founding Fathers*. The three orthodox Christians Holmes examines are Samuel Adams, Elias Boudinot, and John Jay. Brooke Allen, *Moral Minority: Our Skeptical Founding Fathers* (Chicago: Ivan R. Dee, 2006).

Frank Lambert, *The Founding Fathers and the Place of Religion in America* (Princeton: Princeton University Press, 2003), 161, and, generally, 159–296 (Lambert moves easily from the proposition that Franklin, Jefferson, Paine, Adams, Hamilton, Madison, and Jay "rejected the faith of their Puritan fathers" to the claim that the "significance of the Enlightenment and Deism for the birth of the American republic, and especially the relationship between church and state within it, can hardly be overstated." Leaving aside the fact that Paine was born an English Quaker and Hamilton was a bastard from the West Indies, thus making one wonder whose faith they rejected, Lambert's account of "the founders" rests almost entirely on the writings of Jefferson, Madison, Adams, and Franklin. Although he mentions Jay, he gives no evidence that he rejected orthodox Christianity.); Richard T. Hughes, *Myths America Lives By* (Urbana: University of Illinois Press, 2003), 50–57 (supporting his claim that "most of the American founders embraced some form of Deism, not historically orthodox Christianity," with extensive quotations from Jefferson, two quotations from Paine, and one quotation each from Franklin, Madison, and John Adams), 50–57; and, similarly, Hughes, *Christian America and the Kingdom of God* (Urbana: University of Illinois Press, 2009), 109–118; Steven J. Keillor, *This Rebellious House: American History and the Truth of Christianity* (Downers Grove: InterVarsity Press, 1996), 85 (supporting the assertion that "[m]any of America's 'Founding Fathers' were not Christians in any orthodox sense," with references to Adams, Franklin, Paine, and Allen [and, by implication, Washington and Jefferson]); and Stone, "The World of the Framers," *University of California Law Review* 56 (October 2008): 7–8. Darryl G. Hart writes that "most of the so-called Founding Fathers, from Jefferson and

Adams to George Washington, Benjamin Franklin, and James Madison were generally indifferent to most of the claims of the denominations, from the vicarious atonement to the real presence of Christ in the Lord's Supper." *A Secular Faith: Why Christianity Favors the Separation of Church and State* (Chicago: Ivan R. Dee: 2006), 73.

23. Wiley Rutledge, in *Everson v. Board of Education*, 330 U.S. 1, 33 (1947); Mark David Hall, "Jeffersonian Walls and Madisonian Lines: The Supreme Court's Use of History in Religion Clause Cases," *Oregon Law Review*, 85 (2006): 572, 568–569.

24. Daniel L. Dreisbach, "Famous Founders and Forgotten Founders: What's the Difference, and Does the Difference Matter," in *The Forgotten Founders on Religion and Public Life*, ed., Daniel L. Dreisbach, Mark David Hall, and Jeffry H. Morrison (Notre Dame: University of Notre Dame Press, 2009), 1–25. Madison and Jefferson were critical participants in Virginia's debates about disestablishment, but the influence of Virginia's example or Madison's and Jefferson's roles in these debates upon the nation in the founding era is regularly assumed but has never been demonstrated. See Mark J. Chadsey, "Thomas Jefferson and the Establishment Clause," *Akron Law Review*, 40 (2007): 623–646; and Mark David Hall "Madison's Memorial and Remonstrance, Jefferson's Statute for Religious Liberty, and the Creation of the First Amendment," *American Political Thought*, 3 (Spring 2014): 32–63.

25. For further discussion see Donald Lutz, *A Preface to American Political Theory* (Lawrence: University Press of Kansas, 1992), 7–17.

26. Josiah Sherman served as a chaplain at Valley Forge and wrote a response to Ethan Allen's *Reason the Only Oracle of Man* with the creative title *Oracles of Reason, As Formed by the Deists, are Husks for Deistical and Heathen Swine: But the Truths of the Gospel are Bread for God's Children* (Litchfield: T. Collier, 1787). The pamphlet was published under the pseudonym "Common Sense." He also published a sermon entitled "God in No Sense the Author of Sin: Being an Attempt to Reconcile the Divine Pre-Ordination of All Events with Human Liberty, and the Praise and Blame-Worthiness of Moral Actions" (Hartford: Hudson and Goodwin, 1784). On Josiah Sherman and his response to Allen see Christopher Grasso, "Deist Monster: On Religious Common Sense in the Wake of the American Revolution," *Journal of American History*, 95 (June 2008): 61–64.

27. Rommel, *Connecticut's Yankee Patriot*, 28.

28. Sherman and Law had to revise, update, or reject previous statutes—and in some cases they composed entirely new laws. Sherman took statutes beginning with the letters A–L and Law took the rest, although they consulted together before submitting the final draft to the legislature where the proposed laws were amended and passed or, occasionally, rejected. The draft code is available in the Connecticut State Library (hereinafter "Draft Code"). The final version of the

code was printed in 1784 and reprinted in John D. Cushing, ed., *The First Laws of the State of Connecticut* (Wilmington: Michael Glazier, 1982).

29. Sherman's five "Letters of a Countryman" were published from November 15 to December 20, 1787. They are reprinted in *Essays on the Constitution of the United States*, ed. Paul Leicester Ford (1892; reprint, New York: Burt Franklin, 1970), 211–228. His "A Citizen of New Haven" essay was published on January 7, 1788. It is available in Merrill Jensen, ed., *Documentary History of the Ratification of the Constitution*, vol. 3, *Ratification of the Constitution by the States: Delaware, New Jersey, Georgia, Connecticut* (Madison: State Historical Society of Wisconsin, 1978), 524–527.

30. Timothy Dwight, *A Statistical Account of the City of New Haven*, A Statistical Account of the Towns and Parishes in the State of Connecticut (New Haven: Connecticut Academy of Arts and Sciences, 1811), 76–77.

CHAPTER 2

1. Jack Rakove, *Original Meanings: Politics and Ideas in the Making of the Constitution* (New York: Alfred A. Knopf, 1997), 7, 18; Hall, "Faith and the Founders of the American Republic."

2. Like Franklin, Jefferson and Adams lived for extended periods of time in Europe. Franklin was raised in the Reformed tradition but rejected it at an early age. For details on the religious views of these founders see Daniel L. Dreisbach, Mark D. Hall, and Jeffry H. Morrison, eds., *The Founders on God and Government* (Lanham: Rowman and Littlefield, 2004) (containing essays on Washington, Adams, Jefferson, Madison, and Franklin); and Dreisbach, Hall, and Morrison, *The Forgotten Founders on Religion and Public Life* (containing essays on Paine and Hamilton).

3. John M. Murrin, "Religion and Politics in America from the First Settlements to the Civil War," in *Religion and American Politics*, ed., Mark A. Noll (New York: Oxford, 1990), 29, 31.

4. See, for instance, George H. Sabine, *A History of Political Theory*, 3rd ed. (New York: Holt, Rinehart, and Winston, 1961), especially 180–328; W. M. Spellman, *Monarchies 1000–2000* (London: Reaktion Books, 2001), 10–23; 147–187. Of course, some Christians eventually came to reject doctrines like original sin, but they were virtually nonexistent in America prior to the nineteenth century.

5. The analogy is not perfect because by definition liberal political thinkers all embrace liberalism whereas some Reformed Christians embraced or embrace political views at odds with what I earlier described.

6. John Calvin, *Institutes of the Christian Religion*, 2 vols., trans. Ford Lewis Battles (Westminster: John Knox Press, 1960). An excellent overview of Calvin's thought is William J. Bouwsma, *John Calvin: A Sixteenth Century Portrait* (New York: Oxford University Press, 1988).

7. Kenneth A. Lockridge, *Literacy in Colonial New England* (New York: W. W. Norton, 1974), 98.

   Lockridge calculates that 60% of males in New England were literate in 1660, and that this percentage rose to 85% by 1760 (13). For a higher estimate of literacy rates for colonial New England, see Samuel Eliot Morison, *Puritan Pronaos: The Intellectual Life of Colonial New England* (New York: New York University Press, 1936), 82–85. Particularly relevant for this study, Christopher Collier states that "virtually every" Connecticut voter in 1787 could read. Collier, *All Politics Is Local*, 83.

8. On New England churches and ecclesiology, see especially James F. Cooper, Jr., *Tenacious of Their Liberties: The Congregationalists in Colonial Massachusetts* (New York: Oxford University Press, 1999); and David A. Weir, *Early New England: A Covenanted Society* (Grand Rapids: Eerdmans, 2005).

9. Max Weber famously noted the connection between Protestantism and capitalism in *The Protestant Ethic and the Spirit of Capitalism*, 3rd ed., ed. and trans. Stephen Kalberg (Los Angeles: Roxbury, 2002). Although his analysis is flawed in important ways, Weber deserves credit for noticing the significant impact Protestantism had on economic growth. See generally W. Stanford Reid, ed., *John Calvin: His Influence in the Western World* (Grand Rapids: Zondervan, 1982).

10. John Witte Jr., *The Reformation of Rights: Law, Religion, and Human Rights in Early Modern Calvinism* (Cambridge: Cambridge University Press, 2007), 1–80. There is a debate among students of Reformed thought concerning the extent to which early Reformers believed civic government could be redeemed. David VanDrunen provides an excellent overview of this literature and makes a good, but in my mind not persuasive, case that early Reformed leaders adhered to the two kingdom doctrine of Augustine and Luther in *Natural Law and the Two Kingdoms: A Study in the Development of Reformed Social Thought* (Grand Rapids: Eerdmans, 2010).

11. Peter Martyr Vermigli (1499–1562) is one of the few Reformed thinkers who was more conservative than Calvin with respect to resisting ungodly rulers. See Robert M. Kingdon, *The Political Thought of Peter Martyr Vermigli: Selected Texts and Commentary* (Geneva: Librairie Droz, 1980), 9–11, 99–100.

12. The development of Protestant resistance theory is told in concise form by Quentin Skinner in *The Foundations of Modern Political Thought*, vol. 2: *The Age of Reformation* (Cambridge: Cambridge University Press, 1978), especially chapters 7–9. See also Bouwsma, *John Calvin*, 204–213; Richard L. Greaves, *Theology and Revolution in the Scottish Reformation: Studies in the Thought of John Knox* (Grand Rapids: Christian University Press, 1980); and his "The Nature and Intellectual Milieu of the Political Principles in the Geneva Bible Marginalia," *Journal of Church and State*, 22 (Spring 1980): 233–249; Michael Walzer, *The Revolution of the Saints: A Study in the Origins of Radical Politics* (Cambridge: Harvard University Press, 1965); and Stephen E. Lucas, "The *Plakkat van*

Verlatinge: A Neglected Model for the American Declaration of Independence," in *Connecting Cultures: The Netherlands in Five Centuries of Transatlantic Exchange,* ed. Rosemarijn Hoefte and Johanna C. Kardux (Amsterdam: Vu University Press, 1994), 187–207.

13. Stephanus Junius Brutus, *Vindiciae, Contra Tyrannos,* ed. George Garnett (Cambridge: Cambridge University Press, 1994), 149, 92, 37–40, 129–131; Skinner, *Foundations of Modern Political Thought,* 2: 329 (quoting Brutus). David VanDrunen emphasizes that a mixture of biblical and natural law arguments was very common in Reformed resistance literature after the St. Bartholomew's Day massacre of 1572. *Natural Law and the Two Kingdoms,* 119–148.

14. The exact nature of these covenants was hotly contested among New England ministers. See generally Miller, "From Covenant to Revival"; Sacvan Bercovitch, *The Puritan Origins of the American Self* (New Haven: Yale University Press, 1975) and *The American Jeremiad* (Madison: University of Wisconsin Press, 1978); Christopher Grasso, *A Speaking Aristocracy: Transforming Public Discourse in Eighteenth Century Connecticut* (Chapel Hill: University of North Carolina Press, 1999), 24–85; Jonathan D. Sassi, *A Republic of Righteousness: The Public Christianity of the Post-Revolutionary New England Clergy* (New York: Oxford University Press, 2001), 19–83; and Glenn A. Moots, *Politics Reformed: The Anglo-American Legacy of Covenant Theology* (Columbia: University of Missouri Press, 2010).

15. Skinner, *Foundations of Modern Political Thought,* 2: 321. But see Walzer, *Revolution of the Saints.* George Garnett argues that Roman law is critical to Brutus's argument. See "Editor's Introduction," Garnett, *Vindiciae,* xix–liv. But see Anne McLaren, "Rethinking Republicanism: *Vindiciae, Contra Tyrannos* in Context," *Historical Journal,* 49 (2006): 23–52; and the response by George Garnett, "Law in the *Vindiciae, Contra Tyrannos*: A Vindication," *Historical Journal,* 49 (2006): 877–891.

16. Eric Nelson, *The Hebrew Republic: Jewish Sources and the Transformation of European Political Thought* (Cambridge: Harvard University Press, 2010). The extent to which later Calvinists were faithful to the teachings of John Calvin and/or the Bible are questions that goes beyond the scope of this book.

17. Daniel L. Dreisbach and Mark David Hall, eds., *The Sacred Rights of Conscience: Selected Readings on Religious Liberty and Church-State Relations in the American Founding* (Indianapolis: Liberty Fund Press, 2009), 86. For further discussion see Kendall and Carey, *Basic Symbols of the American Political Tradition,* 30–42.

18. Weir, *Early New England.* See also Daniel J. Elazar, *Covenant and Commonwealth: From Christian Separation through the Protestant Reformation* (New Brunswick: Transaction, 1996); Elazar, *Covenant & Constitutionalism;* and Moots, *Politics Reformed.*

19. Perry Miller, ed., *The American Puritans: Their Prose and Poetry* (New York: Columbia University Press, 1956), 89. See also Baldwin, *New England Clergy,*

26–27; and Richard L. Bushman, *From Puritan to Yankee: Character and the Social Order in Connecticut, 1690–1765* (Cambridge: Harvard University Press, 1967), 154–159. Not all Puritan colonies were grounded on the consent of the governed. See, for instance, Karen Ordahl Kupperman, *Providence Island, 1630–1641: The Other Puritan Colony* (New York: Cambridge University Press, 1993).

20. John Winthrop, "Speech to the General Court," (1645), in Miller, *The American Puritans*, 90–93; Bushman, *From Puritan to Yankee*, 12; Joy B. Gilsdorf and Robert R. Gilsdorf, "Elites and Electorates: Some Plain Truths for Historians of Colonial America," in *Saints and Revolutionaries: Essays on Early American History*, ed. David D. Hall, John M. Murrin, and Thad W. Tate (New York: W. W. Norton: 1984), 207–244; Collier, *All Politics Is Local*, 13–15, 163; Robert E. Brown, *Middle-Class Democracy and the Revolution in Massachusetts, 1691–1780* (Ithaca: Cornell University Press, 1955); Kenneth A. Lockridge, *A New England Town: The First Hundred Years, Dedham, Massachusetts* (New York: W. W. Norton, 1970); David D. Hall, *A Reforming People: Puritanism and the Transformation of Public Life in New England* (New York: Alfred A. Knopf, 2011), 90; and Perry Miller, "Hooker and Connecticut Democracy," in *Errand Into the Wilderness* (New York: Harper and Row, 1956), 16–47. Jonathan Edwards emphasized the necessity of civic authorities having ability and wisdom in his 1748 sermon, "God's Awful Judgment in the Breaking and Withering of Strong Rods of Community," in *The Works of President Edwards* (New York: Robert Carter and Brothers, 1879), 3: 604–614. Bruce C. Daniels notes that "society committees" assigned pews based on three criteria: "estate, age, and usefulness to the community." Daniels, *The Connecticut Town: Growth and Development, 1635–1790* (Middletown: Wesleyan University Press, 1979), 115. J. S. Maloy argues persuasively modern notions of democratic accountability can be traced to colonial New England, and that Calvinist ecclesiology encouraged the development of democratic political institutions and practices. Maloy, *The Colonial American Origins of Modern Democratic Thought* (New York: Cambridge University Press, 2008), esp. 86–170.

21. *The Public Records of Connecticut* (Hartford: Case, Lockwood and Brainard, 1894), 2: 568 [hereafter *PRC*]; Dreisbach and Hall, *Sacred Rights*, 83–213; Edmund S. Morgan, *Puritan Political Ideas, 1558–1794* (Indianapolis: Bobbs-Merrill, 1965), xiii–xlvii. The Fundamental Orders of Connecticut (1639) stipulated that the governor be a member of "some approved congregation," and required all magistrates to take an explicitly religious oath of office. Bruce Frohnen, *The American Republic* (Indianapolis: Liberty Fund Press, 2002), 13–14.

In *Myth of American Individualism*, Shain highlights the communal nature of founding era political theory and emphasizes that community goals were defined by Reformed Protestant ends. In his introductory chapter, he provides a long list of historians, political scientists, and law professors who believe the overriding concern of America's founders was to promote individualism.

22. Frohnen, *American Republic*, 15–22; Hall, *A Reforming* People, 107, 148, and passim; *The Laws and Liberties of Massachusetts* (1648; reprint, San Marino: Huntington Library, 1998), 46, 50. For a brief overview of rights in early Connecticut see Christopher Collier, "The Connecticut Declaration of Rights Before the Constitution of 1818: A Victim of Revolutionary Redefinition," *Connecticut Law Review*,15 (1982–1983): 87–98.

23. John Davenport, "A Sermon Preach'd at The Election of the Governour" (Boston, 1670), 4. See generally Baldwin, *New England Clergy*,13–21. Similarly, two years earlier Jonathan Mitchel declared in his election sermon that "the Law of Nature, is part of the Eternal Law of God." Mitchel, "Nehemiah on the Wall in Troublesome Times..." (Cambridge, 1671), 11. Note that in these examples (and numerous others could be given) indisputably orthodox clergy appealed to "the law of nature" as a source of authority.

24. Samuel Nowell, "Abraham in Arms" (Boston, 1678), 10–11. T. H. Breen ranks this sermon, along with John Wise's "A Vindication of the Government of New England Churches" (1717) and Jonathan Mayhew's "A Discourse Concerning Unlimited Submission and Non-Resistance to Higher Powers" (1750) as among the most important statements of Puritan political theory. Breen, *The Character of the Good Ruler: A Study of Puritan Political Ideas in New England, 1630–1730* (New Haven: Yale University Press, 1970), 117. Mayhew was theologically more liberal than most of his fellow ministers, but there was widespread agreement among these clergy on basic political principles. On the latter point see Baldwin, *New England Clergy*; and Martha Louise Counts, "The Political Views of the Eighteenth Century New England Clergy as Expressed in Their Election Sermons"(PhD diss., Columbia University, 1956).

Some scholars consider any hint of a right of self-preservation to be evidence of the influence of Thomas Hobbes and/or John Locke. However, the right to protect oneself had long been a part of the natural law tradition, and it is clearly present in Reformed works written well before Hobbes's *Leviathan*.

25. Scholars differ as to the origins of subjective natural rights. John Witte provides a brief overview of this literature in his introduction to *Reformation of Rights*. It should be evident that I agree with him that subjective natural rights existed well before Hobbes and Locke, and that Calvinists contributed significantly to their development. For further discussion see Georg Jellinek, *The Declaration of the Rights of Man and of Citizens: A Contribution to Modern Constitutional History*, trans. Max Farrand (1901; reprint, Westport: Hyperion Press, 1979); and Witte, *Reformation of Rights*.

Christopher Wolfe demonstrates that natural law is compatible with core principles of liberalism such as human equality, consent, the centrality of rights, limited government, and the rule of law. He recognizes that many of these concepts can be traced to Christian political thought (and in some cases pre-Christian thought), but does not consider their development within the Reformed tradition. Nevertheless, his work offers a useful response to academics who argue that a commitment to universal moral standards is incompatible with a classical liberalism. Wolfe, *Natural Law Liberalism* (New York: Cambridge University Press, 2006).

26. Francis J. Bremer, "In Defense of Regicide: John Cotton on the Execution of Charles I," *William and Mary Quarterly* 37 (1980): 103–124; John Cotton, *The Keyes to the Kingdom of Heaven*...(London 1644; reprint Boston: Tappan and Dennet, 1843), 97–100; Richard Dunn, *Puritans and Yankees: The Winthrop Dynasty of New England, 1630–1717* (1962; reprint, New York: W. W. Norton, 1971), 30–36, 229–257.

27. Shain, *Myth of American Individualism*, esp. 155–288; C. S. Lewis, *Studies in Words* (Cambridge: Cambridge University Press, 1960), esp. 111–132.

28. Hall, *A Reforming People*, 193 and passim.

29. Arguments for and against the declension thesis include Perry Miller, *The New England Mind: From Colony to Province* (Cambridge: Harvard University Press, 1953); and Edmund S. Morgan, "New England Puritanism: Another Approach," *William and May Quarterly*, 3rd ser., 18 (1966). Bushman's *From Puritan to Yankee* is indispensible on this subject, but he overemphasizes the degree and scope of theological change in eighteenth-century Connecticut. See also Weir, *Early New England*, 227; and Breen, *The Character of the Good Ruler*, 240, on the persistence of covenant ideals in New England.

30. Excellent works on American providentialism include Nicholas Guyatt, *Providence and the Invention of the United States, 1607–1876* (Cambridge: Cambridge University Press, 2007); Thomas S. Kidd, *The Protestant Interest: New England after Puritanism* (New Haven: Yale University Press, 2004); Ruth H. Bloch, *Visionary Republic: Millennial Themes in American Thought* (New York: Cambridge University Press, 1985); and Hatch, *The Sacred Cause of Liberty*. Richard Dunn offers an excellent account of late seventeenth-century New England in *Puritans and Yankees*.

31. Thomas S. Kidd, *The Great Awakening: The Roots of Evangelical Christianity in Colonial America* (New Haven: Yale University Press, 2007), passim; Mary Latimer Gambrell, *Ministerial Training in Eighteenth-Century New England* (New York: Columbia University Press, 1937). On the continued influence of clergy in New England into the early nineteenth century see Sassi, *A Republic of Righteousness*, 1–83.

32. Carl Becker, *The Declaration of Independence*, 27; Isaac Kramnick, *Republicanism and Bourgeois Radicalism: Political Ideology in Late Eighteenth-Century England and America* (Ithaca: Cornell University Press, 1990), 293; Scott Douglas Gerber, *To Secure These Rights: The Declaration of Independence and Constitutional Interpretation* (New York: New York University Press, 1995), 199–200; Barbara

A. McGraw, *Rediscovering America's Sacred Ground: Public Religion and Pursuit of the Good in a Pluralistic America* (Albany: State University of New York Press, 2003), xv, 23–24, 61–66. See also Hartz, *The Liberal Tradition in America*; Michael Zuckert, *Natural Rights and the New Republicanism* (Princeton: Princeton University Press, 1994), 15–27; Nathan Tarcov, *Locke's Education for Liberty* (Chicago: University of Chicago Press, 1984), 1. Barry Shain argues persuasively that political scientists and law professors are especially prone to view the American founding in profoundly individualistic terms in *Myth of American Individualism*, 3–18.

The emphasis on Locke is even more pronounced in many textbooks. William Ebenstein, for instance, in his popular political theory text, wrote that the "Declaration [of Independence] is pure Locke, and the main elements of the America constitutional system—limited government, inalienable individual rights, inviolability of property—are all directly traceable to Locke." *Great Political Thinkers: Plato to the Present*, 4th ed. (New York: Holt, Rinehart and Winston, 1969), 400.

33. See, for instance, Jeremy Waldron, *God, Locke, and Equality: Christian Foundations in Locke's Political Thought* (Cambridge: Cambridge University Press, 2002); Joshua Foa Dienstag, "Serving God and Mammon: The Lockean Sympathy in Early American Political Thought," *American Political Science Review*, 90 (September 1996): 497–511; Richard L. Greaves, "Radicals, Rights, and Revolution: British Nonconformity and Roots of the American Experience," *Church History*, 61 (June 1992): 151–168; John Dunn, *The Political Thought of John Locke: An Historical Account of the Argument of the "Two Treatises of Government"* (Cambridge: Cambridge University Press, 1969), 256; Winthrop S. Hudson, "John Locke: Heir of Puritan Political Theorists," in *Calvinism and the Political Order*, ed. George L. Hunt and John T. McNeill (Philadelphia: Westminster Press, 1965), 108–129; Morgan, *Puritan Political Ideas*, xli; J. N. Figgis, *The Divine Right of Kings*, 2nd ed. (Cambridge: Cambridge University Press, 1934), 113–115; Herbert D. Foster, "International Calvinism through Locke and the Revolution of 1688," *American Historical Review*, 32 (April 1927): 475–499.

There are indisputably tensions between Locke's theological views and Calvinism. See, for instance, W. M. Spellman, *John Locke and the Problem of Depravity* (New York: Oxford University Press, 1988). The broader literature on Locke and Christianity is far too extensive to review here, but a good overview of it and an excellent account of how religion and politics are related in Locke's thought may be found in Greg Forster, *John Locke's Politics of Moral Consensus* (Cambridge: Cambridge University Press, 2005).

34. See, for instance, Leo Strauss, *Natural Right and History* (Chicago: University of Chicago Press, 1958); C. B. Macpherson, *The Political Theory of Possessive Individualism* (London: Oxford University Press, 1962); Pangle, *Spirit of Modern Republicanism*; Peter Myers, *Our Only Star and Compass: Locke and the Struggle for*

Political Rationality (Lanham: Rowman and Littlefield, 1998); Michael Zuckert, *Launching Liberalism: On Lockean Political Philosophy* (Lawrence: University Press of Kansas, 2002). Some of these scholars understand Locke to be a secret atheist, although others recognize that he may have been *some* sort of Christian.

35. Zuckert, *Natural Rights Republic*, passim. Zuckert also offers a close reading of the text of the Declaration, and on occasion he refers to a few other founders, but he focuses disproportionately on the sage of Monticello. Engeman and Zuckert, *Protestantism and the American Founding* contains a restatement of Zuckert's thesis, essays criticizing it, and a response to those essays by Zuckert.

Like Zuckert, Steven K. Green believes that "[t]he 'Nature's God' of Jefferson's declaration was thus not a Calvinist God but a deistic god of natural religion discovered through reason." He contends that America's founding documents were heavily influenced by the Enlightenment, as evidenced by their statements that government must be based on consent and that people have rights. Green, *The Second Disestablishment: Church and State in Nineteenth-Century America* (New York: Oxford University Press, 2010), 54, 32, and, generally, 3–77. Perhaps the most extreme example of an attempt to understand the Declaration almost solely in light of Jefferson's views is Alan Dershowitz's *Blasphemy: How the Religious Right is Hijacking Our Declaration of Independence* (Hoboken: John Wiley, 2007).

36. Zuckert, *Natural Rights Republic*, 1–89; Jefferson to Henry Lee, May 8, 1825, in *The Life and Selected Writings of Thomas Jefferson*, ed. Adrienne Koch and William Peden (1944, reprint, New York: Random House, 1993), 656–657. Pauline Maier argues effectively that "Jefferson had been appointed not as an author in the modern sense but as a draftsman," in *American Scripture: Making the Declaration of Independence* (New York: Alfred A. Knopf, 1997), 124 and generally 97–153.

37. Bruce P. Stark, *Connecticut Signer: William Williams* (Hartford: American Revolution Bicentennial Commission of Connecticut, 1975); Larry R. Gerlach, *Connecticut Congressman: Samuel Huntington* (Hartford: American Revolution Bicentennial Commission of Connecticut, 1976), esp. 13, 88; and Frederick Calvin Norton, "Biographies of the Governors of Connecticut," *Connecticut Magazine*, 7 (March–April 1901): 175–177.

Of course, some of the founders listed earlier (and in the following lists) were better Calvinists than others—e.g., John Adams was a lifelong Congregationalist, but privately he came to embrace Unitarian theology. On the other hand, he specifically claimed to be heavily influenced by Reformed political theory (see pp. 24 of this chapter). As well, some joined other denominations late in life (e.g., Wilson eventually became an Anglican). And of course delegates may have had other ideological concerns, to say nothing of practical interests. Nevertheless, there is little reason to believe any of the Reformed founders listed here would share Zuckert's views regarding the Declaration.

38. Zuckert, *Natural Rights Republic*, 76, 141. *District of Columbia v. Heller*, 128 S. Ct. 645 (2008), at 648.

    Richard Hughes argues that Jefferson wrote a deistic Declaration of Independence and that "it took some time for the Calvinists—and other orthodox Christians as well—to discern the fundamental differences between themselves and the author of the Declaration." Hughes, *Christian America and the Kingdom of God*, 113.

    I find Zuckert's interpretation of Jefferson to be plausible, if not fully persuasive. However, anyone trying to understand the Declaration (or any public document), should, in addition to carefully reading the text in question, consult the views of those who drafted, amended, and, critically, approved it. For example, if scholars are interested in the scope of right to "liberty" proclaimed by the Declaration, they should not simply look very hard at Jefferson's views, but consider his views alongside the other fifty-five men who signed the document. Of course, scholars might go beyond this group to explore how the concept was generally understood at the time, how the Declaration's readers interpreted it, how state legislators received it, etc. Helpful here is J. G. A. Pocock's distinction between the "history of authorship" and the "history of readership" in his introduction to Edmund Burke, *Reflections on the Revolution in France* (Indianapolis: Hackett, 1987), ix. Cf. H. Jefferson Powell, "The Original Understanding of Original Intent," *Harvard Law Review*, 98 (March 1985): 935–937.

39. John Dunn, "The Politics of Locke in England and America in the Eighteenth Century," in *John Locke: Problems and Perspectives: A Collection of New Essays*, ed. John Yolton (Cambridge: Cambridge University Press, 1969), 45–80, see esp. 69–71. Dunn concludes with respect to the American Revolution, "[f]or the American population at large the revolution may have been about many things, but in a very few cases can it possibly have been thought to have been in any sense about the *Two Treatises of Government* of John Locke" (80).

40. Clinton Rossiter, *Seedtime of the Republic: The Origin of the American Tradition of Political Liberty* (New York: Harcourt, Brace, 1953), 491, note 111; John Locke, *A Letter on Toleration*, 3rd ed. (Boston: Rogers and Fowle, 1743); M. Louise Greene, *The Development of Religious Liberty in Connecticut* (Boston: Houghton, Mifflin, 1905), 121; Franklin Bowditch Dexter, *Biographical Sketches of the Graduates of Yale College, October, 1701–May, 1745* (New York: Henry Holt, 1885), 698–722. Of course Lockean ideas could be transmitted through other means, but the relative inaccessibility of his works on politics must be taken into account when assessing his influence on the American founding.

41. Donald S. Lutz, "The Relative Influence of European Writers on Late Eighteenth-Century American Political Thought," *American Political Science Review*, 78 (1984): 189–197, esp. 192–193; John Locke, *An Essay Concerning the True Original Extent and End of Civil Government* (Boston: Edes and Gill, 1773); J. C. D. Clark,

The Language of Liberty, 1660–1832 (Cambridge: Cambridge University Press, 1994), 26. There are a variety of problems with relying on citations, and accounts of which books were available at what time are woefully incomplete. Responses to scholars questioning the availability of Locke's works and his influence in colonial America include Zuckert, *Natural Rights and the New Republicanism*, 18–25; and Dworetz, *Unvarnished Doctrine*.

42. Daniel L. Dreisbach, "The Bible and the Political Culture of the American Founding" in *Faith and the Founders of the American Republic* (New York: Oxford University Press, 2014); Benjamin Franklin to Samuel Cooper, May 15, 1781, in *The Works of Benjamin Franklin*, ed. John Bigelow (New York: G. P. Putnam's Sons, 1904), 423–424. Similarly, Joyce Appleby writes that the "most important source of meaning for eighteenth-century Americans was the Bible." "The American Heritage—The Heirs and the Disinherited," *Journal of American History*, 74 (1987): 809. Compare with, for example, Wilson Carey McWilliams, "The Bible in the American Political Tradition," in *Religion and Politics*, ed. Myron J. Aronoff (New Brunswick: Transaction, 1984), 11–45 ("the founding generation rejected or deemphasized the Bible and biblical rhetoric," 21).

     In 1842, a ninety-one-year-old veteran of the War for Independence was asked if he had "been reading Harington or Sidney and Locke about the eternal principles of liberty?" He responded, "Never heard of 'em. We read only the Bible, the Catechism, Watts' Psalms and Hymns, and the Almanac." The veteran went on to insist that the patriots' primary motivation was self-government. Quoted in Samuel Eliot Morison, *The Oxford History of the American People* (New York: Oxford University Press, 1965), 212–213.

43. Herbert D. Foster, *Collected Papers of Herbert D. Foster: Historical and Biographical Studies* privately printed, 1929), 77–105. See also, Perry Miller, *The New England Mind: The Seventeenth Century* (1939; reprint, Boston: Beacon Press, 1961), 89–108; Charles F. Robinson and Robin Robinson, "Three Early Massachusetts Libraries" *Publications of the Colonial Society of Massachusetts* 28 (Boston: Colonial Society of Massachusetts, 1935), 107–185; Arthur Orlo Norton, "Harvard Text-Books and Reference Books of the Seventeenth Century," *Publications of the Colonial Society of Massachusetts* 28 (Boston: Colonial Society of Massachusetts, 1935), 361–437. David W. Hall points out numerous similarities between classic Reformed works and texts written by colonial and founding era political and ecclesiastical leaders. Although similarities in and of themselves do not constitute proof of intellectual influence, given the context in which New England elites were raised they are at least suggestive. See Hall, *The Genevan Reformation*, 285–446.

44. Cotton Mather, *Magnalia Christi Americana* (Hartford: Silas Andrus and Son, 1885), 1: 274; Miller, *The New England Mind*, 1: 93.

45. Morrison, *John Witherspoon*, 81; *Works of John Adams*, 6: 4. In the same discussion, Adams also refers to "Machiavel," "the great restorer of the true

politics," and other thinkers. One should not read too much into Adams's brief discussion, but I reference it to help show that works of Reformed political theory were read and discussed by American elites, and that at least one prominent founder clearly articulated the position that Reformed ideas had a significant impact on Locke's political theory.

46. John Adams to F. C. Schaeffer, November 25, 1821, in *The Founders on Religion: A Book of Quotations*, ed. James H. Hutson (Princeton: Princeton University Press, 2005), 15–16. See also John Adams, "A Dissertation on Canon and Feudal Law," in *The Political Writings of John Adams*, ed. George A. Peek (New York: Macmillan, 1985), 3–21.

47. Gary Scott Smith, "Samuel Adams: America's Puritan Revolutionary," in Dreisbach, Hall, and Morrison, *Forgotten Founders*, 40–64; Stoll, *Samuel Adams*, 23; *The Writings of Samuel Adams*, ed. Harry Alonzo Cushing (New York: G. P. Putnam's Sons, 1904), 1: 201–212; Bell, *War of Religion*, 100–101; George Buchanan, *De Jure Regnie: Or the Due Right of Government* (Philadelphia, 1766); Farrand, *Records of the Federal Convention*, 1: 438.

48. Judah Champion, "Christian and Civil Liberties" (Hartford: E. Watson, 1776), 6, 8. See also Foster, "International Calvinism through Locke," 475. One of the earliest and most famous examples of a cleric's use of Locke is found in Elisha Williams's sermon, "The Essential Rights and Liberties of Protestants" (1744), in *Political Sermons of the American Founding Era: 1730–1805*, ed. Ellis Sandoz, 2nd ed., 2 vols. (Indianapolis: Liberty Fund Press, 1998), 1: 55–65.

49. Zuckert, *Natural Rights Republic*, 172. Cf. Paul A. Rahe, *Republics Ancient and Modern: Classical Republicanism and the American Revolution* (Chapel Hill: University of North Carolina Press, 1992), 3: 10.

50. Of course, some clergy from Reformed denominations moved toward deism anyway, (e.g., Ebenezer Gay, Charles Chauncy, Jonathan Mayhew, and Elihu Palmer), but there is little reason to doubt that the vast majority of clergy in the era were anything other than orthodox Christians. Noll, *America's God*, 138–145. Scholars who argue that deism flourished in this era are often misled by contemporary critics of deism lamenting its perceived rise. See, for instance, Kerry S. Walters, *Rational Infidels: The American Deists* (Durango: Longwood Academic, 1992). In their study of the availability of European Enlightenment works in America, David Lundberg and Henry F. May note that "[t]he Deists, who appear relatively seldom in this or any period [between 1700 and 1813], were apparently known more through anti-Deist tracts and sermons than directly." Lundberg and May, "The Enlightened Reader in America," *American Quarterly*, 28 (Summer 1976): 286, 267. Moreover, liberal Congregationalists such as Chauncy and Mayhew seem to have been heavily influenced by Reformed *political* ideas.

51. Steven Dworetz makes a similar point about the American clergy's use of Locke in *Unvarnished Doctrine*, 32–34, 135–183.

This is not to say that Locke and the patriots were never criticized from a Christian or biblical perspective. See, for instance, Jonathan Boucher, "On Civil Liberty, Passive Obedience, and Non-resistance" (1775) in Frohnen, *American Republic*, 159–178. Boucher was an Anglican Loyalist who was born in England. Shortly after preaching this sermon in a Maryland parish he returned to the land of his birth. For an account of an Anglican Loyalist from Connecticut, see Sheldon S. Cohen, *Connecticut's Loyalist Gadfly: The Reverend Samuel Andrew Peters* (Hartford: American Revolution Bicentennial Commission of Connecticut, 1976). On the education of ministers in the era, see Gambrell, *Ministerial Training in Eighteenth-Century New England*. With the exception of the Swiss born Presbyterian John Joachim Zubly and a few Old Lights, I have found very few Reformed ministers in America who opposed the War for Independence. Randall M. Miller, ed., *"A Warm and Zealous Spirit": John J. Zubly and the American Revolution* (Macon: Mercer University Press, 1982); Adrian C. Leiby, *The Revolutionary War in the Hackensack Valley: The Jersey Dutch and the Neutral Ground, 1775–1783* (New Brunswick: Rutgers University Press, 1962), esp. 20–25; and Mark A. Noll, *Christians in the American Revolution* (Washington, DC: Christian University Press, 1977), 120–121. This is not to say that all patriots who were members of Reformed congregations were motivated by religion or Calvinist political thought. Ethnicity, interests, and other factors wholly unrelated to the Reformed tradition undoubtedly played a role with some individuals and groups. For further discussion see chapter 3 of this volume.

Unlike Calvinist clergy, Anglican ministers in America were more equally divided. Among those in American from 1775 to 1783, 128 were Loyalists, 130 were patriots, 71 fled, and the opinions of 59 are unknown. One might expect these men to be loyal to the king, who was, after all, the head of their church. Their country of origin may also have been a significant factor. In 1775, 141 Anglican ministers were born in America, 134 were born outside of what became the United States (primarily England and Scotland), and the birthplace of 36 is unknown. James B. Bell, *A War of Religion: Dissenters, Anglicans, and the American Revolution* (Houndmills: Palgrave MacMillan, 2008), 240, 244.

52. Scholars who argue for the influence of the Scottish Enlightenment include Garry Wills, *Inventing America: Jefferson's Declaration of Independence* (Garden City: Doubleday, 1978); Allen Jayne, *Jefferson's Declaration of Independence: Origins, Philosophy, and Theology* (Lexington: University Press of Kentucky, 1998); and Jean Yarbrough, *American Virtues: Thomas Jefferson and the Character of a Free People* (Lawrence: University Press of Kansas, 1998). In *The Political and Legal Philosophy of James Wilson*, I show that the version of Scottish moral sense theory that was most influential in America is compatible with orthodox Christian convictions, if not Reformed theology per se.

53. Robert Middlekauff, *The Glorious Cause: The American Revolution: 1763–1789*, rev. ed. (New York: Oxford University Press, 2005), 52. Middlekauff repeatedly refers to the cultural influence of Christianity, but rarely describes it as an intellectual influence (e.g., 134–136, 244–246, and 504). However, in an interview with the *Claremont Review of Books*, he remarked that "I do think that religion is supremely important, and I wouldn't limit it just to the period of the Revolution. I think that at least up to the Civil War and perhaps after, you can understand American history only if you have an understanding of American religion. It's like trying to understand the 20th century without some understanding of economics. This is a terribly rough equation, but Calvin is to the 17th and maybe the 18th century what John Maynard Keynes is to the 20th century." "Is America Still a Glorious Cause? A Conversation with Historian Robert Middlekauff," *Claremont Review of Books*, 2 (December 1983): 10.

54. On the classical republican tradition, see Bernard Bailyn, *The Ideological Origins of the American Republic* (Cambridge: Harvard University Press, 1967); Gordon Wood, *The Creation of the American Republic, 1776–1787* (Chapel Hill: University of North Carolina Press, 1969); and J. G. A. Pocock, *The Machiavellian Moment: Florentine Political Thought and the Atlantic Republican Tradition* (Princeton: Princeton University Press, 1975).

55. In his magisterial volume, *Republics Ancient and Modern*, Rahe demonstrates that eighteenth-century republicanism is far different from classical republicanism, but he overestimates the influence of a modern, secularized Locke in the founding era. Like other Strausseans, he defends this view by paying disproportionate attention to founders like Madison, Jefferson, Hamilton, and virtually ignoring statesmen such as Sherman, Ellsworth, Huntington, Trumbull, Williams, and Wolcott.

56. James Cooper notes that Congregational "ministers frequently addressed questions of church government in their sermons." James F. Cooper, *The Tenaciousness of Their Liberties: The Congregationalists in Colonial Massachusetts* (New York: Oxford University Press, 1999), 31. It is somewhat ironic given my argument in this paragraph that Sherman read Jean-Jacque Rousseau's *Social Contract* sometime between 1775–1780, and he even copied select passages into an account book. Most of the excerpts concerned the social contract, the importance of consent, and popular sovereignty. "Papers of Roger Sherman," Account Book, n.d., The Library of Congress.

57. Roger Sherman to François de Marbois, November 18, 1782, in Miscellaneous Bound Manuscripts, Massachusetts Historical Society. The text is a copy or draft of the letter sent to Marbois written in Sherman's hand. On Marbois's project and the responses to it, see Merrill D. Peterson, *Thomas Jefferson and the New Nation* (New York: Oxford University Press, 1970), 247–265; Jefferson, *Notes on Virginia*, in Koch and Peden, *Life and Selected Writings of Thomas Jefferson*, 173–267.

58. Ahlstrom, *Religious History*, 1: 426; Harry S. Stout, "Preaching the Insurrection," *Christian History*, 15 (1996): 17. Presumably both figures are for white Americans. See also William Hutchison, *Religious Pluralism in America* (New Haven: Yale University Press, 2003), 21 (who writes that "the colonists [were] at least 85 percent English-speaking Protestants"). According to Charles O. Paullin, 56% of churches in America in 1776 were in the Reformed tradition. Paullin, *Atlas of the Historical Geography of the United States* (Washington, DC: Carnegie Institution, 1932), 50. Roger Finke and Rodney Stark rely heavily on his study when they discuss denominations in the era in *The Churching of America, 1776–1990: Winners and Losers in Our Religious Economy* (New Brunswick: Rutgers University Press, 1992), 25. According to Edwin Gaustad and Philip Barlow, 63% of the churches in 1780 were in the Reformed tradition. Gaustad and Barlow, *New Historical Atlas of Religion in America* (New York: Oxford University Press, 2001), 8. The two estimates for 1776 (56% and 75%) are not necessarily contradictory if Reformed churches had larger congregations than non-Reformed churches. If one counts Anglicans as being in the Reformed tradition (a disputable but plausible assessment), then 75% of America's churches in 1776 were Reformed. Although Lutherans are closely related to Calvinists on many theological matters, they are not usually considered to be a part of the Reformed tradition.

59. Finke and Stark, *Churching of America*, 29; Grasso, *A Speaking Aristocracy*, 105, 349. Christopher Collier reports that of the delegates to Connecticut's ratification convention whose religious affiliation is known, 92 percent of the Federalists and 95 percent of the anti-Federalists were Congregationalists. Collier, *All Politics Is Local*, 99. This is not to deny that toward the end of the eighteenth century a small minority of New Englanders embraced strange and heterodox beliefs and practices. See especially Stephen Marini, *Radical Sects of Revolutionary New England* (Cambridge: Harvard University Press, 1982).

60. Finke and Stark, *Churching of America*, 45; Frederick Lewis Weis, *The Colonial Clergy and the Colonial Churches of New England* (Lancaster: Society of the Descendants of the Colonial Clergy, 1936); Gambrell, *Ministerial Training*.

61. Harry S. Stout, "Preaching the Insurrection," *Christian History*, 15 (1996): 12. On the orthodoxy of these Congregational clergy see Stout, *The New England Soul: Preaching and Religious Culture in Colonial New England* (New York: Oxford University Press, 1986), passim. On the significance and influence of Reformed clergy in southern New England between 1783–1799, see Sassi, *A Republic of Righteousness*, 1–83.

62. William Warren Sweet, "The American Colonial Environment and Religious Liberty," *Church History*, 4 (March 1935): 43–56. Sidney E. Mead offered a similar figure in "From Coercion to Persuasion: Another Look at the Rise of Religious Liberty and the Emergence of Denominationalism," *Church History*, 25 (1956): 317–337. However, both of these estimates are simply based upon

conjecture. Finke and Stark, *Churching of America*, 15. Isaac Kramnick and R. Laurence Moore, *The Godless Constitution: The Case Against Religious Correctness* (New York: W. W. Norton, 1996), 17.

63. James Hutson, "The Christian Nation Question," in his *Forgotten Features of the Founding: The Recovery of Religious Themes in the Early American Republic* (Lanham: Lexington Books, 2003), 111–132.

Scholars who argue for a lack of religiosity among Americans in the founding era are also led astray by laments about the lack of denominational commitments among Americans or jeremiads decrying what was perceived to be insufficient attention to religious and moral concerns. See, for instance, Ezra Stiles's analysis of Connecticut's 1794 election returns, where he concluded that only thirty of the eighty-five men earning more than one hundred votes were "religious Characters." Ezra Stiles, *The Literary Diary of Ezra Stiles*, ed. Franklin Bowditch Dexter (New York: Charles Scribner's Sons, 1901), 3: 546. The point applies with equal force to claims by Calvinists that other ministers, university professors, or parishioners were embracing "Arminianism" or "Arianism." Of course, some of these laments were accurate, but often they were overstated. For further discussion of these issues and an excellent overview of Christianity in eighteenth-century America see Bonomi, *Under the Cope of Heaven*, 1–127.

64. Hutson, "The Christian Nation Question," 118. Hutson also provides an excellent critique of historian Jon Butler's work, which purports to build upon and offer additional evidence for Finke and Stark's figures (120–125). See Jon Butler, "Why Revolutionary America Wasn't a 'Christian Nation,'" in *Religion and the New Republic*, ed. James H. Hutson (Lanham: Rowmanand Littlefield, 2000), 187–202; and *Awash in a Sea of Faith: Christianizing the American People* (Cambridge: Harvard University Press, 1990).

65. Patricia U. Bonomi and Peter R. Eisenstadt, "Church Adherence in the Eighteenth Century British Colonies," *William and Mary Quarterly*, 3rd ser., 39 (April 1982): 275.

66. Finke and Stark, *Churching of America*, 29; David Hackett Fisher, *Albion's Seed: Four British Folkways in America* (New York: Oxford University Press, 1989), 431, 606, 608; Howard Miller, "The Grammar of Liberty: Presbyterians and the First American Constitutions," *Journal of Presbyterian History*, 54 (1976): 151–152; Clark, *The Language of Liberty*, 351–363; Tiedemann, "Presbyterianism and the American Revolution"; Fred J. Hood, *Reformed America: The Middle and Southern States, 1783–1837* (University: University of Alabama Press, 1980); and G. S. Rowe, *Thomas McKean: The Shaping of an American Republicanism* (Boulder: Colorado Associated University Press, 1978), esp. 61–63; Archibald Henderson, "The Mecklenburg Declaration of Independence," *Mississippi Valley Historical Review*, 5 (September 1918): 207–215.

An Anglican minister wrote to London that "after a strict inquiry" he could find no Presbyterian minister "who did not, by preaching and every effort in their power, promote all the measures of the Congress, however extravagant." Quoted in Leiby, *The Revolutionary War in the Hackensack Valley*, 228. However, some southern Presbyterians may have been exceptions to this rule, as indicated by the July 10, 1775, letter from four Presbyterian ministers in Philadelphia (Francis Alison, James Sprout, George Duffield, and Robert Davidson) to their co-religionists in North Carolina urging them to join the patriot cause. Clark, *The Language of Liberty*, 123.

67. A few scholars have contended that *The New England Primer* became significantly less Calvinist as the eighteenth century progressed. However, Stephanie Schnorbus argues persuasively that although some versions of the primer printed after 1780 shifted in a Lockean direction, that they all "remained secure in Calvinist orthodoxy." Stephanie Schnorbus, "Calvin and Locke: Dueling Epistemologies in *The New England Primer*, 1720–1790," *Early American Studies*, 8 (Spring 2010): 250–287, 287; *The New-England Primer*, ed. Paul Leicester Ford (1727; reprint, New York: Dodd, Mead, 1897).

68. Ralph Ketcham, *James Madison: A Biography* (Charlottesville: University Press of Virginia, 1971), 17–50; Morrison, *John Witherspoon and the Founding of the American Republic*, 4; Joseph S. Tiedemann, "Presbyterianism and the American Revolution in the Middle Colonies," *Church History*, 74 (June 2005): 339; Gideon Mailer, "Anglo-Scottish Union and John Witherspoon's American Revolution," *William and Mary Quarterly*, 3rd ser., 67 (October 2010): 709–746.

69. Frohnen, *American Republic*, 12. Paul Lucas demonstrates that Congregationalists in the Connecticut Valley had significant and acrimonious disputes even in the seventeenth century. However, as an intellectual matter, disagreements were clearly within the bounds of Reformed theology, particularly with respect to political theory and church-state relations. See Paul R. Lucas, *Valley of Discord: Church and Society along the Connecticut River, 1636–1725* (Hanover: University Press of New England, 1976).

70. There is a voluminous literature on the New Light-Old Light controversy, but works particularly relevant to this book include Heimert, *Religion and the American Mind*; Valeri, *Law and Providence in Joseph Bellamy's New England*; and Samuel Harrison Rankin, Jr., "Conservatism and the Problem of Change in the Congregational Churches of Connecticut, 1660–1760" (PhD diss., Kent State University, 1971), 296 (arguing for New Light majorities by 1754). Christopher Grasso points out that Old Lights in Connecticut were generally "conservative Calvinists trying to preserve church order and political power," whereas those in Massachusetts are "usually characterized as Boston 'liberals' straying from Calvinist orthodoxy." Grasso, *A Speaking Aristocracy*, 106.

71. Bernard C. Steiner claimed that Connecticut election sermons may be traced to the formation of the colony, but the first recorded sermon is from 1674. Steiner,

"Statistics of the Connecticut Election Sermons,"*New England Historical and Genealogical Register*, 46 (1892): 123; Baldwin, *New England Clergy*; Counts, *The Political Views of the Eighteenth Century New England Clergy*; William G. McLoughlin, *New England Dissent: 1630–1883: The Baptists and the Separation of Church and State* (Cambridge: Harvard University Press, 1971), 2: 915–1062, 1018–1019. McLoughlin provides an excellent account of the demise of the Standing Order.

72. *Acts and Laws of His Majesties Colony of Connecticut in New-England* (New London, 1715), 207. For the 1784 version of this statute, see Cushing, *First Laws*, 258. For a more extensive list of Connecticut laws reflecting the influence of Christianity, see chapter 6. Collier, *All Politics Is Local*, 83.

73. This list emphasizes Connecticut leaders closest to Sherman; it is not exclusive. See Michael Toth, *Founding Federalist: The Life of Oliver Ellsworth* (Wilmington: ISI Books, 2011); William F. Willingham, *Connecticut Revolutionary: Eliphalet Dyer* (Hartford: American Revolution Bicentennial Commission of Connecticut, 1976); Casto, *Oliver Ellsworth*; W. D. McCrakean, *The Huntington Letters* (New York: Appleton, 1905); David M. Roth, *Connecticut's War Governor: Jonathan Trumbull* (Chester: Pequot Press, 1974); Morgan, *Gentle Puritan: A Life of Ezra Stiles*; Louis Leonard Tucker, *Connecticut's Seminary of Sedition: Yale College* (Hartford: American Revolution Bicentennial Commission of Connecticut, 1974); Sassi, *A Republic of Righteousness* (on Stiles, Dwight, and other clergy); and Grasso, *A Speaking Aristocracy*, esp. 24–26, 84–85, 230–278 (on Griswold and Stiles).

74. Collier, *Roger Sherman's Connecticut*, 75, 323–324, 31–37; Rommel, *Connecticut's Yankee Patriot*, 12; and James D. German, "The Social Utility of Wicked Self-Love: Calvinism, Capitalism, and Public Policy in Revolutionary New England," *Journal of American History*, 82 (December 1995): 966. German concedes that Sherman took elements of Christianity seriously but contends that he was able to reconcile his faith with "the frankest pursuit of self interest" (973–974, 970). Bushman makes a similar claim in *From Puritan to Yankee*, 255. Other scholars, relying on these earlier accounts, have repeated them. See, for instance, Bonomi, *Under the Cope of Heaven*, 167; and Murrin, "Religion and Politics in America from the First Settlements to the Civil War," 31, 41.

75. Stiles, *Literary Diary*, 3: 500.

76. Daniel T. V. Huntoon, *History of the Town of Canton* (Cambridge: John Wilson and Son, 1893), 134–135.

77. Ibid., 188–189.

78. Ibid., 192–194; Sandoz, *Political Sermons*, 1: 208–232; Samuel Dunbar, "Righteousness by the Law Subversive of Christianity," (Boston: S. Kneeland, 1751).

79. Records of New Milford/First Congregational Church, Connecticut Church Records, reel #582, 5, Connecticut State Library.

    The Massachusetts Historical Society has a copy of the important Old Light "Resolves of the General Consociation Convened at Guilford, November 24th,

1741," that was written in Sherman's handwriting in 1746. In 1742, Connecticut's General Assembly responded to the Resolves by passing anti-itinerancy laws that remained in place until 1750. Both documents are in Stephen Nissenbaum, ed., *The Great Awakening at Yale College* (Belmont: Wadesworth, 1972), 128–132, 136–139. That Sherman would copy this eight-page document in 1746 suggests an interest in the proper scope of religious liberty, but it is unclear whether he supported or opposed the Resolves. General Consociation of Connecticut Churches Collection, Massachusetts Historical Society.

80. Records of the Congregational Church at White Haven, Connecticut Church Records, reel #577, 24, Connecticut State Library; Stiles, *Literary Diary*, 3: 344; Robert L. Ferm, *Jonathan Edwards the Younger: 1745–1801: Colonial Pastor* (Grand Rapids: Eerdmans, 1976), 139. See especially Roger Sherman to David Austin, March 1, 1790, Roger Sherman Collection, box 1, folder 12, Yale University.

81. Brooks Mather Kelly, *Yale: A History* (New Haven: Yale University Press, 1974), 34, 61; Stiles, *Literary Diary*, 3: 500, 490–491.

82. Exact titles of each almanac varied, but all concerned "the year of our Lord Christ."

83. Collier, *Roger Sherman's Connecticut*, 11. All aphorisms taken from Victor Hugo Paltsits, *The Almanacs of Roger Sherman: 1750–1761* (Worcester: Davis Press, 1907), 40–48.

84. Roger Sherman to Joseph Bellamy, July 23, 1772, Jonathan Edwards Collection, Gen. mss. 151, box 28, folder 1538, Beinecke Library, Yale University. Roger Sherman to John Witherspoon, July 10, 1788 and John Witherspoon to Roger Sherman, July 25, 1788, Miscellaneous Bound Manuscripts, Massachusetts Historical Society.

85. Stiles, *Literary Diary*, 3: 500; Roger Sherman, "A Short Sermon on the Duty of Self Examination, *Preparatory to Receiving the* Lord's Supper," (New Haven: Abel Morse, 1789), 10–11.

86. Sherman, "Short Sermon," 5, 8. Cf. Jonathan Edwards, *On the Nature of True Virtue* (1765).

87. Sherman, "Short Sermon," 16–17.

88. Dr. Nathan Williams to Roger Sherman, September 23, 1791, Sherman Collection, box 1, folder 14, Yale University.

89. Roger Sherman to Dr. Nathan Williams, December 17, 1791, Society Collection, Historical Society of Pennsylvania. Roger Sherman to Samuel Hopkins, June 28, 1790, in *Correspondence Between Roger Sherman and Samuel Hopkins*, ed. Andrew P. Peabody (Worcester: Press of Charles Hamilton, 1889), 10. Sherman's language here is similar to that of the answer to Question 3 of the Westminster Larger Catechism, which refers to the Old and New Testaments as "the only rule of faith and obedience."

90. Roger Sherman to Samuel Hopkins, June 28, 1790 and October 1790, in Peabody, *Correspondence*, 8, 24.

91. No theologian was better represented in Sherman's library than Jonathan Edwards, Sr. His collection included (using the short citations used in the inventories): *Life [of David Brainerd?]*, *On the Will*, *History of Redemption*, *Religious Affections*, *Edwards Against Chauncey*, and 15 *Sermons by President Edwards*. "Division of the Books belonging to the Estate of Roger Sherman Esq. Made November 14, 1794," photostatic copy in the Sherman Collection, box 1, folder 16, Yale University. There is also an "Inventory of Pamphlets belonging to the Estate of the Late Roger Sherman, Esq. Including bound Book[s]," in Sherman Papers, Library of Congress. Ahlstrom, *Religious History*, 1: 492.

    See also Justus Mitchell to Roger Sherman, January 26, 1790; Roger Sherman to Justus Mitchell, February 8, 1790; and Justus Mitchell to Roger Sherman, March 17, 1790, in Roger Sherman Papers, Library of Congress. Mitchell (1752–1806) was Sherman's brother-in-law and a Congregational minister in New Canaan, Connecticut. In the letters, the two discussed, among other things, the nature of human depravity and moral obligation.

92. Quoted in Collier, *Roger Sherman's Connecticut*, 93; Benjamin Rush, *Autobiography*, ed. George W. Corner (Princeton: Princeton University Press, 1948), 146. The reference is actually to Jeremiah 3:23, not 12:23.

93. Dwight, "A Statistical Account," 77.

CHAPTER 3

1. Frohnen, *American Republic*, 12–14. On the development of Connecticut's government see Elizabeth Beaumont, "The Slow Evolution of the 'Constitution State,'" in *The Constitutionalism of America State*, ed. George E. Connor and Christopher W. Hammons (Columbia: University of Missouri Press, 2008), 3–22; Roger J. Taylor, *Colonial Connecticut: A History* (Millwood: KTO Press, 1979), esp. 20–48; David M. Roth, *Connecticut: A Bicentennial History* (New York: W. W. Norton, 1979); and Richard J. Purcell, *Connecticut in Transition: 1775–1818* (1918; reprint, Middletown: Wesleyan University Press, 1963), esp. 113–145. The Privy Council disallowed a Connecticut law banning Quakers in 1705 and 1706. The Connecticut Assembly altered the offending legislation but refused to recognize that the law had been disallowed. See Dunn, *Puritans and Yankees*, 349.

2. *The Public Records of the State of Connecticut*, ed. Charles Hoadley (Hartford: Press of The Case, Lockwood, and Brainard Co., 1894) [hereafter PRSC], 5: 323–324. The act did not prohibit Superior Court judges from simultaneously holding lower offices, so Sherman remained mayor of New Haven until his death. In 1784, Connecticut created a Supreme Court of Errors consisting of the

governor and Council to hear select appeals, although it was still possible to appeal to the General Assembly in certain cases.

A good overview of both the impact on Puritan ideas on law and the judiciary in early Connecticut, as well as the development of each, may be found in Everett C. Goodwin, *The Magistracy Rediscovered: Connecticut, 1636–1818* (Ann Arbor: UMI Research Press, 1981). See also Christopher Collier, "The Common Law and Individual Rights in Connecticut Before the Federal Bill of Rights," *Connecticut Bar Journal,* 76 (2002): 1–70.

3. See generally Bushman, *From Puritan to Yankee,* 147–288. However, he argues New Light separatists wanted greater separation between church and state than I believe they did (see especially 228–232). See also Grasso, *A Speaking Aristocracy;* Gildsdorf and Gilsdorf, "Elites and Electorates"; and Jackson Turner Main's fact filled, *Society and Economy in Colonial Connecticut* (Princeton: Princeton University Press, 1985).

4. Lawrence Henry Gipson, *American Loyalist: Jared Ingersoll* (1920; reprint, New Haven: Yale University Press, 1971), 18. I make no attempt to provide an exhaustive account of Sherman's political service. Instead, I focus on his more significant contributions and on issues that shine light on his political theory.

   In 1766 Sherman wrote to William Samuel Johnson, then in London, noting that he owned *Hawkins's Pleas of the Crown* and *Abridgement of Coke on Littleton, Jacob's Law Dictionary* and *Attorneys Practice, Lord Raymond's Reports, Law of Evidence, Hale's History of the Common Law, Attorney's Pocket Companion, Prussian Laws* (2 vols.), and *Conductor Generals.* He then asked Johnson to purchase for him "*Bacon's Abridgement* if compleat & such others on Law & Politicks as you shall think most beneficial to the amount of £20." Sherman to Johnson, December 5, 1766, William Samuel Johnson Papers, box 1, Connecticut Historical Society.

5. Philoeunomos [Roger Sherman], "A Caveat against Injustice, or an Inquiry into the Evil Consequences of a Fluctuating Medium Of Exchange" (New York: Henry De Forest, 1752), 3–5.

6. Ibid., 5–6.

7. Ibid., 10, 8.

8. Ibid. 13, 14.

9. Ibid., 15. See generally, W. J. Rorabaugh, *The Alcoholic Republic: An American Tradition* (New York: Oxford University Press, 1979), 5–57. According to Rorabaugh, between 1722 and 1738, the price of a gallon of rum in Boston fell from 3 shillings 6 pence to 2 shillings. Overall, consumption of distilled spirits per capita almost doubled between 1710–1770 (28, 8).

10. Sherman, "A Caveat," 5, 7.

11. *PRC,* 10: 352–404, 460, 484.

12. *PRC,* 10: 406–409. Unfortunately for students of the era, *The Public Records of Connecticut* do not contain records of legislative debates or individual votes, and

newspaper coverage of the legislative sessions was spotty. Moreover, legislative sessions were closed to outside observers for virtually all of Sherman's career in colonial and state politics. The Connecticut State Library has a journal kept by the lower house that records votes taken on legislation, but not who voted for what. There is not a similar journal for the upper house. Grasso, *A Speaking Aristocracy*, 451. Christopher Collier agrees that Sherman's pamphlet likely influenced the General Assembly. Collier, *Roger Sherman's Connecticut*, 19.

It is noteworthy that Connecticut's 1708 excise act applied to a variety of alcoholic beverages, although "wine, rhum, brandy and distilled liquors" were taxed at higher rates than "cyder" and metheglin (spiced mead). The 1755 act applied only to distilled liquors. Cf. *PRC*, 5: 56–58. The Connecticut Assembly apparently agreed with Sherman that distilled spirits were becoming a particular problem, a view that became widespread among American elites after the publication of Benjamin Rush's 1784 essay *An Enquiry into the Effects of Spirituous Liquors upon the Human Body, and Their Influence upon the Happiness of Society* (1784; reprint, Boston: Thomas and Andrews, 1790). For further discussion see Rorabaugh, *Alcoholic Republic*, 25–57.

13. *PRC*, 11: 493.

14. Ibid., vols. 10–11, passim, 12: 137. Sherman was not a member of the legislature when it issued this call for thanksgiving.

15. Ibid., 12: 454–455.

16. Ibid., 12: 467, 497; 13: 335, 360, 463; 15: 22, 282, 450–453. Of course, the claim is not that *only* a commitment to Reformed Protestantism could lead legislators to support these laws, but that an important reason these laws were adopted in this context was because of such a commitment.

17. Ibid., 12: 495.

18. On this controversy, see Julian P. Boyd, *The Susquehannah Company: Connecticut's Experiment in Expansion* (New Haven: Yale University Press, 1935). See also *Susquehannah Company Papers*, 1: 28, 25.

19. Roger Sherman, "Legal Brief," January 1774, in Boutell, *Life* 70–74; Boyd, *Susquehannah Company Papers*, 5: 268–270. Sherman's essay in the *Connecticut Journal*, April 8, 1774, is reprinted in *Susquehannah Company Papers*, 6: 179–183. The phrase "every *kingdom divided against itself is brought to desolation*" is from Mathew 12: 25. For discussion of Ingersoll's role in the controversy, see Gipson, *American Loyalist*, 314–336.

20. *Susquehannah Company Papers*, 7: 245–246. Sherman played an important but backroom role in negotiating this settlement. See Collier, *All Politics Is Local*, 26–28.

21. Relatively early in his service on the Superior Court, Sherman was joined by William Samuel Johnson. Johnson kept notes on the 130 cases the two heard together between December 1772 and March 1773. In many instances, Johnson

did little more than note the decision of the court, but in twenty-two cases he specifically stated that Sherman dissented or joined a fractured majority. In 1785 the General Assembly required Superior Court judges to issue written opinions, many of which are available in the Connecticut State Library. However, many of these manuscript opinions merely state the decision of the court. Some of these were later published in Kirby's *Reports* (1789), but, as we shall see in the next chapter, he did not always provide a faithful transcription of the handwritten opinions. John T. Farrell, ed., *The Superior Court Diary of William Samuel Johnson, 1772–1773* (Washington, DC: American Historical Association, 1942).

22. *Superior Court Diary of William Samuel Johnson*, 105, 231, 60–61; *Ecclesiastical Society v. Beckwith*, (1786), 1 Kirby 91 (1786). The handwritten opinion for the last case is available in the Connecticut State Library.

23. *Superior Court Diary of William Samuel Johnson*, vii; *Whiting and Frisbie v. Jewel*, 1 Kirby 1 (1786); *Frisbie v. Butler*, 1 Kirby 213 (1787).

24. On the influence of Calvinism and/or Calvinists on the War for Independence, see Charles W. Akers, "Calvinism and the American Revolution," in John H. Bratt, ed., *The Heritage of John Calvin* (Grand Rapids: William B. Eerdmans, 1973), 158–176; Baldwin, *New England Clergy*; Sacvan Bercovitch, "How the Puritans Won the American Revolution," *Massachusetts Review*, 17 (1976): 597–630; Bloch, *Visionary Republic*; Bonomi, *Under the Cope of Heaven*; Heimert, *Religion and the American Mind*; Bridenbaugh, *Mitre and Sceptre*; Griffin, *Revolution and Religion*; Guyatt, *Providence and the Invention of the United States*, 95–172; Hatch, *The Sacred Cause of Liberty*; Miller, "From Covenant to the Revival"; Edmund S. Morgan, "The Puritan Ethic and the American Revolution," *William and Mary Quarterly*, 3rd ser., 24 (1967): 3–43; Royster, *A Revolutionary People at War*; and Kidd, *God of Liberty*.

Bernard Bailyn places too much emphasis on the influence of a secularized Whig ideology, but the essays and primary sources in "Religion and Revolution" support the above argument. See especially Bailyn's essay on Connecticut's Stephen Johnson and the latter's 1765 *New London Gazette* essays in "Religion and Revolution," 125–139, 144–169 and "Some Important Observations, Occasioned by, and Adapted to, the Publick Fast, Ordered by Authority, December 18th, A. D. 1765" (Newport, 1766).

25. Paul Johnson, *A History of the American People* (New York: HarperCollins, 1997), 133; *PRC*, 12: 422, 425. See generally Edmund S. Morgan and Helen M. Morgan, *The Stamp Act Crisis: Prologue to Revolution* (Chapel Hill: University of North Carolina Press, 1953). While firmly opposing the act, Sherman did not approve of the most radical proposals and actions for resisting Parliament. See Roger Sherman to Matthew Griswold, January 11, 1766, in Boardman, *Roger Sherman*, 91–92. G. A. Gilbert, "The Connecticut Loyalists," *American Historical Review*, 4 (January 1899): 276–279; Oscar Zeichner, "The Rehabilitation of Loyalists in Connecticut," *New England Quarterly*, 11 (June 1938): 308–309; Bushman, *From*

Puritan to Yankee, 281; Robert A. East, *Connecticut's Loyalists* (Chester: Pequot Press, 1974), 16.

26. Roger Sherman to William Samuel Johnson, June 25, 1768, in Collier, *Roger Sherman's Connecticut*, 70.

27. Quoted in Boutell, *Life of Roger Sherman*, 58–59.

28. Roger Sherman to Thomas Cushing, April 30, 1772, Society Collection, Historical Society of Pennsylvania.

29. Wilson, "Consideration on the Nature and Extent of the Legislative Authority of the British Parliament," in *Collected Works of James Wilson*, ed. Kermit L. Hall and Mark David Hall, 2 vols. (Indianapolis: Liberty Fund Press, 2007), 1: 3–31; John Adams, "Novanglus" essays, in *The Political Writings of John Adams*, ed. George A. Peek (New York: Macmillan, 1954), 26–79; Thomas Jefferson, "A Summary View of the Rights of British America," in *The Papers of Thomas Jefferson*, ed. Julian P. Boyd et al. (Princeton: Princeton University Press, 1950), 1: 121–137.

30. *Works of John Adams*, 2: 343.

31. *Minutes of the Convention of Delegates from the Synod of New York and Philadelphia and from the Associations of Connecticut; Held Annually from 1766 to 1775, Inclusive* (Harford: E. Gleasonm, 1843); Bridenbaugh, *Mitre and Sceptre*, 207–287, 256; Frohnen, *American Republic*, 110; Joseph J. Ellis, *The New England Mind in Transition: Samuel Johnson of Connecticut, 1696–1772* (New Haven: Yale University Press, 1973), 249; Roger Sherman to William Samuel Johnson, 1768, in Boutell, *The Life of Roger Sherman*, 65, 66. A letter virtually identical to the one in Boutell's volume was printed in *Minutes of the Convention Delegates*, 13–14. The editor notes that "it was annexed to the forgoing Minutes [of the General Association of Connecticut, and the Convention at Elizabethtown], in the hands of the Register of New Haven East Association." It is unclear if Sherman wrote this letter, or if he copied it.

The specter of Archbishop Laud served to remind Americans in this era of the dangers of religious tyranny. For instance, in 1764, the *Newport Mercury* reprinted the commission Charles I gave to Archbishop Laud giving him the power to revoke colonial charters. Middlekauff, *Glorious Cause*, 102; Bridenbaugh, *Mitre and Sceptre*, 235; Roth, *Connecticut's War Governor*, 29–30. For further discussion of the connection between the Stamp Act and ecclesiastical courts see Bell, *A War of Religion*, 215–218.

32. Bailyn, *Ideological Origins*, 95–96; Heimert, *Religion and the American Mind*, 351–352; Bridenbaugh, *Mitre and Sceptre*. William M. Hogue contends that Bridenbaugh overstates the interest Church of England leaders had in establishing an American episcopate and the impact the issue had on the American Revolution. See Hogue, "The Religious Conspiracy Theory of the American Revolution: Anglican Motive," *Church History*, 45 (1976): 277–292. Hogue is likely correct that the threat of an episcopate was never as serious as some

Americans thought, but the fact remains that in the minds of many Americans—particularly those who worshiped in Reformed churches—it was a clear and present danger. Although this issue alone would not have led to the War for Independence, it was seen by New England patriots as an important part of the pattern of tyrannical activity by Great Britain against the colonists.

33. Bridenbaugh, *Mitre and Sceptre*, 194 and passim. See also Bell, *A War of Religion*.

34. Noah Welles, "A Vindication of the Validity and Divine Right of Presbyterian Ordination as Set Forth in Dr. Chauncy's Sermon at the Dudleian Lecture; and Mr. Welle's Discourse upon the Same Subject in Answer to the Exceptions of Mr. Jeremiah Leaming, Contained in His Late Defense of the Episcopal Government of the Church" (New Haven: Samuel Green, 1767). See Bridenbaugh, *Mitre and Sceptre*, 308–311.

35. Welles in 1764 and Stiles in 1783. Noah Hobart preached the election day sermon in 1750, but this was before Sherman had been elected to the General Assembly.

36. John Adams to Jedediah Morse, December 2, 1815, in *Works of John Adams*, 10: 185; Bridenbaugh, *Mitre and Sceptre*, especially 256–259. John Ragosta argues persuasively that dissenters' fears that Great Britain would appoint a bishop if it defeated the patriots does much to explain why the British had such a difficult time recruiting them to fight for the Crown. John A. Ragosta, *Wellspring of Liberty: How Virginia's Religious Dissenters Helped Win the American Revolution & Secured Religious Liberty* (New York: Oxford University Press, 2010), esp. 71–86.

37. Roger Sherman, *Almanack* (1758), quoted in Paltsits, *Almanacs of Roger Sherman*, 14–15.

38. Kidd, *The Protestant Interest*, passim, and *God of Liberty*, esp. 67–74; Samuel Sherwood, "The Church's Flight into the Wilderness…" (1776), in Sandoz, *Political Sermons*, 1: 514; and Martin I. J. Griffin, ed., *Catholics and the American Revolution* (Rideley Park: self-published, 1907), 1: 1–40; 3: 384–392. The latter volume contains a host of excerpts from newspaper articles, pamphlets, and the *Journals of the Continental Congress* associating British tyranny with Roman Catholicism.

39. Six months later, when contemplating returning to Philadelphia with Sherman and Deane in the latter's "Leathern Coveniency," Dyer wrote that "we can Chatt, we can sing, we can dispute everything, Scold and make friends again every half hour, which will make the time pass away easily and ye road smoothly." Quoted in Willingham, *Connecticut Revolutionary: Eliphalet Dyer*, 23.

   Dyer's pastor as a young man was Thomas Clap, later the president of Yale who appointed Sherman to be treasurer of the college. Dyer was a Calvinist's Calvinist. See Willingham, *Connecticut Revolutionary*, passim. Deane, on the other hand, came from a Congregationalist background, but as Congress's agent to France was accused of profiteering. Recalled in 1777, he was unable to clear his name. He returned to Europe in 1781, where one of his main consolations was "escapes into drink and debauchery" until his death from illness, suicide, or poison in 1789. Sherman believed that Deane was guilty. Julian P. Boyd, "Silas Deane: Death by a Kindly Teacher of Treason?" *William and Mary Quarterly*, 3rd ser., 16 (1959): 165–187 (quote at 170), 319–342, 515–550; George L. Clark, *Silas Deane: A Connecticut Leader in the American Revolution* (New York: G. P. Putnam's Sons, 1913); Collier, *Roger Sherman's Connecticut*, 130–137.

40. *Works of John Adams*, 2: 370–377, 371.
41. Benjamin Kent to Samuel Adams, August 20, 1774, in *Life and Times of Joseph Warren*, ed. Richard Frothingham (Boston: Little, Brown, 1865), 342.
42. *Journals of the Continental Congress, 1774–1789*, ed. Worthington C. Ford et al. (Washington, DC: GPO, 1904–37), 1: 33–35 [hereinafter *JCC*].
43. *Works of John Adams*, 2: 16; Merrill Jensen, *The Articles of Confederation: An Interpretation of the Social-Constitutional History of the American Revolution, 1774–1781* (Madison: University of Wisconsin Press, 1940), 61–62. Jensen generally neglected the influence of religion, so it is telling that he highlights the significance of the Suffolk Resolves.
44. *JCC*, 1: 66, 67.
45. Ibid., 1: 68–70, 72.
46. Ibid., 1: 75–80; Collier, *Roger Sherman's Connecticut*, 100–101; Middlekauff, *Glorious Cause*, 238; Gideon Mailer, "Anglo-Scottish Union and John Witherspoon's American Revolution," 709.
47. *JCC*, 1: 83, 87–88. See also Congress's letter to the inhabitants of the colonies, ibid., 99.
48. On the decline of anti-Catholicism in the era, see Charles P. Hanson, *Necessary Virtue: The Pragmatic Origins of Religious Liberty in New England* (Charlottesville: University Press of Virginia, 1998).
49. Immediately following this paragraph he wrote: "These questions may serve for speculation but it is not likely they will need to be Resolved in our Day, and I hope not till the time comes when the Nations shall learn war no more [Isaiah 2:4]." Roger Sherman to William Samuel Johnson, December 5, 1766, William Samuel Johnson Papers, box 1, Connecticut Historical Society.
50. *JCC*, 2: 140–141.
51. Ibid., 2: 146, 150–155, 157. Of course these passages are general enough to be accepted by Christians in general, and Dickinson himself came from a Quaker background. Jane Calvert, "The Quaker Contributions of John Dickinson to the Creation of the American Republic," in Dreisbach and Hall, *Faith and the Founders of the American Republic*.
52. *JCC*, 5: 431, 433, 438.
53. John Adams, *Autobiography*, and John Adams to Timothy Pickering, August 6, 1822, both in *Works of John Adams*, 2: 512–514. Thomas Jefferson to James Madison, August 30, 1823, in *The Writings of Thomas Jefferson*, ed. Paul L. Ford (New York: G. P. Putnam's Sons, 1899), 10: 266–269.

54. Julian P. Boyd and Gerard W. Gawalt, eds., *The Declaration of Independence: The Evolution of the Text*, rev. ed. (Hanover: University Press of New England, 1999), 30.
55. Maier, *American Scripture*, 98 and generally 97–153.
56. Koch and Peden, *Life and Selected Writings of Thomas Jefferson*, 24.
57. Thomas Jefferson to Henry Lee, May 8, 1825, in ibid., 656–657; Zuckert, *Natural Rights Republic*, 76, 141. For a good discussion of different intellectual influences and how they could be mutually reinforcing, see Hans L. Eicholz, *Harmonizing Sentiments: The Declaration of Independence and the Jeffersonian Idea of Self-Government* (New York: Peter Lang, 2001).
58. See, for instance, Holmes, *Faiths of the Founding Fathers*, 47, 65; Fea, *Was America Founded as a Christian Nation?* 131–133, 136; Lambert, *Founding Fathers*, 163; Dershowitz, *Blasphemy*, 11–12; and Green, *Second Disestablishment*, 31–32, 53–54. Westminster Standards, 1: 10; 5: 1, 2, 6; 19: 5; 23: 1; 1: 1, 7; 5; 21: 5; *The Works of the Late Reverend and Learned Isaac Watts* (London, 1753), 4: 356; cf. *The Windham Herald*, April 15, 1797, 4. Such examples could be multiplied almost indefinitely. Jeffry H. Morrison, "Political Theology in the Declaration of Independence" (paper delivered at a conference on the Declaration of Independence, Princeton University, April 5–6, 2002). I am grateful to Daniel L. Dreisbach for pointing me to the language of the Standards.
59. *PRC*, 15: 414–415.
60. Collier, *Roger Sherman's Connecticut*, 125. One reason for the unanimity is that the relatively few Loyalists in the state had been effectively silenced by the General Assembly in 1775. *PRC*, 15: 192–195.
61. *PRC*, 15: 450–453. As a young man Trumbull prepared for the ministry and was licensed to preach, and in his retirement he returned to the study of Hebrew and wrote sermons. He was, according to Connecticut historian David M. Roth, a Puritan's Puritan. It is thus striking that Roth describes the proclamation's language as "Lockean" without even considering the possibility that it is better characterized as flowing from the Reformed political tradition. Roth, *Connecticut's Wartime Governor*, passim, 39. According to Bruce Stark, the proclamation was drafted by William Williams. See Stark, *Connecticut Signer*, 53. The final handwritten draft of the document is in the Jonathan Trumbull Sr. Papers, box 3, Connecticut Historical Society.
62. Edmund Burke, "On Moving His Resolutions for Conciliation with the Colonies," in Edmund Burke, *Conciliation with the Colonies*, ed. Cornelius Beach Bradley (Boston: Allyn and Bacon, 1895), 20; John Leach, "A Journal Kept by John Leach, During His Confinement by the British, in Boston Gaol, in 1775," *New England Historical and Genealogical Register*, 19 (1865): 256; Douglass Adair and John A. Schutz, eds., *Peter Oliver's Origin and Progress of the American Rebellion* (Stanford: Stanford University Press, 1961), 41; Johnson, *History of the American People*, 173; Johann Heinrichs to Herr H, January 18, 1778, in "Extracts from the Letter Book of Captain Johann Heinrichs of the

Hessian Jäger Corps," *Pennsylvania Magazine of History and Biography*, 22 (1898): 137; Clergy of New York, October 28, 1780, quoted in Patricia Bonomi, "'Hippocrates' Twins': Religion and Politics in the American Revolution," *History Teacher* 29, no. 2 (February 1996): 142; Baldwin, *New England Clergy*, 91. In his 1793 *The History of the American Revolution*, David Ramsey noted the "presbyterians and independents, were almost universally attached to the measures of Congress. Their religious societies are governed on the republican plan" (London, 1793), 2: 312–313. PRSC, 1: 3–4, 367–370.

CHAPTER 4

1. One reason scholars interested in political theory spend little time on the era is that the *Journals of the Continental Congress* record only the bare-bone decisions of the Congress, not the debates that preceded them. Although letters and diaries can flesh these out, the lack of recorded debates give theorists relatively little material with which to work.

2. Collier, *Roger Sherman's Connecticut*, 164, 173, 164; JCC, 14: 728–730; 16: 205–207.

3. PRSC, 1: 592–599; Collier, *Roger Sherman's Connecticut*, 350, note 47, 176; PRSC, 1: 606

4. PRSC, 1: 612. Sherman, Hillhouse (sometimes Hilhouse), Huntington, and Paine were by all accounts serious Calvinists, and Paine had even seriously considered entering the ministry. Peabody was a medical doctor who held a variety of offices in New Hampshire. Toward the end of his life he was confined to the "prison yard" in Exeter (roughly the town limits) because of indebtedness, and in his private diary he referred to the deity in terms not often used by Calvinists, including "the great Occult Primary." Richard Bartlett, *A Sketch of the Life and Public Service of the Hon. Nathaniel Peabody* (Concord: Jacob B. Moore, 1824), 13, 14.

5. Sherman Account Book, Sherman Papers, box 1, folder 4, Yale University, 60–61 [hereafter Sherman Account Book]; PRSC, 1: 613. The report printed in PRSC is virtually identical to Sherman's draft, although there are differences of capitalization and punctuation. I quote Sherman's draft but cite both sources.

6. Sherman does not attribute the lines to Pope, nor does he quote them verbatim. They include two of the last four lines in the poem, lines that famously sum up the poet's argument. They read:

    That reason, passion, answer one great aim;
    That true self-love and social are the same;
    That virtue only makes our bliss below;
    And all our knowledge is, ourselves to know.
    The Poetical Works of Alexander Pope (1733–34; reprint, Boston: Phillips, Sampson, 1819), 268.

7. German, "The Social Utility of Wicked Self-Love," 965–998, 970; Paltsits, *Almanacs*, 45; Peabody, *Correspondence between Roger Sherman and Samuel Hopkins*, 8, 24. Compare Sherman's views with those presented by Jonathan Edwards in *Two Dissertations: I. Concerning the End for Which God Created the World; II. The Nature of True Virtue* (Boston: S. Kneeland, 1765).

8. Sherman Account Book, 60, 62; *PRSC*, 1: 613, 614.

9. Sherman Account Book, 62; *PRSC*, 1: 614.

10. *PRSC*, 1: 521–528. Connecticut appointed any two of its delegates to Congress to attend a similar convention held in Philadelphia in January 1780. Sherman and Ellsworth represented the state, but no substantive work was accomplished. *PRSC*, 2: 572–579.

11. Christopher Collier suggests that some of Sherman's interest in this issue may have stemmed from his friends' investments in the Grants, although there is no evidence that he speculated in the region. Collier, *Roger Sherman's Connecticut*, 150–153; *JCC*, 8: 497; Sherman to Elisha Payne, October 31, 1778, Society Collection, Historical Society of Pennsylvania.

12. *JCC*, 21: 836–838; 27: 481–484. The report is in Sherman's handwriting. Farrand, *Records*, 2: 462–463. Collier, *All Politics Is Local*, 73–75.

13. Collier, *Roger Sherman's Connecticut*, 181–188; *JCC*, 26: 118–121, 248–279, 22–29.

14. John Sullivan to George Washington, July 2, 1781, in *Letters of the Members of the Continental Congress*, ed. Edmund C. Burnett (Washington, DC: Carnegie Institution, 1933), 6: 133.

15. *JCC*, 21: 1074–1076; Dreisbach and Hall, *Sacred Rights of Conscience*, 215–238; Morrison, *John Witherspoon*; John Montgomery Forster, *A Sketch of the Life of the Rev. Joseph Montgomery* (Harrisburg: Privately printed, 1879); Derek H. Davis, *Religion and the Continental Congress, 1774–1789: Contributions to Original Intent* (New York: Oxford University Press, 2000), 83–88. James Varnum seems to have come from a Congregationalist background, but his adult views and commitments are unclear. See A. C. Varnum, *History of the Pawtucket Church and Society* (Lowell: Morning Mail Press, 1888), 37–41; and Daniel Howland Green, *History of the Town of East Greenwich and Adjacent Territory: From 1677 to 1877* (Providence: J. A. and R. A. Reid, Printers, 1877), 174–176.

16. *JCC*, 11: 474–481. George Washington repeatedly referred to Micah 4:4 throughout his writings without citation. See Daniel L. Dreisbach, "The 'Vine and Fig Tree' in George Washington's Letters: Reflections on a Biblical Motif in the Literature of the American Founding Era," *Anglican and Episcopal History*, 76 (September 2007): 299–326.

17. *JCC*, 26: 145; 2: 185; 5: 530; 6: 887; 2: 112; 12: 1001–1003. The Continental Congress's *recommendation* that officers attend divine services was weaker than a similar law passed by Connecticut a month earlier which began: "That all officers and soldiers, not having just impediment, shall diligently frequent divine

service and sermon in the places appointed for the assembling the regiment, troop or company" *PRC*, 15: 22. Connecticut's Articles of War were patterned after those passed by Massachusetts in April. See *Journal of the Provincial Congress of Massachusetts* (April 5, 1775): 121.

18. *JCC*, 8: 734–735; 19: 91; 23: 573–574. See generally Davis, *Religion and the Continental Congress, 1774–1789*, 25–198; and Ann Fairfax Withington, *Toward a More Perfect Union: Virtue and the Formation of America Republics* (New York: Oxford University Press, 1991).

19. *JCC*, 4: 159, 216. Worthington Ford, editor of these volumes, usually noted who penned particular documents, but there is no notation for this text.

20. A major exception to this generalization is the historian Merrill Jensen's 1940 book, *The Articles of Confederation*, which provides an excellent overview of the creation and ratification of the document. Jensen takes the ideological motivations of those involved with this endeavor seriously, although his insistence on forcing founders into his neoprogressive categories of "conservatives" and "radicals" lacks nuance. Jack Rakove raises questions about Jensen's conceptual categories in *The Beginnings of National Politics: An Interpretive History of the Continental Congress* (Baltimore: Johns Hopkins University Press, 1979), esp. xiv–xvii, 135–136. See also Calvin C. Jillson and Rick K. Wilson, *Congressional Dynamics: Structure, Coordination, and Choice in the First American Congress, 1774–1789* (Stanford: Stanford University Press, 1994); Robert W. Hoffert, *A Politics of Tensions: The Articles of Confederation and American Political Ideas* (Niwot: University Press of Colorado, 1992); and Richard B. Morris, *The Forging of the Union: 1781–1789* (New York: Harper and Row, 1987).

21. *JCC*, 5: 431, 433, 438.

22. Jensen, *Articles*, 250.

23. Josiah Bartlett to John Langdon, June 17, 1776, in *Letters of the Members of the Continental Congress*, 4: 256.

24. *JCC*, 5: 547, 552, 553.

25. *Works of John Adams*, 2: 499, 550.

26. Jensen, *Articles*, 141; *Works of John Adams*, 2: 499.

27. Jensen, *Articles*, 161–238. Sherman signed the Articles July 9, 1778, along with delegates from the states that had agreed to ratify it. Representatives from New York and Georgia were not present at the time; Maryland, Delaware, and New Jersey had not yet agreed to ratify the document.

28. A Citizen of Philadelphia [Pelatiah Webster], "A Dissertation on the Political Union and Constitution of the Thirteen United States, of North-America" (1783; reprint, Hartford: Hudson and Goodwin, 1783); Hannis Taylor, "The Designer of the Constitution of the United States," *North American Review*, 99 (August 1907): 813–824; Taylor, "Pelatiah Webster: The Architect of Our Federal Constitution," *Yale Law Journal*, 27 (December 1907): 73; Taylor, *The Origin and Growth of the American Constitution: An Historical Treatise* (Boston: Houghton

Mifflin, 1911). Webster wrote one of the first essays defending the Constitution, "Remarks on the Address of Sixteen Members of the Assembly of Pennsylvania," which was published on October 12, 1787 (Philadelphia: Eleazer Oswald at the Coffee House, 1787). A revised version of the essay is reprinted in Taylor, *Origin and Growth of the American Constitution*, 603–609. Edward S. Corwin, "The Pelatiah Webster Myth," *Michigan Law Review*, 10 (June 1912): 619–626.

29. Webster, "Dissertation," 3–30.

30. Ibid., 22, 23, 26, 11, 16; Taylor, *Origin and Growth of the American Constitution*, 153–154. Edward Corwin demolished Taylor's claims about Webster's contributions to the creation of the federal judiciary in "The Pelatiah Webster Myth," 622–626.

31. The full title is "Remarks on a Pamphlet Entitled 'A Dissertation on the political Union and Constitution of the Thirteen United States of North America by a Citizen of Philadelphia' With some brief OBSERVATIONS, Whether all the Western Lands, not actually purchased or conquered by the Crown of GREAT BRITAIN, antecedent to the late Cession, made to the Thirteen Unites States of NORTH-AMERICA, ought not to be considered as ceded to the Thirteen States *jointly*—And whether all the confiscated Estates of those People, by some termed *Loyalists*, are to be considered as forfeited to the States in which they were resident, or to all the States included in the Confederation" (New Haven: T. S. Green, 1784). On Sherman's authorship see Joseph Sabin, *A Dictionary of Books Relating to America* (New York: Sabin, 1891), 461; and Charles Evans, *American Bibliography* (New York: Columbia Press, 1890), 6: 326.

32. Sherman, "Remarks," ix, 18–20.

33. Ibid., 15–22, vi, 38.

34. Roger Sherman to John Franklin, February 21, 1784, in *Susquehannah Company Papers*, 7: 364–365; Pelatiah Webster to Roger Sherman, April 20, 1784, in Ibid., 7: 392–393; Sabin, *A Dictionary*, 461.

35. Sherman, "Remarks," 13–14, ix, 38; cf. Webster, "A Dissertation," 5.

36. *PRSC*, 3: 21–23, 29–31. Like other states, Connecticut also passed acts aimed at restraining or punishing Loyalists. See, for instance, "An Act for Assessing Certain Inimical Persons," ibid., 3: 234–235.

37. Collier, *Roger Sherman's Connecticut*, 169. Connecticut complied with 77% of Congress's requests for soldiers between 1777 and 1783, more than any other state and significantly more than the 54% total compliance rate. Keith L. Dougherty, *Collective Action under the Articles of Confederation* (Cambridge: Cambridge University Press, 2001), 89. See also Chester Destler, *Connecticut: The Provisions State* (Chester: Pequot Press, 1973).

38. *PRSC*, 1: 253–254; 2: 18, 287; 4: 1782.

39. *PRSC*, 5: 122, 281; Roger Sherman to Richard Law, July 25, 1783, Roger Sherman Papers, Connecticut Historical Society. Sherman and Law's draft, with alterations by the Assembly, was bound and is available in the Connecticut State

Library. The final version of the code was printed in 1784 and is reprinted in Cushing, *First Laws.*

40. *Acts and Laws of His Majesty's English Colony of Connecticut, in New England, in America* (New London: Timothy Green, 1969), 1.

41. Draft Code, 1–2; Cushingo; *First Laws,* 1–2; Frohnen, *American Republic,* 15–16; *PRC,* 1: 509. For further discussion see Collier, "The Connecticut Declaration of Rights Before the Constitution of 1818," 87–98.

42. For instance, Bernard Schwartz refers to this text as Connecticut's "Declaration of Rights" and states that it was enacted in 1776. He acknowledges that many scholars do not consider it to be a "bill of rights," but insists that "[b]rief though it was, it does deserve a place in the catalogue of Bills of Rights of the period. There were thus nine state Bills of Rights during the Revolutionary period—not eight (as virtually all commentators tell us)." *The Bill of Rights: A Documentary History* (New York: Chelsea House Publishers, 1971), 1: 289. On the other hand, Robert Allen Rutland did not consider Connecticut to have a "declaration of rights." *The Birth of the Bill of Rights, 1776–1791* (1955; reprint, New York: Collier-Macmillan, 1962), 81, 104.

   Benjamin Perley Poore identified this law as having been adopted in 1776 in *The Federal and State Constitutions, Colonial Charters and Other Organic Laws of the United States* (Washington, DC: GPO, 1877), 1: 257–258. Other scholars and editors had made this mistake earlier, e.g., E. Fitch Smith *Commentaries on Statute and Constitutional Law* (Albany: Gould, Banks, and Gould, 1848), 99. However, most authors and editors who contend that Connecticut adopted a bill of rights in 1776 cite Poore's volume as their source.

43. Draft Code, 1–2; Cushing, *First Laws,* 2.

44. Draft Code, 1; Cushing, *First Laws,* 1; Collier, *Roger Sherman's Connecticut,* 195.

45. Draft Code, 100–101, 45–50, 100; *PRSC,* 5: 323–324. As a result of a campaign spearheaded by Connecticut's Noah Webster, Connecticut passed the first copyright law in the nation. Sherman was serving as an assistant at the time, and in 1790, he was on one of the congressional committees that helped craft the first national copyright law. Although votes were not recorded for either measure, there is no reason to doubt that he supported the statutes. The Connecticut copyright act had tremendous influence on subsequent state and national acts. *PRSC,* 5: 13–15; Cushing, *First Laws,* 133–134; *Documentary History of the First Federal Congress, 1789–1791,* ed. Linda Grant De Pauw et al. (Baltimore: Johns Hopkins University Press, 1972-?), 3: 283 [Hereafter *DHFFC*]; Bruce W. Bugbee, *Genesis of American Patent and Copyright Law* (Washington, DC: Public Affairs Press, 1967), 106–148.

   Noah Webster (1758–1843) of Hartford, Connecticut, is best known for his dictionary, but he also wrote political works influenced by the Reformed political tradition (although his theological views prior to his 1808 conversion experience leaned in the direction of deism). See, for example, Webster,

The Revolution in France, Considered in Respect to its Progress and Effects (New York: George Bunce, 1794), which was printed and published according to an act of Congress.

46. Draft Code, 369; Cushing, *First Laws*, 233–235; Sherman, "Remarks," 41, 16–17; Kidd, *God of Liberty*, 134. Constitutions, statutes, or judicial decisions were made in every state north of Maryland that provided for immediate or graduate emancipation: Vermont (1777), Massachusetts (1780), Pennsylvania (1780), New Hampshire (1783), Rhode Island (1784), New Jersey (1799), and New Jersey (1804). David Menschel, "Abolition Without Deliverance: The Law of Connecticut Slavery, 1784–1848," *Yale Law Journal*, III (October 2001): 184–185. See generally, Arthur Zilversmit, *The First Emancipation: The Abolition of Slavery in the North* (Chicago: University of Chicago Press, 1967); and Joanne Pope Melish, *Disowning Slavery: Graduate Emancipation and "race" in New England*, 1780–1860 (Ithaca: Cornell University Press, 1998).

47. *PRC*, 14: 329. Sherman may not have returned from serving in the Continental Congress when the act was debated and passed. However, the *PRC* does list him as being "present" at the October 13–November 4 session, with an editor's note that the Continental Congress adjourned on October 26. The General Assembly did occasionally approve petitions to allow masters to return slaves they already owned to the state. See, for example, *PRSC*, 5: 46; 2: 427–428, 402.

48. Ibid., 4: 375–376; 1: 415–416.

49. Menshal, "Abolition Without Deliverance," 190; *PRSC*, 6: 472–473; 7: 71.

50. *Arabas v. Ivers*, 1 Root 92 (1784), 92–93; Menschel, "Abolition Without Deliverance," 200–201. The assumption that Arabas was freed simply because of his service is widely repeated by authors who discuss his case. See, for instance, Ray Raphael, *A People's History of the American Revolution* (New York: Harper Perennial, 2002), 360 and David O. White, *Connecticut's Black Soldiers: 1775–1783* (Chester: Pequot Press, 1973), 21.

51. *Connecticut Superior Court Records*, Connecticut State Library, 24: 7, 11–12. In the original manuscript "Arabas" appears as "Arabass," and in his company's rolls it is spelled "Arabus." *Collections of the Connecticut Historical Society* (Hartford: Connecticut Historical Society, 1909), 12: 338, 58.

52. *JCC*, 4: 60; Benjamin Quarles, *The Negro in the American Revolution* (Chapel Hill: University of North Carolina Press, 1961), 15–18, 51–67, 182–185; B. C. Steiner, *History of Slavery in Connecticut* (Baltimore: Johns Hopkins Press, 1893), 24–38; White, *Connecticut's Black Soldiers*, esp. 20–29; Gary B. Nash, *The Forgotten Fifth: African Americans in the Age of Revolution* (Cambridge: Harvard University Press, 2006).

Sherman was also on the Superior Court when it determined in 1773 that a slave was properly manumitted because his owner concluded that the slave was a Christian and that slavery unlawful. *Superior Court Diary of William Samuel Johnson*, 172, 182–193, 209–210.

53. Kirby reports the case as *Wilson [sic] v. Hinkley*, 1 Kirby 199 (1787). He notes that the opinion was by "the whole Court," without mentioning specific justices. The manuscript of the opinion in the Connecticut State Library lists the case as *Hinkley v. Willson* and contains the signatures of the five judges. On the Pitkins, see Bruce Colin Daniels, *Connecticut's First Family: William Pitkin and His Connections* (Chester: Pequot Press, 1975).

54. Farrand, *Records*, 2: 220, 374; Collier, *Roger Sherman's Connecticut*, 271–272; *DHFFC*, 6: 1559–1563. The Northwest Ordinance passed unanimously in the Confederation Congress in 1787, and it was reauthorized with minor changes but without a recorded vote. Assuming that Sherman voted in favor of this important piece of legislation, he had a hand in crafting and approving all four of America's major organic laws.

55. *PRC*, 1: 303; 4: 546; 5: 50, 87, 130.

56. Ibid., 7: 106–107, 237, 257.

57. Ibid., 8: 454–457; 13: 360.

58. *Connecticut Archives: Ecclesiastical Affairs*, series 1, 10: 66a–67; *PRSC*, 1: 232–233. For further discussion of church-state relations in Connecticut between 1636 and 1784, see Sheldon Samuel Cohen, *The Connecticut Colony Government and the Polity of the Congregational Churches, 1708–1760* (PhD diss., New York University, 1963); Greene, *The Development of Religious Liberty in Connecticut*; and Bushman, *From Puritan to Yankee*, 147–288. However, Bushman overemphasizes the extent to which "the Separates advocated that the civil authority abandon all interest in religion," 228.

59. Draft Code, 34–35; Cushing, *First Laws*, 20–21, 235–237; Greene, *The Development of Religious Liberty in Connecticut*, 338–341; McLoughlin, *New England Dissent*, 2: 923–924. The statute regulating societies fell into Richard Law's revisions, but Sherman drafted a significant portion of it. Roger Sherman to Richard Law, July 25, 1783, Roger Sherman Papers, Connecticut Historical Society.

60. Draft Code, 34; Cushing, *First Laws*, 21. The opening sentence is similar to Article III of the Massachusetts Constitution of 1780. Francis Newton Thorpe, *The Federal and State Constitutions* (Washington, DC: GPO, 1909), 3: 1889.

61. Specifically, the syllogism refers to the connection between virtue and morality, republican institutions, and religion—and by religion the founders meant some version of Christianity. See James H. Hutson, *Religion and the Founding of the American Republic* (Washington: Library of Congress, 1998), 81; Hutson, *Forgotten Features*, 1–44.

62. Roger Sherman to Simeon Baldwin, November 26, 1791, Roger Sherman Collection, box 1, folder 14, Yale University.

63. Cushing, *First Laws*, 213–214, 21–22, 157–160, 235–237, 258–259, 182–187, 196–197, 101, 8, 41, 43, 87, 89, 97, 67; Isaac Backus "An Appeal to the Public For Religious Liberty," (1773) in Sandoz, *Political Sermons*, 1: 329–368; John Leland, "The Rights of Conscience Inalienable," (1791) in Dreisbach and Hall, *Sacred Rights of Conscience*, 335–344; William G. McLoughlin, ed., *Isaac Backus on Church, State, and Calvinism: Pamphlets, 1754–1789* (Cambridge: Harvard University Press, 1968).

     A 1777 statute allowed Quakers to "affirm" rather than swear oaths. When Sherman revised "An Act for Enjoyning an Oath of Fidelity to This State," he suggested permitting "Quakers, and others who conscientiously scruple the lawfulness of taking an Oath in any case, to take an affirmation of the same." When the General Assembly revised his proposal, it limited the exemption to Quakers. Draft Code, 112.

64. Cushing, *First Laws*, 213–214, 22; Draft Code, 35; "Secret Committee Minutes," February 5, 1776, in *Letters of the Delegates to Congress*, 3: 205. In spite of Sherman's objection, Congress agreed to employ the Papist "Dohicky Arundel." Arundel was killed in action on July 8, 1776, by an exploding cannon. Griffin, *Catholics and the American Revolution*, 1: 240.

65. *JCC*, 4: 159, 216; Stiles, *Literary Diary*, 2: 297–298. Years later, Sherman's concern for French Roman Catholics is evident when he wrote to William Ellery on June 29, 1790 that: "I hope France will not be involved in a war. before they have Settled a free & effective Government. I think it will be an important event to the European Nations in general, as well as to us. These States, I hope will enjoy peace, until the time when the Nations Shall learn war no more [Isaiah 2:4, Micah 4:3]." *DHFFC* 19: 1961–1962.

66. Cushing, *First Laws*, 182, 213–214. According to Christopher Collier, there "were only a handful of Catholics in late-18th century Connecticut and a half-dozen Jews." Collier, "Common Law and Individual Rights in Connecticut," 44. Even a theologically liberal Zephaniah Swift believed that "where the people in general acknowledge the truth of a particular religion, and the duty of public worship, the legislature may step in to their aid, and enact laws that are necessary to enable them to support public worship in a manner agreeable to their consciences." Swift, *A System of Laws for the State of Connecticut* (Windham: John Byrne, 1795), 1: 144. On Swift see Donald F. Gerardi, "Zephaniah Swift and Connecticut's Standing Order: Skepticism, Conservativism, and Religious Liberty in the Early Republic," *New England Quarterly*, 67 (June 1994): 234–256.

     It is noteworthy that Sherman's views on religious liberty and church-state relations are similar to those contained in Ezra Stiles's famous 1783 election sermon, which was preached the same year Sherman wrote his religious liberty statute. Sherman and Henry Daggett were charged by the Assembly to "return the Thanks of this assembly for his Sermon." See Stiles, "The

United States Elevated" (New Haven: Thomas and Samuel Green, 1783), esp. 53–71; *Connecticut Archives: Ecclesiastical Affairs*, series I, 15: 389.

67. *PRSC*, 7: 256.

68. (New London, 1791); reprinted Dreisbach and Hall, *Sacred Rights of Conscience*, 335–344.

69. *PRSC*, 7: 311–313. Connecticut retained its system of multiple establishments until 1819. An excellent account of church-state relations in the state between 1791–1818 may be found in McLoughlin, *New England Dissent*, 915–1062.

70. *Connecticut Superior Court Records*, Connecticut State Library, 24: 11–12.

CHAPTER 5

1. Unidentified author, "Constitutional Convention, 1787," *Historical Magazine*, 5 (January 1861): 19.

2. I make no attempt to provide a comprehensive account of the Convention and ratification debates or even Sherman's contributions in them. Excellent works on the Convention include Richard Beeman, *Plain, Honest Men: The Making of the Constitution* (New York: Random House, 2009); Clinton Rossiter, *1787: The Grand Convention* (1966; reprint, New York: W. W. Norton, 1987); and Rakove, *Original Meanings*. Christopher Collier downplays the significance of ideas and believes Sherman was duped by the nationalists, an assessment with which I disagree. Nevertheless, his *All Politics Is Local* is required reading for anyone interested in Connecticut's contributions to the creation and ratification of the Constitution.

   My treatment of the Federal Convention relies heavily on Farrand's *Records*, but of course this is not an ideal source as Madison, Yates, and others offer only a selective account of the delegates' arguments. Moreover, Madison, the main source of notes on the convention, has been accused of altering his notes for political purposes. For the purposes of readability, I treat speeches recorded in Farrand as being the delegates' actual speeches—i.e., instead of writing "Madison recorded Sherman as saying" I write "Sherman said." James H. Hutson, ed., *Supplement to Max Farrand's The Records of the Federal Convention of 1787* (New Haven: Yale University Press, 1987), xx–xxxi.

3. Rakove, *Original Meanings*, 92.

4. Collier, *All Politics Is Local*, 163, 12. Richard Dunn contends that although the Connecticut Assembly altered that anti-Quaker law, it refused to recognize that the law had been disallowed. Dunn, *Puritans and Yankees*, 349.

5. Wolcott, who had never been exposed to small pox, made a wise choice. Oliver Ellsworth's servant apparently contracted the disease in Philadelphia during the Convention. Hutson, *Supplement*, 3, 4; Collier, *Roger Sherman's Connecticut*, 228; *PRSC*, 6: 292–293.

6. Farrand, *Records*, 1: 20–23.

7. Rakove, *Original Intentions*, 50–51; *Federalists*, 10 and 51, in *The Federalist Papers*, ed. Clinton Rossiter (New York: Mentor, 1961); Hall, *Political and Legal Philosophy of James Wilson*. Madison, Hamilton, and Wilson were all educated, at least in part, by Reformed teachers. Madison was a life-long Anglican, and Hamilton and Wilson eventually joined this denomination. Garrett Ward Sheldon, "Religion and Politics in the Thought of James Madison," and Mark David Hall, "James Wilson: Presbyterian, Anglican, Thomist, or Deist? Does it Matter?" in Dreisbach, Hall, and Morrison, *Founders on God and Government*, 83–116, 181–206; Gregg Frazer, Alexander Hamilton, Theistic Rationalist," in Dreisbach, Hall, and Morrison, *Forgotten Founders on Religion and Public Life*, 101–124.

8. Farrand, *Records*, 3: 33–34.

9. Ibid., 1: 48–50, 53–54. Sherman also wanted state legislatures to pay national representatives to increase their accountability to the states. Ibid., 1: 373.

10. Ibid., 1: 133, 134.

11. Ibid., 1: 48. For examples of scholars who use Sherman's statement to portray the founders as undemocratic, see Charles A. Beard, *An Economic Interpretation of the Constitution* (1913; reprint, New York: Free Press, 1965), 214; Marci A. Hamilton, "The Calvinist Paradox of Distrust and Hope at the Constitutional Convention," in *Christian Perspectives on Legal Thought*, ed. Michael W. McConnell, Robert F. Cochran, Angela C. Carmella, and Harold Joseph Berman (New Haven: Yale University Press, 2001), 300; Gary J. Kornblith and John M. Murrin, "The Dilemma of Ruling Elites in Revolutionary America," in *Ruling America: A History of Wealth and Power*, ed. Steve Fraser and Gary Gerstele (Cambridge: Harvard University Press, 2005), 40; and Ray Raphael, *Founders: The People Who Brought You a Nation* (New York: New Press, 2009), 455–456.

12. Farrand, *Records*, 1: 49, 132–133; *Works of John Adams*, 6: 440.

13. Farrand, *Records*, 1: 347–348. By "experimental ground," Sherman meant what would today be called "experience." Cf. John Dickinson's comment on August 13, "Experience must be our only guide. Reason may mislead us." Ibid., 2: 278.

14. Ibid., 1: 136–137, 150.

15. Ibid., 1: 196, 201–202; 3: 615; 1: 242–245, 450.

16. Ibid., 2: 6–7; 1: 511, 516, 526; 2: 3.

17. In terms of geography, only two states were smaller than Connecticut in 1790, so Sherman may also have been looking toward the future when the state would have a smaller percentage of the nation's population. Collier, *All Politics Is Local*, 179.

18. Farrand, *Records*, 2: 5, 13–15.

19. Ibid., 2: 27. Almost a month later, Pinckney proposed that the legislature should be able to negate state laws with a two-thirds vote of each house. The proposal was supported by Madison and Wilson (who called it a "key-stone wanting to compleat the wide arch of Government we are raising"), but opposed by Sherman as being "unnecessary; the laws of the General Government being Supreme &

paramount to the State laws according to the plan, as it now stands." The proposal failed 5–6. Farrand, *Records*, 2: 390.

20. Sherman virtually always favored states' rights, but his hatred of paper money
overrode this commitment as seen by his support for what became Article 1,
Section 10's prohibition on states issuing bills of credit. Ibid., 2: 439.

21. Ibid., 1: 133; 2: 25–26. Jack Rakove suggests that the "proposals Sherman presented on July 17 are almost certainly those which Farrand reprinted in
Appendix E of the *Records*, III, 615–616. It is puzzling that Farrand failed to
identify this document with Sherman's motion, but linked it instead with the
preparation of the New Jersey Plan." Rakove, *Original Intentions*, 380.

22. Farrand, *Records*, 2: 25–26, 106, 181–183. Ellsworth's letter is quoted in Rakove,
Original Intentions, 83. William Samuel Johnson records in his diary that he and
Sherman left Philadelphia on July 20. William Samuel Johnson, Letterbooks &
Diaries, William Samuel Johnson Papers, Connecticut Historical Society.
Sherman was back in Philadelphia by August 5, as indicated by a letter from
Jedidiah Morse to Simeon Baldwin, noting that he had called upon Simeon's
father-in-law in Philadelphia and had received "such *Data* as left me to con-
clude that you are at present very happy." *Life and Letters of Simeon Baldwin*,
264–265.

   In the final days of the Convention, Sherman caught Gouverneur Morris's
attempt to replace the comma at the end of the following line with a semi-
colon: "To lay and collect taxes, duties, imposts and excises," in penultimate
draft of Article I, Section 8. Doing so would have turned the phrase "to pay the
debts and provide for the common defence and general welfare of the United
States" into a virtually unlimited grant of power. The comma was retained.
Farrand, *Records*, 3: 379, 483–494; Forrest McDonald, *E Pluribus Unum: The
Formation of the American Republic, 1776–1790* (Boston: Houghton Mifflin,
1965), 187.

23. Farrand, *Records*, 2: 344–345; cf. the debate on defining treason, 2: 345–350.
Notably, justices have allowed Congress to use the necessary and proper
clause in conjunction with the commerce clause to significantly expand its
power. See, for instance, *McCulloch v. Maryland*, 17 U.S. 316 (1819); *United
States v. Darby Lumber*, 312 U.S. 100 (1941); and *Wickard v. Filburn*, 317 U.S.
111 (1942).

24. Farrand, *Records*, 2: 629, 650–651.

25. Ibid, 1: 65, 68; cf. 1: 85.

26. Ibid., 1: 97.

27. Ibid., 1: 98–99; 2: 300, 103, 587.

28. Ibid., 2: 29–32.

29. Ibid., 2: 33–34, 57–59, 497–499, 522–529; cf. 1: 98.

30. Ibid., 2: 405, 318, 419, 426–427.

31. Ibid., 1: 578, 214, 218, 423.

32. See, for instance, *United States v. Curtiss-Wright Export Corp.*, 299 U.S. 304 (1936); and John Yoo, *The Powers of War and Peace: The Constitution and Foreign Affairs After 9/11* (Chicago: University of Chicago Press, 2006).

33. Farrand, *Records*, 1: 124–125 (emphasis added); 2: 46.

34. Ibid., 1: 232–233.

35. Ibid., 2: 41–46.

36. *Symsbury Case*, 1 Kirby 444 (1785); Farrand, *Records*, 2: 27, 28. "Sysmbury Case," *Connecticut Supreme Court Historical Society*, 1 (2006): 27–48; Wesley W. Horton, *The History of the Connecticut Supreme Court* (Thomson West, 2008), 17. On judicial review prior to *Marbury*, see Charles Grove Haines, *The American Doctrine of Judicial Supremacy* (New York: MacMillan, 1914), 63–121. William Winslow Crosskey and William Jeffrey deny that *Symsbury* is properly categorized as a case of judicial review because the General Assembly could have overturned the Superior Court decision. See Crosskey and Jeffrey, *Politics and the Constitution in the History of the United States* (Chicago: University of Chicago Press, 1980), 3: 961. With the exception of James Iredell, every justice prior to John Marshall believed the Supreme Court could declare an act of Congress void if it violated natural law. See Scott Douglas Gerber, ed. *Seriatim: The Supreme Court Before John Marshall* (New York: New York University Press, 1998).

37. Farrand, *Records*, 1: 21, 97–98, 138–140; 2: 73–80, 298–300.

38. Ibid., 2: 431–432, 551.

39. Ibid., 2: 220, 221; 1: 201, 586–587; 2: 220–221, 374, 416–417.

40. Richard Barry, *Mr. Rutledge of South Carolina* (New York: Duell, Sloan and Pearce, 1942), 332. According to Barry, before dinner "[t]he southern Episcopalian asked the northern Congregationalist to say grace. Roger Sherman bowed his head and prayed for ten minutes" (ibid.). McDonald, *E Pluribus Unum*, 176–178, 298–299.

41. Barry's work does not contain footnotes, but it has a section on "Notes and Sources," where he commented that the *Massachusetts Centinel* noted the dinner Rutledge gave Sherman (Barry, *Mr. Rutledge*, 397). Christopher Collier suggests Barry's account may have been based on Rutledge's diary, to which Barry apparently had access. However, the whereabouts of the diary are currently unknown. Collier, *Roger Sherman's Connecticut*, 259. A reviewer of the book noted that "Mr. Barry [is] a former newsman, a novelist and playwright," which may help explain the author's cavalier use of evidence and the book's lack of citations. W. Neil Franklin, review of *Mr. Rutledge of South Carolina*, in *Journal of Southern History*, 9 (May 1943): 264. See also James H. Hutson, "Riddles of the Federal Convention," *William and Mary Quarterly*, 3rd ser., 44 (July 1987): 415–418.

42. Farrand, *Records*, 2: 375, 400, 415–419, 449–453. Christopher Collier writes that South Carolina and Connecticut shared an interest in prohibiting Congress from taxing imports, and he provides a useful reminder that Connecticut had virtually no commercial interest in the slave trade. He concludes

that Sherman and Rutledge "probably" helped craft the compromises on the slave trade and navigation acts. Collier, *All Politics Is Local*, 63–73. Richard Beeman agrees that a bargain was struck, but he does not identify Sherman and Rutledge as its authors, *Plain, Honest Men*, 325–329. David O. Stewart argues that Rutledge agreed to support proportional representation in exchange for Wilson agreeing to support the three-fifths compromise. He also suggests that delegates from South Carolina agreed to give up the two-third requirement for navigation acts if "Sherman and the New Englanders" supported the fugitive slave clause. Stewart, *The Summer of 1787* (New York: Simon and Schuster, 2007), 59–85, 203.

43. Farrand, *Records*, 2: 364.
44. Ibid., 2: 369–370, 416–417.
45. Zilversmit, *The First Emancipation*, passim.
46. Farrand, *Records*, 2: 219, 364, 370, 417, 372. Much has been written on the extent to which critics of slavery were hypocritical. George Mason, for instance, owned more than three hundred slaves whom he did not free, and he gave speeches in the Virginia ratification convention threatening his fellow slave owners with the possibility that the national government might interfere with the institution. Luther Martin was appointed "Honorary-Counselor" of the Maryland Society for promoting the Abolition of Slavery, and the Relief of Free Negroes and others unlawfully held in Bondage, which was established on September 8, 1789. The society's charter justifies opposing slavery in part because the "common Father of mankind created all men free and equal; and his great command is, that we love our neighbor as ourselves." However, Martin continued to own slaves, and he represented both African Americans asserting their claims of freedom and slave owners. Although John Dickinson manumitted forty-seven slaves in 1777, he indentured them for twenty-one years of additional service. Yet some founders simply freed their slaves, and only twenty-five of the fifty-five delegates to the Federal Convention owned slaves in 1787. Beeman, *Plain, Honest Men*, 308–336; Bill Kauffman, *Forgotten Founder, Drunken Prophet: The Life of Luther Martin* (Wilmington: ISI Books, 2008), 92–93; Gary B. Nash and Jean R. Soderlund, *Freedom by Degrees: Emancipation in Pennsylvania and Its Aftermath* (New York: Oxford University Press, 1991), 145–146.
47. Hall, *Political Philosophy of James Wilson*, 59–60. Wilson and Sherman were the only delegates to object to an early version of the fugitive slave clause. They temporarily succeeded in defeating the provision, but Convention delegates later agreed "nem. con." to a version of the clause that did not contain the word "slave." Farrand, *Records*, 2: 443, 453–454. See also Thomas G. West, *Vindicating the Founders: Race, Sex, Class, and Justice in the Origins of America* (Lanham: Rowman and Littlefield, 1997), 1–36.

Richard Beeman points out that William Few, William Pierce, and William Blount took a break from the Federal Convention to attend the Confederation

Congress, which was then meeting in New York City. Their visit provided a quorum that allowed the body to pass the Northwest Ordinance. Blount returned to Philadelphia on August 7, Few returned to sign the Constitution, but Pierce never returned. Madison's former personal secretary Edward Coles wrote in 1856 that James Madison told him that members of Congress and the Convention communicated with each other during the summer over the issue of slavery. The Ordinance is mentioned twice in Convention documents and debates dated after July 26. Beeman, *Plain, Honest Men*, 215–218; Hutson, *Supplement*, 321; Farrand, *Records* 2: 148, 439. For an entertaining and provocative account of this compromise see Stewart, *The Summer of 1787*, 137–149.

48. Farrand, *Records*, 1: 452–453. Franklin wrote a note on his speech stating, "The Convention, except three or four persons, thought Prayers unnecessary." Ibid., 452. Given the background and regular practices of most delegates, it seems more likely that they were convinced by Hamilton's arguments.

49. For example, Peter Marshall and David Manuel, *From Sea to Shining Sea* (Grand Rapids: Felming H. Revell, 1986), 18–20.

50. For example, Kramnick and Moore, *The Godless Constitution*, 34; Morton Keller, *America's Three Regimes: A New Political History* (New York: Oxford University Press, 2007), 40.

51. See, for instance, the founders profiled in Dreisbach, Hall, and Morrison, *The Forgotten Founders on Religion and Public Life*; Dreisbach, Hall, and Morrison, *The Founders on God and Government*; and Dreisbach and Hall, *Faith and the Founders of the American Republic*. See also texts authored or approved by Convention participants in Dreisbach and Hall, *The Sacred Rights of Conscience*, 215–620. These sources do not *prove* my assertion with respect to every delegate at the Convention, but they help create a strong prima facie case. After he left public life, Madison concluded that congressional chaplains and presidential calls for prayer were unconstitutional. See Madison, "Detached Memoranda," in Dreisbach and Hall, *Sacred Rights of Conscience*, 589–593.

52. Farrand, *Records*, 2: 181, 302; 1: 20; 2: 185. The three oath provisions are in Article I, Section 3; Article II, Section 1; and Article VI. Sherman objected to the Virginia Plan's oath provision on the grounds that it "unnecessarily intrud[ed] into the State jurisdictions." Farrand, *Records*, 1: 203. See also ibid., 2: 87–88.

The first appearance of an exemption is found in James Wilson's Committee of Detail draft of what became the Article II oath. His draft of Article VI did not contain an exemption, perhaps because the former spells out the oath whereas the latter does not. Delegates agreed to add an exemption to the Article VI exemption on August 30. The exemption from the oath requirement for what became Article I, Section 3 was added sometime between the draft presented by the Committee of

Style on September 12 and the engrossed version approved on September 17. Ibid., 2: 172, 468, 592, 610, 653.

53. Ibid., 2: 468.

54. Charles R. King, ed., *The Life and Correspondence of Rufus King* (New York: G. P. Putnam's Sons, 1894), 1: 420. Sherman must have been chagrined that his protégé Ellsworth voted for Morris.

    In 1766, Sherman, as a justice of the peace, issued an arrest warrant for Benjamin Arnold for inciting a riot. Roger Sherman Collection, box 1, folder 5, Yale University; Collier, *Roger Sherman's Connecticut*, 54.

55. For further discussion and a range of relevant documents, see Dreisbach and Hall, *Sacred Rights of Conscience*, 366–404; Daniel L. Dreisbach, "The Constitution's Forgotten Religion Clause: Reflections on the Article VI Religious Test Ban," *Journal of Church and State*, 38 (Spring 1996): 261–296.

56. Farrand, *Records*, 3: 78–79. An excellent treatment of this sequence of events may be found in Jonathan D. Sarna and David G. Dalin, *Religion and State in the American Jewish Experience* (Notre Dame: University of Notre Dame Press, 1997), 69–75.

57. Kramnick and Moore, *The Godless Constitution*; Daniel J. Elazar, *The American Constitutional Tradition* (Lincoln: University of Nebraska Press, 1988), 144; Shain, afterword in Dreisbach, Hall, and Morrison, *The Founders on God and Government*, 274–277; Hamilton, "The Calvinist Paradox of Distrust and Hope at the Constitutional Convention," 293–306. Michael Toth reports that after Count de Voleny "shared his plans for restructuring the French government," Ellsworth observed that "'there is one thing for which you have made no provision—the selfishness of man.'" Toth, *Founding Federalist*, 10–11.

58. For instance, Sherman argued against adding a proposal to protect the liberty of the press by noting that the "power of Congress does not extend to the Press." Farrand, *Records*, 2: 617–618, 637; Mark David Hall, "Religion and the American Founding," in *A History of the U.S. Political System: Ideas, Interests, and Institutions*, ed. Richard A. Harris and Daniel J. Tichenor (Santa Barbara: ABC-Clio, 2010), 1: 99–112.

59. Farrand, *Records*, 1: 122; 2: 468–469.

60. Jensen, *Documentary History*, 3: 351–353; 13: 470–472.

61. Ibid., 3: 363.

62. Ibid., 3: 372–373, 456–457.

63. All of Sherman's essays were originally published in the *New Haven Gazette*, but were reprinted nationally. His "A Citizen of New Haven" essay was published on January 7, 1788. Sherman published "Observations on the Alterations Proposed as Amendments to the New Federal Constitution," on December 4, 1788, and signed it "A Citizen of New Haven, I." He then published a slightly revised version of the January 7, 1788, essay as "A Citizen of New Haven II," on

December 25, 1788 (this essay begins with a second title: "Observations on the New Constitution"). All seven letters are republished in Paul Leicester Ford, ed., *Essays on the Constitution of the United States* (1892; reprint, New York: Burt Franklin, 1970), 211–241, but Ford used the December 1788 versions of the "Citizen" essays. I discuss Sherman's "Observations on the Alterations Proposed as Amendments" essay in the next chapter.

64. Ford, *Essays on the Constitution*, 228, 216.

65. Ibid., 218–221. The essay by Centinel was not published in Connecticut papers. Pauline Maier, *Ratification: The People Debate the Constitution, 1787–1788* (New York: Simon and Schuster, 2010), 132.

66. Ford, *Essays on the Constitution*, 222–223, 223–226, 227–228.

67. Jensen, *Documentary History*, 3: 524–525. A draft of the essay is available in the Roger Sherman Collection, box 1, folder 9, Yale University. Notably, several paragraphs were deleted that were critical of the Articles of Confederation.

68. Jensen, *Documentary History*, 3: 524–527.

69. Ibid., 3: 526, 524–527.

70. Ibid., 3: 527.

71. Ibid., 3: 554. For details about the ratification of the Constitution in Connecticut see ibid., 3: 315–614; and Collier, *All Politics Is Local*, passim; Maier, *Ratification*, 125–139; Donald Lutz, "Connecticut: Achieving Consent and Assuring Control," in *Ratifying the Constitution*, ed. Michael Allen Gillespie and Michael Lienesch (Lawrence: University Press of Kansas, 1989), 117–137.

72. Jensen, *Documentary History*, 3: 462–463, 514, 556–557, 468. Examples could be multiplied. See, for instance, ibid., 3: 357, 360–362, 370–371, 401, 402–403.

73. Ibid., 3: 498–500.

74. Ibid., 3: 558, 587–593.

75. Ibid., 3: 351, 502–503, 353; Collier, *All Politics Is Local*, 99, 154–155. As well, seven members of the convention were ministers, of whom six voted to ratify the Constitution. According to Collier, four of the seven ministers were "nonpracticing." Jensen, *Documentary History*, 360–362.

76. Dreisbach and Hall, *Sacred Rights of Conscience*, 351–364 (for different views of the significance of the lack of references to the deity in the U.S. Constitution).

77. Rossiter, *1787*, 247–250. Richard Beeman concludes that there were only three "indispensible men of the convention": Madison, Washington, and Franklin, and places Sherman along with Morris, Wilson, and Charles Pinckney in the second rank of "men who helped shape the Constitution." Beeman, *Plain, Honest Men*, xix–xxi.

78. Robertson, "Madison's Opponents and Constitutional Design," 225–243, 242; and *The Constitution and America's Destiny*; Rakove, *Original Meanings*. Keith L. Dougherty and Jac C. Heckelman agree with Robertson and Rakove that "Sherman was an effective delegate that historians have traditionally overlooked," but they suggest that his "influence at the Convention was partly the

result of the voting scheme and partly his position relative to others." See, "A Pivotal Voter from a Pivotal State: Roger Sherman at the Constitutional Convention," *American Political Science Review*, 100 (May 2006): 297–302, 302.
79. Collier, *Roger Sherman's Connecticut*, 237–282; *All Politics Is Local*, passim, 78, 79, 77–78.
80. Farrand, *Records*, 1: 132–133. For an excellent discussion of the 17th Amendment and its impact see Todd Zywicki, "Beyond the Shell and Husk of History: The History of the Seventeenth Amendment and its Implications for Current Reform Proposals," *Cleveland State Law Review*, 45 (1997): 165–234.
81. See, for instance, *Federalist*, 39, where Madison argues for the virtues of a partly federal and partly national government of enumerated powers.

CHAPTER 6

1. *DHFFC*, 14: 508–512; 16: 781; Collier, *Roger Sherman's Connecticut*, 316. The House and Senate kept journals, but these contain only sparse records of motions and contested votes. Accordingly, I rely heavily on newspaper accounts of congressional speeches, but the Senate's proceedings were secret and media coverage of both bodies was spotty, so there are relatively few records of important debates. Several papers covered congressional proceedings, including the *Congressional Register*, and the *Gazette of the United State*, the *Daily Advertiser*, and the *New York Gazette*. None of these recorded speeches verbatim, and their accounts sometimes vary. Unless there is an obvious contradiction or problem, I draw freely from these sources and, for the sake of simplicity, I treat the accounts as accurate records of the representatives' words (i.e., instead of writing "Thomas Lloyd recorded Sherman as saying" I simply write "Sherman said"). It is noteworthy that Sherman thought these papers were "[l]iable to make some mistakes," but he did "not think them guilty of unfairness." *DHFFC*, 13: 1015.
2. Even appointed positions were often held by elected officials. So, for instance, although Sherman was appointed to the Superior Court in 1766, every single member of this court was first elected. Beginning in 1785, he was simply appointed to this body, hence the qualification "for virtually all of…"
3. *DHFFC*, 10: 580.
4. Ibid., 11: 1267–1268.
5. Heimert, *Religion and the American Mind*, 512.
6. *DHFFC*, 10: 725–726. See especially *Myers v. U.S.*, 272 U.S. 52 (1926); *Humphreys' Executor v. U.S.*, 295 U.S. 602 (1935); and *Morrison v. Olson*, 487 U.S. 654 (1988). Alexander Hamilton, that great advocate of executive power, had written in "Federalist #77" that the "consent of that body [the Senate] would be necessary to displace as well as to appoint [executive branch officers]." Rossiter, *The Federalist Papers*, 459. After William Smith quoted "Federalist #77" in debates on the issue, he received a note from Egbert Benson reporting that

"*Publius* had informed him since the preceding day's debate, that upon mature reflection he *had changed his opinion* & now was convinced that the President alone should have the power of removal at pleasure," in Rakove, *Original Meanings*, 350. Seth Barrett Tillman points out that this account is "akin to triple hearsay," and offers an intriguing way to reconcile Hamilton's apparently contradictory positions in "The Puzzle of Hamilton's *Federalist* No. 77," *Harvard Journal of Law and Public Policy*, 33 (Winter 2010): 149–166, 164.

7. *DHFFC*, 11: 917, 977, 1024.

8. Sherman had published a revised version of this essay on December 25, 1788, but the quote with which Adams starts his essay is clearly from the earlier essay. Charles Francis Adams erroneously suggests that a letter from Sherman, not Sherman's essay, started this correspondence. *Works of John Adams*, 6: 437.

9. *Works of John Adams*, 6: 427–429.

10. Ibid., 6: 429–436.

11. Ibid., 6: 437–442. Adams dates Sherman's first letter as July 20 and provides no date for the second letter. In 1826, someone made a handwritten copy of these five letters, which were then in the possession of Roger Sherman Baldwin. These copies reveal that Sherman's first letter was written on July 18 and the second on July 27. The three letters written by John Adams are substantially the same as those printed in *Works of John Adams*, but those of Sherman differ significantly. However, the differences do not affect the above analysis. The Papers of Roger Sherman, box 1, Library of Congress.

12. Collier, *Roger Sherman's Connecticut*, 307.

13. *Works of John Adams*, 6: 442.

14. *DHFFC*, 12: 71, 79.

15. Louis Fisher, *Presidential War Power*, 2nd rev. ed. (Lawrence: University Press of Kansas, 2004), passim.

16. *DHFFC*, 10: 568.

17. Sherman, "A Caveat against Injustice," 15; "Remarks on a Pamphlet," iii, vi–viii; e.g., *PRC*, 10: 406–409.

18. *DHFFC*, 10: 568, 581; 14: 247; Rorabaugh, *The Alcoholic Republic*, 52–53; William B. Barber, "'Among the Most Techy Articles of Civil Police': Federal Taxation and the Adoption of the Whiskey Excise," *William and Mary Quarterly*, 3rd ser., 25 (January 1968): 58–84.

19. *DHFFC*, 10: 644.

20. Ibid., 12: 284, 289, 772, 649; 8: 335–337; 3: 340–341.

21. Steiner, *History of Slavery in Connecticut*, 69–70; Edwards, "The Injustice and Impolicy of the Slave Trade, and of the Slavery of Africans," 3rd ed. (New Haven: New Haven Anti-Slavery Society, 1833); Collier, *Roger Sherman's Connecticut*, 272; Roger Sherman to Samuel Huntington, March 7, 1792, Sprague Collection, Historical Society of Pennsylvania (copy of a letter that had been sold to a private individual).

22. *DHFFC*, 12: 223–224.
23. Ibid., 13: 1148–1149.
24. Ibid., 13: 1419–1424; Abigail Adams to Cotton Tuffs, May 30, 1790 in DHFFC, 19: 1638; Farrand, *Records*, 2: 327. Sherman cited Adam Smith's *Wealth of Nations* when discussing the cost of collecting tariffs (*DHFFC*, 13: 1395).
25. *JCC*, 17: 915–916; *DHFFC*, 12: 2612; Collier, *Roger Sherman's Connecticut*, 291–296.
26. *DHFFC*, 13: 1498–1506.
27. Ibid., 14: 382. A handwritten copy of the note is in the Sherman Collection, box 1, folder 21, Yale University. On the bottom of the note, in a different script, there is a sentence dated February 14, 1791, which records that Madison returned the note to Sherman with a "smile." On the debate over the constitutionality of a national bank, see especially *McCulloch v. Maryland*, 17 U.S. 316 (1819).
28. *DHFFC*, 8: 216; 13: 1539–1541.
29. Ibid., 13:1221; "Benefactors of Yale College," notebook, Office of the Treasurer Records, c. 1701–1971, Yale University.

    A final note on currency: according to Christopher Collier, "the dollar was divided into ninety pennies until Sherman—with the aid of Secretary of State Jefferson—introduced the decimal system as a congressman in 1790." *Roger Sherman's Connecticut*, 163.
30. Farrand, *Records*, 2: 588. In this section, I focus on Sherman's contributions to the creation of the Bill of Rights. Those unfamiliar with the history of the Bill of Rights may be surprised to find how little time Congress spent debating each right and how poorly these debates were recorded. In many cases, it is not possible to discuss Sherman's arguments for or against specific proposals because no records exist on the subject.

    Good general discussions of the creation of the Bill of Rights include Rutland, *Birth of the Bill of Rights*; and Akhil Reed Amar, *The Bill of Rights: Creation and Reconstruction* (New Haven: Yale University Press, 1998). Richard Labunski offers a readable account in *James Madison and the Struggle for the Bill of Rights* (New York: Oxford University Press, 2006), although, as the title implies, he highlights Madison's contributions. A useful collection of primary source documents on the subject is Neil H. Cogan, ed., *The Complete Bill of Rights: The Drafts, Debates, Sources, and Origins* (New York: Oxford University Press, 1997).
31. Ford, *Essays on the Constitution*, 215–228; Jensen, *Documentary History*, 524–527.
32. *DHFFC*, 4: 12–26.
33. Ford, *Essays on the Constitution*, 233–236.
34. Ibid., 235; Cushing, *First Laws*, 182–183.
35. Ford, *Essays on the Constitution*, 235.
36. *DHFFC*, 11: 811, 815, 821–827, 836; 4: 3–4, 9–12; Collier, *Roger Sherman's Connecticut*, 297; *DHFFC*, 16: 682, 975, 1041.
37. *DHFFC*, 11: 1158–1163; 4: 4.

38. "Library of Congress Confirms Discovery of Bill of Rights Draft by Roger Sherman," *Library of Congress Information Bulletin,* 46 (August 10, 1987): 349. Gerber, "Roger Sherman and the Bill of Rights," 532–540.

39. *DHFFC,* 11: 821–827; 4: 9–12. Wilson, "Remarks in the Pennsylvania Convention," in Hall and Hall, *Collected Works of James Wilson,* 195.

40. *DHFFC,* 4: 9–12; 16: 1099–1100. The draft in Sherman's hand was apparently penned between July 21 and July 28. The Select Committee's printed report dated July 28, 1789, differs significantly from this draft. It may be found at *DHFFC,* 4: 27–31.

41. *DHFFC,* 4: 9–12; 16: 1099–1100. Gerber provides a useful table comparing Madison's speech, the draft in Sherman's hand, and the final version of the Bill of Rights in "Roger Sherman and the Bill of Rights," 534–540. Randy E. Barnett argues that the second amendment in Sherman's draft incorporates Madison's draft of what eventually became the Ninth Amendment. It seems more likely that Sherman's amendment was simply listing specific natural rights that could not be violated by the national government. Randy E. Barnett, "Introduction: James Madison's Ninth Amendment," in *The Rights Retained by the People,* ed. Barnett (Fairfax: George Mason University Press, 1989), 1:7. Cf. Cogan, *Complete Bill of Rights,* 627–628. *DHFFC,* 4: 11, 39, 47; 11: 1291.

42. *DHFFC,* 11: 1289. For examples of scholars who refer to provisions in this draft as being made by Sherman, see Cogan, *Complete Bill of Rights,* 1, 83; Barnett, *The Rights Retained by the People,* 7, 351–352.

43. *DHFFC,* 11: 1208, 1212, 1233; 4: 27–31. Sherman's reference to "brass, iron, and clay" is an allusion to Daniel 2:31–35.

44. *DHFFC,* 11: 1239, 1249. Sherman makes a similar point in a letter to Samuel Huntington, November 21, 1791, Gratz Collection, Historical Society of Pennsylvania.

45. *DHFFC,* 11: 1249–50, 1313; 4: 46. Akhil Amar offers an enlightening discussion of the original "First Amendment" in *The Bill of Rights,* 8–17. The second of the original proposed amendments was not ratified until 1992.

46. *DHFFC,* 11: 1260–1262; 3: 149–150. The various versions of what became the First Amendment's religion clauses are conveniently laid out in Dreisbach and Hall, *Sacred Rights of Conscience,* 637–639.

47. Ibid., 11: 1285–1288. Connecticut's 1784 militia statute did not contain an exemption for conscientious objections. The statute would have been revised by Richard Law, not Sherman. There is no record of whether Sherman attempted to amend the proposed statute or not. Cushing, *First Laws,* 144–145.

48. *DHFFC,* 11: 1292; 4: 39.

49. Ibid., 11: 1296–1297, 1301, 1310.

50. Ibid., 11: 1285–1288. Cf. Roger Sherman to Samuel Huntington, November 21, 1791, Gratz Collection, Historical Society of Pennsylvania (noting that "the jurisdiction of Congress is limited to a few objects that concern the States in general").

51. *DHFFC*, 11: 1283, 1296, 1313, 1323.
52. Ibid., 4: 7.
53. Ibid., 4: 6–9; 35–48; 3: 216–218, 228–229; Rutland, *Birth of the Bill of Rights*, 194–221. In light of my argument about the influence of the Reformed tradition on America's founders, it is worth quoting John Witte's observation that "every one of guarantees in the 1791 Bill of Rights had already been formulated in the prior two centuries—by Calvinist theologians and jurists among others." *Reformation of Rights*, 31.
54. It is sometimes asserted that Jefferson's Virginia Statute for Religious Liberty influenced the authors and ratifiers of the First Amendment. I argue that there is little evidence to support this proposition in "Madison's Memorial and Remonstrance, Jefferson's Statute for Religious Liberty, and the Creation of the First Amendment" *American Political Thought*, 3 (Spring 2014): 32–63.
55. *Everson v. Board of Education*, 330 U.S. 1 (1947), at 33; Hall, "Jeffersonian Walls and Madisonian Lines," 563–614.
56. *DHFFC*, 11: 1292, 19: 1430, 1827. For a fine discussion of Ellsworth's role on the conference committee see William R. Casto, "Oliver Ellsworth's Calvinist Vision of Church and State in the Early Republic," in Dreisbach, Hall, and Morrison, *The Forgotten Founders on Religion and Public Life*, 65–100.
57. See, for instance, Dreisbach and Hall, *Sacred Rights of Conscience*. 426–433, 441–487; Dreisbach, Hall, and Morrison, *The Forgotten Founders on Religion and Public Life*, 65–100, 248–277 (on Sherman and Ellsworth); Dreisbach and Hall, *Faith and the Founders of the American Republic* (on Baldwin and Boudinot); John E. O'Connor, *William Paterson: Lawyer and Statesman, 1745–1806* (New Brunswick: Rutgers University Press, 1986); Marc M. Arkin, "Regionalism and the Religion Clauses: The Contribution on Fisher Ames," *Buffalo Law Review*, 47 (Spring 1999): 763–828.
58. *DHFFC*, 11: 1500–1501.
59. George Washington, "Thanksgiving Proclamation," October 3, 1789, in Dreisbach and Hall, *Sacred Rights of Conscience*, 453–454.
60. *DHFFC*, 11: 1501.
61. Ibid., 3:9, 39, 44; 10: 332, 391. Dreisbach and Hall, *Sacred Rights of Conscience*, 472; Andy G. Olree, "James Madison and Legislative Chaplains," *Northwestern Law Review* (Winter 2008): 174–176, 203–206.
62. Ibid., 3:116–117; Dreisbach and Hall, *Sacred Rights of Conscience*, 237–238; Cord, *Separation of Church and State*, 17–82.
63. *DHFFC*, 14: 127, 162–163, 149. Sherman also spoke in favor of exempting "students at college," because it was an "indulgence in favour of literature, which it justly merited, and what had been extended to them by all enlightened nations where such establishments as a national militia obtained, it was the practice of these states before the revolution, and one worthy, in his opinion[,] of being continued." Ibid., 14: 107–108.

64. Mark David Hall, "The Sacred Rights of Conscience: America's Founders on Church and State," *Oregon Humanities* (Fall–Winter 2005): 40–46; Donald L. Drakeman, *Church, State, and Original Intent* (Cambridge: Cambridge University Press, 2009), passim.

65. Hall, "Jeffersonian Walls and Madisonian Lines," 568–569.

66. DHFFC, 19: 1507–1509; *Connecticut Journal*, October 13, 1790, 2. The Biblical references, italicized in the original, are from Psalm 12:8, Matthew 7:12, and I Timothy 1:6.

67. Collier, *Roger Sherman's Connecticut*, 314–315. See also Roger Sherman to Samuel Huntington, November 21, 1791, Gratz Collection; and Roger Sherman to Samuel Huntington, March 7, 1792, Sprague Collection, Historical Society of Pennsylvania; Roger Sherman to Benjamin Trumbull, January 2, 1792, Miscellaneous Bound Manuscripts, Massachusetts Historical Society. The Sherman-Baldwin correspondence is in the Roger Sherman Collection, Yale University.

68. Collier, *Roger Sherman's Connecticut*, 317–323, 329–332.

69. Roger Sherman Collection, box 1, folder 16, Yale University. Roger Sherman was also the grandfather of George Frisbie Hoar, senator from Connecticut; Ebenezer R. Hoar, judge and senator from Massachusetts; and William Maxwell Evarts, U.S. secretary of state, U.S. attorney general, and U.S. senator from New York.

   On May 6, 1844, James Kent, the great legal scholar, jurist, and chancellor of New York, wrote to Simeon Baldwin noting that he had just read an address by Roger Sherman Baldwin, then governor of Connecticut. He commented that the "Doctrines of the Message are just & admirable, & they recall the bright days of the Trumbulls, Ellsworths and Shermans, who threw such a Lustre on the golden annals of your State." Kent was a friend of Simeon's and a student at Yale from 1777–81, so he may have known Sherman, and he undoubtedly was well acquainted with his character and political activities. *Life and Letters of Simeon Baldwin*, 2, 20–23.

70. Tryon Edwards, ed., *The Works of Jonathan Edwards, D. D.: Late President of Union College* (Boston: John P. Jewett, 1854), 2: 183.

CHAPTER 7

1. Daniel L. Dreisbach, "Famous Founders and Forgotten Founders: What's the Difference, and Does the Difference Matter?" in Dreisbach, Hall, and Morrison, *The Forgotten Founders on Religion and Public Life*, 1–25, 2. Gregg and Hall, *America's Forgotten Founders*, 1–5.

2. I am grateful to my teaching assistant Jay Miller for providing the data on stamps. For more information, see http://www.postalmuseum.si.edu/u.s.stampsexhibit/US3_010.jpg. Trumbull's painting "The Signing of the Declaration" was featured in full on an 1869, 24-cent stamp and in part on a 1976 sheet (where one of the five stamps on the sheet contains the portraits of Adams, Sherman, and Livingston).

3. Again, Trumbull's "The Signing of the Declaration" saves Sherman from complete obscurity because it is featured on the back of the two dollar bill. It should also be noted that Connecticut chose a statue of Sherman as one of its two contributions to the National Statutory Hall.

4. George Washington's papers are projected to fill ninety volumes, the Adams family papers one hundred, Jefferson's papers approximately seventy-five, and James Madison's and Benjamin Franklin's papers at least fifty volumes each. Even Hamilton's papers required twenty-seven volumes. By contrast, paper collections for most other founders, if they are published at all, are usually between one and three volumes. A collection of Sherman's papers has never been published, but if one were, it would not require more than three volumes. I am currently editing a one-volume collection of Sherman's writings entitled *Collected Works of Roger Sherman*, which will be published by Liberty Fund Press.

5. On *Everson*'s syllogism, see Hall, "Jeffersonian Walls and Madisonian Lines," esp. 563–614. The article addressesand rejects the possibility that Madison's and Jefferson's views were influential enough to justify focusing on them to the exclusion of other founders. See also Hall, "Madison's Memorial and Remonstrance, Jefferson's Statute for Religious Liberty, and the Creation of the First Amendment."

6. Of course some jurists and scholars question whether the founders' views are relevant for contemporary law and politics, a debate much too extensive to be considered here. Some critics of originalism even argue that the founders did not think their views should be used to interpret the Constitution (e.g., Rakove, *Original Meanings*, 339, 365; and Powell, "The Original Understanding of Original Intent," 885–948). Sherman did not hold this position, as indicated by his multiple references to the framers' intentions in congressional debates. For a discussion of the literature on this question, see Dennis J. Goldford, *The American Constitution and the Debate over Originalism* (New York: Cambridge University Press, 2005).

7. Farrand, *Records*, 1: 347–348; Ford, *Essays on the Constitution*, 228. Similarly, late in life, he wrote to his son-in law, "Judges can acquire a knowledge of the rights of the people of these States much better by riding the circuit than by staying at home and reading British and other foreign Laws." Roger Sherman to Simeon Baldwin, January 21, 1791, Roger Sherman Collection, box 1, folder 14, Yale University.

APPENDIX

BY THE HONORABLE
JONATHAN TRUMBULL, Esq.;

Governor and Commander in Chief of the *English* Colony of
Connecticut in *New-England*.

A PROCLAMATION

The race of Mankind was made in a State of Innocence and Freedom, subjected only to the laws of GOD the CREATOR, and through his rich Goodness, designed for virtuous Liberty and Happiness here and forever; and when moral evil was introduced into the World, and Man had corrupted his Ways before GOD, Vice and Iniquity came in like a Flood, and Mankind became exposed, and a prey to the Violence, Injustice and Oppression of one another. GOD, in great Mercy, inclined his People to form themselves into Society, and to set up and establish civil Government for the Protection and Security of their Lives and Properties from the Invasion of wicked Men: But through Pride and Ambition, the King's and Princes of the World, appointed by the People the Guardians of their Lives and Liberties, early and almost universally, degenerated into Tyrants, and by Fraud or Force betrayed and wrested out of their Hands the very Rights and Properties they were appointed to protect and defend. But a small Part of the Human Race maintained and enjoyed any tolerable Degree of Freedom. Among those happy few the Nation of *Great-Britain* was distinguished, by a Constitution of Government wisely framed and modeled, to support the Dignity and Power of the Prince, for the Protection of the Rights of the People; and under which, that Country in long Succession, enjoyed great Tranquility and Peace, though not unattended with repeated and powerful Efforts, by many of it's haughty Kings, to destroy the constitutional Rights of the People, and establish arbitrary Power and Dominion. In one of those convulsive Struggles, our Forefathers having suffered in that, their native Country, great and variety of Injustice and

Oppression, left their dear Connections and Enjoyments, and fled to this then inhospitable Land, to secure a lasting Retreat from civil and religious Tyranny.

The GOD of Heaven favored and prospered their Undertaking—made Room for their Settlement—increased and multiplied them to a very numerous People, and inclined succeeding King's to indulge them and their Children for many Years, the unmolested Enjoyment of the Freedom and Liberty they fled to inherit: But, an unnatural King has risen up—violated his sacred Obligations, and by the Advice of evil Counsellors, attempted to wrest from us, their Children, the sacred Rights we justly claim, and which have been ratified and established by solemn Compact with, and recognized by, his Predecessors and Fathers, King's of *Great-Britain*—laid upon us Burdens too heavy and grievous to be born, and issued many cruel and oppressive Edicts, depriving us of our natural, lawful, and most important Rights, and subjecting us to the absolute Power and Controul of himself, and the *British* Legislature; against which we have sought Relief by humble, earnest and dutiful Complaints and Petitions: But, instead of obtaining Redress, our Petitions have been treated with Scorn and Contempt, and fresh Injuries heaped upon us, while hostile Armies and Ships are sent to destroy and lay waste our Country. In this distressing Dilemma, having no Alternative but absolute Slavery, or successful Resistance; this, and the United American Colonies, have been constrained by the over-ruling Laws of Self-Preservation, to take up Arms for the Defence of all that is sacred and dear to Freemen, and make their solemn Appeal to Heaven for the Justice of their Cause, and resist Force by Force.

GOD ALMIGHTY has been pleased, of his infinite Mercy, to succeed our Attempts, and give us many Instances of signal Success and Deliverance; but the Wrath of the King is still increasing, and not content with before employing all the Force which can be sent from his own Kingdom to execute his cruel Purposes, has procured, and is sending all the Mercenaries he can obtain from foreign Countries, to assist in extirpating the Rights of *America*, and with their's, almost all the Liberty remaining among Mankind.

IN this most critical and alarming Situation, this, and all the Colonies, are called upon, and earnestly pressed, by the honorable CONGRESS of the *American* Colonies, united for mutual Defence, to raise a large additional Number of their Militia and able Men, to be furnished and equipped with all possible Expedition, for Defence against the soon expected Attack and Invasion of those who are our Enemies without a Cause. In chearful Compliance with which Request, and urged by Motives the most cogent and important that can affect the human Mind, the General Assembly of this Colony have freely and unanimously agreed and resolved, that upwards of Seven Thousand able and effective Men be immediately raised, furnished and equipped, for the great and interesting Purposes aforesaid. And not Desirous that any should go to a Warfare at their own Charges, (though equally interested in others) for Defence of the great and all-important Cause in which we are engaged, have granted large and liberal Pay and Encouragements, to all who shall voluntarily undertake for the Defence of themselves and their Country, as by their Acts may appear.

I DO THEREFORE, by and with the Advice of the Council, and at the Desire of the Representatives in General Court assembled, issue this PROCLAMATION, and make the solemn Appeal of said Assembly to the Virtue and public Spirit of the good People of this Colony. Affairs are hastening fast to a Crisis, and the approaching Campaign will, in all Probability, determine forever the Fate of *America*. If this should be successful on our Side, there is little to fear on Account of any other. Be exhorted to rise, therefore, to superior Exertions on this great Occasion; and let all that are able and necessary, shew themselves ready in Behalf of their injured and oppressed Country, and come forth to Help of the LORD against the Mighty, and convince the unrelenting Tyrant of *Britain* that they are resolved to be FREE. Let them step forth to defend their Wives, their little Ones, their Liberty, and every thing they hold sacred and dear, to defend the Cause of their Country, their Religion and their GOD. Let every one to the utmost of their Power, lend a helping Hand to promote and forward a Design on which the Salvation of *America* now evidently depends. Nor need any be dismayed: the Cause is certainly a just and a glorious one: God is able to save us in such Way and Manner as he pleases, and to humble our proud Oppressors. The Cause is that of Truth and Justice: he has already shewn his Power in our Behalf, and for the Destruction of many of our Enemies. *Our Fathers trusted in him and were delivered.* Let us all repent, and thoroughly amend our Ways, and turn to him, put all our Trust and Confidence in him—in his Name go forth, and in his Name set up our Banners, and he will save us with temporal and eternal Salvation. And while our Armies are Abroad, jeopardizing their Lives in the high Places of the Field, let all who remain at Home, cry mightily to GOD for the Protection of his Providence, to shield and defend their Lives from Death, and to crown them with Victory and Success. And in the Name of the said General Assembly, I do hereby earnestly recommend it to all, both Ministers and People, frequently to meet together for social Prayer to ALMIGHTY GOD, for the out-pouring of his blessed Spirit upon this guilty Land—That he would awaken his People to Righteousness and Repentance—bless our Councils—prosper our Arms, and succeed the Measures using for our necessary Self-Defence—disappoint the evil and cruel Devices of our Enemies—preserve our precious Rights and Liberties—lengthen out our Tranquility, and make us a People of his Praise, and the blessed of the LORD, as long as the Sun and Moon shall endure.

AND all the Ministers of the Gospel in this Colony, are directed and desired to publish this Proclamation in their several Churches and Congregations, and to enforce the Exhortations thereof by their own pious Example and public Instructions.

GIVEN under my Hand, at the Council Chamber in Hartford, *the 18th Day of June, Anno Domini* 1776.

JONATHAN TRUMBULL

SELECT COMMITTEE REPORT DRAFT BILL OF RIGHTS

In the Handwriting of Roger Sherman

DRAFT BILL OF RIGHTS

Report as their Opinion, That the following articles be proposed by Congress to the legislatures of the Several States to be adopted by them as amendments of the Constitution of the united States, and when ratified by the legislatures of three fourths (at least) of Said States in the union, to become a part of the Constitution of the united States, pursuant to the fifth Article of said Constitution.

(1)

The powers of government being derived from the people, ought to be exercised for their benefit, and they have an inherent and unalienable right to change or amend their political Constitution, when ever they judge such change will advance their interest & happiness.

(2)

The people have certain natural rights which are retained by them when they enter into Society, Such are the rights of Conscience in matters of religion; of acquiring property and of pursuing happiness & Safety; of Speaking, writing and publishing their Sentiments with Decency and Freedom; of peaceably assembling to consult their common good, and of applying to Government by petition or remonstrance for redress of grievances. Of these rights therefore they Shall not be deprived by the Government of the united States.

(3)

No person Shall be tried for any crime whereby he may incur loss of life or any infamous punishment, without Indictment by a grand Jury, nor be convicted but by the unanimous verdict of a Petit Jury of good and lawful men freeholders of the vicinage or district where the trial Shall be had.

(4)

After a census Shall be taken, each State Shall be allowed one representative for every thirty thousand Inhabitants of the description in the Second Section of the first Article of the Constitution, until the whole number of representatives shall amount to _____ but never to exceed _____.

(5)

The militia shall be under the government of the laws of the respective States, when not in the actual Service of the united States, but such rules as may be prescribed by Congress for their uniform organization & discipline shall be observed in officering and training them, but military Service shall not be required of persons religiously scrupulous of bearing arms.

(6)

No soldier shall be quartered in any private house in time of Peace, nor at any time, but by authority of law.

(7)

Excessive bail shall not be required, not excessive fines imposed, nor cruel & unusual punishments inflicted in any case.

(8)

Congress Shall not have power to grant any monopoly or exclusive advantages of commerce to any person or Company; nor to restrain the liberty of the Press.

(9)

In suits at common law in courts acting under the authority of the united States, issues of fact shall be tried by a Jury if either party request it.

(10)

No law Shall be passed for fixing a compensation for the members of Congress except the first Shall take effect until after the next election of representatives posterior to the passing such law.

(11)

The legislative, executive and judiciary powers vested by the Constitution in the respective branches of the Government of the united States, shall be exercised according to the distribution therein made, so that neither of said branches shall assume or exercise any of the powers peculiar to either of the other branches.

And the powers not delegated to the Government of the united States by the Constitution, nor prohibited by it to the particular States, are retained by the States respectively, nor shall the exercise of power by the Government of the united States particular instances here in enumerated by way of caution be construed to imply the contrary.

Index

federalism, 72–73, 75, 80, 92–100, 120,
131–133, 139–140
Federalist Papers, 7, 113, 121
Floyd, William, 22, 60, 118
founders
famous, 5–7, 12, 149–153, 160–162
forgotten, 3, 7, 13, 149–153, 157,
161–162
Foster, Abiel, 142
Franklin, Benjamin, 5, 12, 23, 57, 59, 71,
108, 120, 129, 149–151

George, King, 53–62
Gerry, Elbridge, 113, 140
Gilman, Nicholas, 111, 142
God, distant words for, 60
Goodman, Christopher, 15
Gorham, Nathaniel, 104, 120
Great Awakening, 20, 31, 34, 84–85
Griswold, Matthew, x, 9, 32, 151
Gwinnett, Button, 71

Haiti, 129
Half-Way covenant, 31, 85
Hall, Lyman, 22, 60
Hamilton, Alexander, 5, 12, 93, 94, 96,
97, 103, 108–109, 121, 130–132,
149–152, 205–206
Hancock, John, x, 9, 22, 60, 113, 151
Harrison, Benjamin, 71
Hart, John, 22, 60
Henry, Patrick, 2, 152
Hewes, Joseph, 71
Hiester, Daniel, 142
Hillhouse, James, 146
Hillhouse, William, 64
Hinkley v. Wilson (1787), 83
Hobart, Noah, 51
Hooker, Thomas, 13, 17, 30
Hopkins, Samuel, 38, 65, 147
Hopkins, Stephen, 71
Houston, William, 111

Huger, Daniel, 142
human nature,
made in image of God, 13
sinful, 13, 64–67, 163, 203
Huntington, Benjamin, x, 9, 32, 64,
142, 151
Huntington, Samuel, x, 9, 32, 60, 82,
112, 117, 129, 151
Hutchinson, Anne, 18

Ingersoll, Jared, 111
*An Inquiry into the Nature of True
Holiness*, 38

Jackson, James, 139, 142
Jay, John, 57, 151
Jefferson, Thomas, 2, 5–7, 12, 21, 27, 50,
53, 59, 71, 141–142, 145–146,
150–152, 162, 170–171
Jews, 89, 111
Johnson, William Samuel, 42, 49, 51,
57, 91, 94, 99, 105, 113, 116, 122,
146, 183–184
Judicial power, 103–106

Kent, James, 210
King, Rufus, 94, 108, 120
Kirby, Ephraim, 48
Knox, John, 13, 15, 158

Langdon, John, 111, 142
Lansing, John, 111
Laud, William, 185
Law, Richard, x, 9, 32, 77–78, 81, 151
Lee, Richard Bland, 126
Lee, Richard Henry, 2, 64, 72, 155
Legislator, role of, 122–124
Leland, John, 90
"Letters of a Landholder," 113
Linn, William, 144
Livermore, Samuel, 138, 152
Livingston, Philip, 22, 60

CPSIA information can be obtained at www.ICGtesting.com
Printed in the USA
BVOW05s0934101114

374402BV00002B/2/P